# NOURISHED

# NOURISHED

## A MEMOIR of FOOD, FAITH
## & ENDURING LOVE

*(with Recipes)*

## LIA HUBER

CONVERGENT

NEW YORK

CONVERGENT BOOKS is a registered trademark and its C colophon
is a trademark of Penguin Random House LLC.

Library of Congress Cataloging-in-Publication Data
Names: Huber, Lia, author.
Title: Nourished : a memoir of food, faith, and enduring love (with recipes) /
Lia Huber.
Description: New York : Convergent Books, 2017.
Identifiers: LCCN 2017003795 | ISBN 9780451498816 (hardback)
Subjects: LCSH: International cooking. | Food security. | Food—Psychological
aspects. | Well-being. | BISAC: COOKING / Health & Healing / General. |
TRAVEL / Special Interest / Adventure. | LCGFT: Cookbooks.
Classification: LCC TX725.A1 H84 2017 | DDC 641.5—dc23
LC record available at https://lccn.loc.gov/2017003795

ISBN 978-0-451-49881-6
Ebook ISBN 978-0-451-49882-3

Printed in the United States of America

*Book design by Anna Thompson*
*Jacket design by Jessie Bright*
*Jacket photograph by Alison Ashton*

10 9 8 7 6 5 4 3 2 1

First Edition

*For Christopher . . .*
*for always being willing to jump out of airplanes with me.*
*For Noemi . . . don't forget.*
*For my parents . . .*
*for teaching me anything is possible.*

# Contents

✦❈✦

# PROLOGUE

They're not going to like the vegetables," the old woman in the corner of the hut mumbled through wrinkled lips and missing teeth. She was speaking in Kaqchikel, the language native to this region of Guatemala, but I understood her nonetheless. I was used to the skeptical, almost goading tenor of that sentence.

The other women, of varying ages, nodded in agreement. I stirred the giant pot perched on a rickety propane burner and pretended not to understand.

I was in Guatemala as part of a team that had traveled there to build a house for a family, and since I was also a professional cook, they had asked me to make lunch for sixty elementary school kids. A soup was strongly suggested. Me being me, I dove into the task by researching traditional soups of the region and settled on a simple chicken soup. Knowing that malnutrition statistics were dire in villages like San Rafael, I also took it upon myself to go heavy on the veggies.

Of course, when I had left our team's compound to procure said veggies the day before, my armful of giant market bags had caused many to ask, "What are you doing?"

"I'm going to buy vegetables for the soup," I answered. Inevitably, whoever they were, they would make the same face the old Guatemalan woman just did, shrug, and say in Spanish, "The kids aren't going to like the vegetables."

So now I knew that sentence in three languages.

When my husband and I had arrived in San Rafael along with our team, the social workers had taken us on a tour. I'd expected poverty. Over half of the people in Guatemala live below the poverty line, and 15 percent—like those in San Rafael—live on the edge of subsistence. That means homes cobbled together from sticks and scraps and corrugated plastic. It means no toilets or potable water. It means that most kids are out working in the fields by the end of elementary school in order to help the family survive.

What caught me off guard was that the people in San Rafael made money by growing vegetables—primarily squash, corn, and green beans—yet kept none of those vegetables for themselves. I watched as a farmer lifted boxes of pristine green beans off his donkey, and then I turned to the social worker. "I don't understand. It seems like there's plenty to have some for his family."

"They have to sell everything they produce just to get by," she replied.

Poverty is a tricky thing, and I'm not going to pretend to know how it feels to live each day on the brink of survival. But the wrappers crunching an inch thick beneath my feet and the sticky hands and faces of nearly every child I met were telling a story too. Surely the junk food that people were buying would cost more than what a farmer would make on the few handfuls of green beans that would feed his family.

The unspoken narrative came to the surface in that dirt-floored kitchen with the grumbled sentence I'd heard in three languages. Moms were concerned their kids wouldn't eat the green beans.

A skinny, dirt-streaked boy appeared in the kitchen doorway and then scurried away—which, apparently, was a sign that the time had come. I ladled out bowl after bowl of steaming soup and sent it off with the helpers into the classroom.

Twenty minutes later, I realized I'd served well beyond sixty bowls. "What's going on?" I asked one of the helpers.

One of the women piped up from the corner with a wry grin on her face. "The kids are asking for seconds." Another woman stood up and took the ladle from me, shooing me out of the room in a manner that appeared brusque. But I knew Guatemalans well enough to detect a note of affection in her gesture.

As I walked toward the classroom, I thought about my own junk-laden childhood. When I was these kids' age, I would come home from school and polish off a bag of Doritos, follow those up with a half dozen Chips Ahoy, and then not touch the carrots in Mom's pot roast. Our economic circumstances might be vastly different, but these kids and I could have been kin, judging from how we felt about vegetables.

The same went for the mothers grumbling in the kitchen. With their skeptical, almost antagonistic posture, they could have been stand-ins for any number of women I've met in the United States. They told me things like, "Of course you roasted a chicken . . . you're a chef. I'm more of a KFC kind of gal." Or, "Of course you made sautéed mushrooms . . . you're such a foodie. Our family's more Hamburger Helper." And on went the explanations about how they didn't have time or training or energy to cook with real food.

But I'm here to tell you that those excuses are a bunch of baloney.

(Which, by the way, I used to love. Fried.) Choosing root vegetables over something out of a box isn't about being a foodie. It's a matter of life and death. I know because fake, convenient, fast food nearly killed me, and real food not only saved my life but made it richer than I ever could have dreamed.

I walked across the cracked cement where the kids had been playing soccer and through the classroom door, expecting to see piles of soggy vegetables sitting beside the bowls. Instead I saw tops of heads as the kids all but lapped up the soup. They looked up with wide, wet smiles and I asked, "*Le gustan el caldo . . . le gustan chayote?*" (Do you like the soup . . . do you like the squash?)

One particularly gutsy boy raised his spoon like the Statue of Liberty raising her torch and declared, "*Rico chayote!*" (Squash is delicious!) Others joined in, and soon the whole room was chanting, "*Rico chayote, rico chayote!*" I hugged each and every one of those children—even the ones who thought hugging was uncool—and walked back to the kitchen in a broth-scented bubble of euphoria.

There, too, the scene had turned convivial. The women were slurping bowls of soup and chatting with one another and, miracle of miracles, they were smiling at me. One handed me a bowl of my own and patted the seat beside her. I took it, savoring the rich stock studded with chicken and squash (it really was good), the intimacy of being hip to hip, and the warmth of the bowl in my hands.

That pot of soup had nourished a roomful of children and then turned "us and them" into "we."

I never tire of seeing miracles like these happen. And they do, because food is so much more than just something we put in our mouths or use to fuel our bodies. It's a blend of memories, emotions, feelings, needs. There's a soul to food, isn't there? Fragrances and flavors intermingle with our life experiences to become wondrously satisfying in ways that stretch far beyond the plate.

Or bowl, in this case.

For me, food went from something I didn't think about to becoming a pivotal part of my life. It was what brought me joy. It was how I healed my body when doctors couldn't. It was how I related to people and gained deeper insight into my life's purpose and the way I serve the world.

Lest you think that sounds highfalutin, let me say that I'm not talking fancy food and foams and names you can't pronounce (although I did go through that stage on my journey). I'm talking real food. I'm talking real experiences. I'm talking a rustic chicken soup made on a rickety propane burner in a dirt-floor kitchen.

Who knows what will happen with the kids in that classroom? One bowl of soup probably won't change their lives, but maybe it will. If one kid—or one parent—notices how much better they feel after that bowl of soup rather than a bag of chips, it could have a ripple effect on generations to come.

Maybe she'll escape the disease that runs rampant among her fellow villagers, which would mean a step away from poverty toward freedom. Maybe she'll gain the energy and vitality to step out in ways she never thought she could, modeling change and inspiring a brighter future. Maybe, just maybe, she'll find her life going in a delightfully different direction than she'd planned.

Can all of that happen to someone because of things as seemingly mundane as soup and chicken and vegetables? I'll let you be the judge.

# PART I
## *SEEDS*

*Inside even the most minute, dustlike grain of seed is a living plant. True, it's in embryonic form, possessing only the most rudimentary parts, but it lives, and it is not completely passive. Thus they maintain their spark of life—dim though it may be— until conditions are right for them to complete their destiny as germinated plants.*

THE NEW SEED-STARTERS HANDBOOK

*"Night and day, whether he sleeps or gets up, the seed sprouts and grows, though he does not know how."*

MARK 4:27

# CHAPTER 1

# THE SUMMER THAT CHANGED EVERYTHING

### JUNE 1991

My heart thumped wildly, thrumming in my ears. What in God's name was I doing?

Above me the sky was molten black, speckled with stars as dazzling as diamonds. I had my unwrinkleable plaid blazer wadded up under my head as a pillow—my long, sun-bleached hair was stringy from the salt air—and I hugged my knees against my chest in the fetal position. I felt small, insignificant, and very alone. The water mirrored the heavens as the high-speed ferry carried me across the Ionian Sea to the island of Corfu.

But what exactly, I asked myself, was I speeding toward?

The short answer was Alexi, a tall, dark Greek man with mischievous green eyes whom I'd met the week before while vacationing on Corfu with my friend Andrea.

The long answer wasn't quite so clear.

The first night Andrea and I had spent on Corfu, we went to a bar where raucous Americans and Australians were slurring, groping, and for some reason breaking plates over people's heads. I'd observed from a distance atop a picnic bench, feeling like I should want to participate (I was twenty, after all) but having no desire to. I knew that wasn't what I'd come to Greece for. Although if you'd asked me to pinpoint what I *had* come for, I wouldn't have been able to. History? Mystery? Something akin to culture? Whatever it was, I was sure it was not at that bar.

Soon after, though, I got a glimpse. A man whom Andrea had met insisted on taking us to a souvlaki stand up the road from the beach for a late lunch. We trudged along the sand and turned up a one-lane road lined with souvenir shops. The road took us to a nondescript restaurant with four orange tables on the covered patio. I was unimpressed . . . until the owner, Alexi, rode up on a yellow motorbike and unfurled his long, swarthy frame. We sparred verbally all afternoon over platters of grilled marinated pork skewers, crispy fries, and a big platter of Greek salad. Then Alexi leaned over to me and said, "There's something I want to show you. Be ready tomorrow morning."

The next day I watched dawn crack on the horizon, spreading a sultry light as smooth as butter over the island. Alexi pulled up on his motorbike, and I climbed on and wrapped my arms around his waist. The wind whipped my hair as he steered up the main road past vineyards, orchards, and cemeteries, then through a little village. "I live there, with my family." He pointed to a whitewashed stone house on the right. As we reached the end of the village and began to zigzag up a steep dirt path, my nose tingled with dust and the scent of minty herbs. I could see snatches of turquoise sea between the gnarled trunks of ancient olive trees.

At the top of the mountain Alexi stopped the bike on a plateau hundreds of feet above the ocean. Bees buzzed in the wildflowers, waves rolled in like pinstripes on the sea below, and the air smelled herbal and fresh, like my mother's spice rack. I was taken aback not just by the beauty but by a sense of peace like I'd never felt before. Then Alexi took me home to that little white house we'd passed in the village where his father, Spiros, was cooking lunch. I was cautious—surely I was but one in a long string of young foreign women who had crossed that threshold—but Spiros put me instantly at ease.

"*Pastitsada,*" he said, pressing into my hands a bowl of long, thick noodles drenched in tomato sauce with shards of meat that smelled like gingersnaps.

We sat at the simple wooden table in the kitchen, Alexi at the head and Spiros and me across from each other. I twirled some noodles around my fork and brought it to my mouth. The sauce tasted nothing like the jarred Ragu I knew so well. It was rich and savory with a swirl of spices and a slightly sweet finish. I sucked on the noodles and, to my horror, found they were hollow. They flapped against my cheeks like Medusa's locks with a loud slurp-flap-flap, leaving tomato sauce all over my face. Mortified, I looked across at Spiros as I wiped away the sauce, but he just chuckled, his blue eyes twinkling.

When Andrea and I left Corfu for another island, I couldn't stop thinking of Alexi and his family. So at the end of the week on Santorini, when Andrea and I had agreed to part ways, she went north to Paris, and I got on a ferry, alone, to Corfu. And now said ferry was pulling into the harbor at 10:00 at night.

I hadn't even tried to sleep. I was too busy second-guessing my decision. Alexi didn't even know I was coming; what would I do if he'd already replaced me? There were umpteen other girls on Corfu who looked better in a bikini than I did (let's just say that I lacked on top yet was given ample provisions on bottom); why *would* he wait for me?

My legs shook as I hailed a cab and pulled my backpack over my shoulder. I felt queasy as the car wound up and over the mountains, through the olive groves and down toward the beach. I could see the lights at the end of the road; the restaurant was open, which was good.

We rolled closer, and I saw that Alexi was alone. The fluorescent light gleamed off his glossy black hair. He looked up at the cab with a quizzical expression. I rolled down my window, and he smiled a wide, genuine smile. He bounded toward the cab and my shoulders felt like they dropped about six inches.

That night, in the Kourtesis' home again, I lay awake trying to pinpoint what had drawn me back. I had just spent a year studying in Paris, the most beautiful city in the world, and while I'd enjoyed it immensely, my default state of being had been a sense of detachment and anxiety. On the other hand, during the week I'd spent on Corfu, I'd felt like I'd sunk knee deep into rich, fertile earth.

The next morning I awoke to Mama Kourtesi sitting on the edge of the bed, beaming down at me. She ushered the two of us upstairs to the kitchen and served us plates of fried eggs. A donkey's bray joined the tick-tock of the pendulum clock on the wall, and a breeze rustled the trees just past the lace curtains on the window. Still groggy, I lifted the fork and a bit of deep golden yolk, as thick as cake batter, dripped from a tine. I'd never seen a yolk do that before. I'd never seen a yolk that color before. The edges of the egg's white were crinkled and browned like parchment. I took a bite and just about fell off my chair. It was rich and peppery, more like eating steak than an egg.

I had eaten plenty of eggs during my twenty years—most of them scrambled or poached—but the eggs on the plate in front of me bore no similarity to the hundreds that had come before them.

Growing up in the American Midwest, I was a meat-and-potatoes girl, quite literally. When my mom would serve the weekly pot roast, I would pick out all of the carrots and peas, pile them on my younger brother Russell's plate, and take his meat and potatoes when Mom wasn't looking. My parents had a beautiful garden, yet I refused to touch any vegetable in it except for raw carrots and cucumbers, and the chives that grew along the border.

Things didn't improve with age. As I alternated between putting on pounds and dieting—as young women tend to do—I was indoctrinated into the torturous penance of plain salads with lemon juice squeezed over the top, plates of mushy steamed vegetables, and a palate of white: mashed potatoes with no gravy, egg-white omelets devoid of yolk, plain rice. These were all fat free and, therefore, virtuous.

Coming from that background, I simply had no frame of reference for this flamboyantly rich egg on my plate that was, quite literally, dripping with pleasure.

"How did you do this?" I asked Mama Kourtesi. "How did you get these eggs to taste like this?"

She glanced in question at Alexi, who translated for his mother. He shrugged and returned her answer, "She fried them in olive oil."

Olive oil and eggs—*just* olive oil and eggs—had produced *those flavors*? I was skeptical. To me, olive oil was just something that made you fat. Something to be avoided, other than the minute little drippy drops you occasionally needed in a pan or on a salad.

*At first*, my days in Greece were simple. The family didn't want to impose on me by asking for my help with the house or the restaurant. So I took long morning walks, winding down the mountain past olive groves with black nets beneath them; past vineyards and fig trees; past meadows speckled with ruby-red ranunculus; past hillsides matted with wild herbs and dotted with grazing sheep. I'd pass chicken coops, donkeys, beehives, and kitchen gardens burdened with tomatoes, zucchini the size of my forearm, and lustrous black eggplant. As ordinary as these pastoral scenes were, they felt exotic to a girl from the Chicago suburbs.

In grade school I had a Greek friend, Liz, whose father owned restaurants. She used to bring fancy things like French dip in her sack lunch. But what I remember most were the pomegranates she'd occasionally pull out of her bag. She'd break open the leathery orb to reveal cluster upon hidden cluster of garnet-colored gems. I was mesmerized each and every time and hadn't seen a pomegranate since those grade school days. Yet on Corfu, they hung by the roadside, as commonplace as apples in Illinois.

*One night,* as we were sitting outside with Alexi's friends listening to a band at the neighboring bar, I noticed a woman with thick, dark hair and come-hither eyes glancing over at Alexi. Over the course of my life I'd developed an uncanny knack for ranking myself in regard to the other women in proximity, a practical response to the worldview instilled by the magazines I read as a kid, which boiled down to something like, "If you're not attractive, no one will want you." All was well if I stacked up to be the prettiest or the smartest or the wittiest. But if someone else placed higher, I'd vex myself, thinking it inevitable that whoever I was with would want to trade up. To be perfectly honest, I played that way too. It's how I thought the world worked.

The night air was as soothing and rich as a cup of Greek coffee, and the waves lapped the shore just a block away. Yet I was obsessed with monitoring how much attention Alexi was giving the raven-haired vixen beside us. I was sure that the conversations he was having with his friends—in Greek—were about her.

A half hour into the set, Alexi got up, grabbed a stack of plates, and whispered something into the lead singer's ear. Then he yelled, "*Opa!*" and sent one plate after another crashing to the ground.

Convinced that he was showing off for the Greek woman, I stomped off to the beach in tears. How could he? Why hadn't he just let me go back to my family, rather than convince me to stay and then flirt with someone else right in front of me?

I trudged through the soft sand and sat on a log near the water-line, hugging my knees to my chest. Moonlight gilded the waves as I tried to dispassionately assess the situation. I wasn't unattractive; I was a bit plump for my average height, with long reddish-brown hair streaked blond by the sun and eyes that defied neat classification between blue, green, or gray. But I wasn't a black-haired bomb-shell. No question, the prettier girl had won.

A few minutes later I heard the swish of sand. "Why did you run away?" Alexi asked, with that grand flourish of the arms that Greek men make.

"Because you were showing off for that woman!"

He scrunched up his eyes. "What woman?"

"The Greek woman, the one you were flirting with when you threw the plates!"

Alexi's face softened, and he nodded. The log jiggled slightly as he sat down beside me. I tried to scoot away, but he leaned close to my ear. "It is Greek custom," he whispered, "to break plates when requesting a song from a band, as a sort of payment." He waited until I met his eyes. "I asked them to play that song for you, Lia," he said. "It was a love song."

I looked out to sea again, feeling hollow. Was it really possible that he didn't want to trade up to the prettier girl? That he was happy just with me? Alexi had just given me a gift and, rashly, from my own distorted reality, I took it and smashed that special moment to pieces. Even worse, I had no one to blame but myself.

*One day* not long into summer, Spiros had a heart attack. I will never forget being in the hospital room with him while Alexi and his mother discussed his condition with the doctor in the hallway. Spiros and I gripped each other's hands and through both our tears I saw his fear and willed him comfort with all the oomph I could muster. His hands tightened on mine, and his eyes softened. I could see that it had gotten through. Neither of us spoke the other's language, yet it was one of the clearest, most vulnerable expressions of love I'd ever encountered.

Once Spiros got home from the hospital, I was put in charge of taking care of him. We would sit in the living room on the chintz sofa with a deck of cards laid out on the lacquered wood coffee table in front of us. Spiros would grunt phrases emphatically in Greek and then motion for me to pick up the cards. I never knew what game we were playing or how to play it, but I always enjoyed seeing how happy Spiros was when he won, which he did every time, since he alone knew the objective of the game.

That was how he taught me numbers. He taught me vocabulary in the kitchen.

One day, he boiled potatoes on the two-burner stove. *"Sompa!"* Spiros smacked the stove as he took the pot off the burner and drained the potatoes in the sink. Then he swiveled to set the pot on the weathered wooden dining table. *"Trapezi!"*

The potatoes were encased in a cloud of steam. He picked one up to peel it without the slightest flinch, then smashed cloves of garlic with the palm of his hand and placed them in the giant mortar and pestle with the potatoes. Next he pounded the mixture, adding spirals of green-yellow olive oil from the ouzo bottle that sat next to the stove. Once it became a paste, he added more potato and more garlic and more oil. The fragrance was so strong it was sticky and almost sweet.

When Spiros wasn't looking, I dragged my finger through the fluffy mass and brought it to my lips. It felt like I'd put on wasabi lipstick. My lips, my tongue, the insides of my cheeks all burned madly. I fanned my mouth and made funny puffing sounds, which sent Spiros into a fit of chortling. I never in a million years would have thought that that kind of chile-hot heat could come from garlic, which, in my experience, consisted of benign, mushy, pale yellow nuggets.

*One week* in late July I noticed whole lambs suspended from high hooks on the side of the road and wondered aloud to Alexi what they were doing there. He grinned. "They're for the festival of Panteleimon. You'll see tonight."

That evening, strings of bare lightbulbs crisscrossed the plane trees that lined the village plaza, and long, wooden tables spilled out onto the road. The air was filled with a seductive scent of live coals and roasted meat. Alexi sat me down at one of the benches and walked toward a cluster of people all holding white squares of butcher paper. I heard a loud *whack!* and, in unison, the crowd lifted the papers to shield their faces from the juice flying over their heads. I surmised the lambs were being carved.

Alexi came back to the table a few minutes later with a neatly wrapped parcel. As he unfolded the paper square, the meaty steam that came from the glistening strands made my mouth water. I picked off a piece and reveled at how the meat—tender and smoky—melted on my tongue. Just a year before I would have recoiled at the thought of eating part of a lamb taken off a carcass still within eyeshot. Now it seemed reverent, almost holy.

The following day, Mama took the family to church, as one did on Corfu, which was up a steep flight of stone stairs and surrounded by olive groves. At the entrance to the church, Mama crossed herself in the orthodox way, from right to left, which I'd seen her do each time we passed a graveyard, or when certain people—presumably those who had passed away—were mentioned. She lit a candle and propped it up in a little box of sand, then motioned for me to do the same.

Once inside we slid into a pew. The light was dim. Incense hung thick as velvet drapes, and faded golden icons stared out with blank expressions. I never knew when to close my eyes or cross myself, and if so which way. I felt awkward and out of place, just as I had at church in my youth.

At age four, I had a persistent, soul-wrenching desire to grasp what eternity was and what life would be like after death, prompted by the stripes of train tracks on my pajamas that seemed to make the train go on forever and ever and ever. A year or so later I awoke out of—or into—a dream and saw six figures in flowing white robes standing peacefully around my bed looking down at me. I was terrified. When I finally squeaked out enough sound to call my mom, they remained, even as she stood in the doorway urging me to go back to sleep. I knew, somehow, that those figures were protecting me, and in the years after I came to think of them as my guardians. Whether they were real angels or not I still couldn't say, but in those experiences God had felt real—sometimes big and comforting like a hug from my father and sometimes scary, like standing at the edge of a high dive, stomach tingling.

My early experiences with church had none of that mystery, none of that authenticity. I was always on the outside of the hardbaked cliques, never on the right page, and feeling like everyone was speaking (or snickering) in a language I didn't understand. Years later in that tiny Greek chapel, my stomach tingled with those same hungry butterflies, feeling like everyone could see that I was a fake and didn't belong.

*Life as* usual resumed on Monday—breakfast, cards, cooking, eating. But on Wednesday night our world turned on its ear once again when Spiros suffered a second heart attack and was flown to Athens with Mama.

With both of them gone, the family needed me to help Alexi's sister, Matina, at the souvlaki stand. We prepped in the morning, sitting on overturned buckets peeling potatoes, cutting the pork into cubes for the marinade, and fitting chickens onto the rotisserie. Then just after noon, a line would form out the door for the chicken; its luscious, lemony scent would draw people like the Pied

Piper all the way from the beach. Alexi would join us in the after-noon, grilling souvlaki skewers while I brushed pitas with olive oil and toasted them on the griddle beside him.

One day after I'd been on Corfu for a couple of months, Alexi and I were having lunch at home alone. He looked at me and said, "You know I have my life here."

"I know," I said. And I did. In addition to owning the souvlaki stand, Alexi and Matina's husband, Yannis, owned a successful car electronics shop in the main town on Corfu. Alexi was, in many ways, the head of his clan and, according to Matina, one of the most sought-after bachelors on the island.

"I have my life here," Alexi repeated, "and I didn't think I had room for anything else." He reached over and took my hand. "But now I can't imagine living without you here."

My heart quickened, wondering if he would say the words. Then, without a ring, without any sort of pomp and circumstance, he did.

"Will you marry me?"

I caught my breath and looked down at the table, my free hand fidgeting in my lap. I wanted to say yes. Truth be told, at that moment I couldn't imagine another plausible future that I'd even want to entertain. Yet some dormant part of me, like a fossil emerging from the silt of years upon years of advice and caution instilled by my parents, came barreling in with the voice of reason. And, strangely enough, I listened.

"I want to," I told Alexi. "I really do. It's just that I don't even know if I can comprehend what 'marriage' means right now." I looked up, expecting to see disappointment on Alexi's face, but he was still smiling. "I'm only twenty, and I've got one more year left to go in school. I'd hate to throw that away when I'm so close."

Alexi stroked my cheek. "I'll wait, then."

As the weeks wore on, the idea of staying on Corfu and settling into the Kourtesi family felt more and more like a reality. I took on odd jobs, creating menus, painting signs, and pondering what kind of career I could build on the island. My *maybe* turned into a de facto *yes* as Alexi and I began to plan for the future. I would go back to finish school and when I came to Corfu the following summer, we would open our own restaurant. Alexi had even begun negotiating for the space.

One night, after closing the souvlaki stand just after midnight, Alexi and I drove to his friend Mihalis's house for dinner. He and his wife ushered us out onto a wide terrace where Alexi's friends and their children were sitting around the table. The air smelled of salt, and the thump of the waves against the bluffs below punctuated the conversation.

As smoky fish roe dip, feta, and Greek salad were passed, I could barely make out individual conversations over the general din, which consisted of both laughter and, I could tell from the cadence alone, well-worn jibes slung back and forth at one another. I admit to being in awe of the women—beautiful, thin, and totally unself-conscious—who were eating feta without batting an eye and dousing their salads with olive oil as if it weren't out to give them thunder thighs.

Just when I was starting to feel like an interloper—everyone was speaking very rapid Greek—Mihalis came out with a sizzling cauldron. My eyes began watering and I sneezed. Everyone turned to look at me mischievously, and I feared I'd failed to cross myself properly. Mihalis's wife ladled out the *bourdetto*, a rich and spicy Venetian fish stew that was a hallmark of Corfu, and I took a bite. My eyes bulged from what felt like the heat of a million chile peppers.

"I have put much cayenne pepper in this *bourdetto*, my dear,"

Mihalis chimed. There was a chuckle at the end of the table, and Mihalis's smile widened. "Here on Corfu we have a saying that pepper makes babies."

The snickers intensified, and my defenses deployed, but my curiosity got the best of me. "How's that?" I asked, wiping my nose.

"You eat pepper, you drink wine, you make babies," he answered, and the table erupted in laughter. As I looked around at the faces of the people raising toasts in our direction and saw Alexi beaming at me, I realized they weren't belittling me—they were welcoming me. This meal was a rite of passage. In their special way Alexi's friends were inviting me not just to the table, but into their lives, their families, their future.

*The end* of August drew near, and I left for the States for my cousin's wedding and to finish my senior year of college. As the plane lifted up and over the cobalt-blue Ionian Sea, I felt strangely and uncomfortably uprooted, and dubious about returning to America.

I'd been raised to believe that love and attention were hitched precariously to appearance and achievement. Yet the Kourtesis taught me that I could be loved for being compassionate, imaginative, and outspoken. In America, I fought with food, while in Greece I saw food and joy stitched together as natural companions, like garlic and olive oil.

At the time, though, those fledgling thoughts were only cloudy observations, like little specks in a bucket of mud. Little did I know they were settling deep into my soul, the seeds of whom I would become.

⟡

# SKORDALIA

*Skordalia will always remind me of cooking with Spiros. You can serve it as the Greeks do, as a sort of dip for Mama's Salt Cod Fritters from Chapter 16, or as a pungent, garlicky spin on mashed potatoes. Use a nice, big mortar and pestle that will hold at least 4 cups.*

Sea salt
1$\frac{1}{2}$ pounds Yukon Gold potatoes, peeled
    and cut into 1$\frac{1}{2}$-inch chunks
5 or 6 garlic cloves (depending on how
    spicy you'd like it), smashed
$\frac{1}{2}$ cup extra virgin olive oil
Freshly ground black pepper

Bring a medium pot of salted water to a boil. Boil the potatoes for 10 minutes, until a fork easily pierces a chunk. Drain well.

Meanwhile, using a mortar and pestle, pound the garlic to a paste with a pinch of salt. Add the potato pieces, one by one, mashing each until it turns to a paste, drizzling in a bit of oil after every few pieces. Add salt and pepper to taste, scrape into a bowl, and serve.

MAKES 2 CUPS / SERVES 4

# CHAPTER 2

# BREAD AND WINE

AUGUST 1991

The day after I returned from Greece to my parents' home in Connecticut, my mom took me shopping at Stew Leonard's, an iconic grocery store that was on her "must see" list for visitors. Picture Costco meets Disney.

Inside, the floor plan was like a maze. You couldn't simply go to the aisle you were looking for, you had to wind through the whole warehouse of a store, which was a good twenty- to thirty-minute affair, depending on foot traffic.

That day, I wove past the bakers in their hairnets and came to an aisle of hundreds upon hundreds of stacked cartons, all of them filled with pristine white eggs. While I stood stupefied by the sheer volume, a kid to my right pushed a big red button and a fake chicken with a banjo popped out above the cartons and, with a trio of chicks, sang a bluegrass ditty.

"Aren't you glad to be home?" Mom squeezed my shoulder.

I didn't tell her, but the truth was, I was horrified.

Now that I had eaten eggs that were freshly plucked from beneath real, non-bluegrass-singing hens on Corfu, this display—

everything about this place—seemed ghastly. It was as if these
had been neutered of everything that eggs could and should be,
therefore needed a bluegrass band to either elevate their valu
distract you from what was lacking.

A bit farther on, we came to the chicken aisle. Cases a good thi
feet long were filled with meat in cellophane-wrapped foam tra
plump, uniform pink shapes that were in no way similar to th
chickens they once were. Trays of lamb chops were given the sam
treatment in the next aisle, bearing no resemblance whatsoever to
the lambs at the village festival on Corfu.

The first time I'd seen whole animal carcasses—rabbits and
ducks in France—I was disgusted. It felt almost too raw, so to
speak, in the sense that it was in the form of the animal itself. Before that, the closest I'd come to seeing a whole slaughtered animal
was a drumstick.

But now, the opposite was true. Staring at these plastic-wrapped
trays of sanitized animal parts—parts that had long since left their
whole without a trace—it felt disrespectful to proffer these pieces
without acknowledging the animals from which they came. I hurried through the aisles, sick to my stomach, and left the store.

*Despite my* phobia over the summer that feta and olive oil and fatty
meats and egg yolks would turn me into the Michelin woman,
I'd actually lost weight in Greece. Yet I fell right back into my old
guilt-deprivation eating cycle when I returned to school in New
Orleans—caught between Lucky Dogs and steamed broccoli—
and gained the weight right back. By that time, my body had begun
to hurt too. Yes, I was living like a college kid—staying up way too
late and making poor decisions about what I was consuming—yet

I always seemed to pay a much higher price than my friends. I can almost guarantee that the other people vying for bar stools weren't doing it because it hurt too much to stand. I didn't understand what was happening to me, and I didn't talk about it. I just tried to grin and keep up.

Alexi and I remained engaged throughout my senior year. He would call me near the end of his workday to wake me up, and I would call him after midnight just as he was starting his day. We would share what was going on in each other's lives, before the conversation turned to discussing what our collective life would look like when we were together again.

I felt suspended between two worlds. Part of me was a woman engaged to a Greek man, preparing to wrap up school and start my life on Corfu. This reality made the rituals of my sorority—let alone the letters on my shirt—feel absurd, as surreal and removed as the chicken parts in cellophane. But another part of me was an American college student, winning awards for my writing, and being told by teachers and counselors (and parents) that I'd be crazy to throw away what lay ahead in America to go back to Corfu. Finally, five days before graduation, I decided that I couldn't pass up the reality of a future ripe with opportunity and called Alexi to break off the engagement.

At first, it was like a shock wave hit both of our lives, knocking out the transmission of the future we had so clearly envisioned together. We both hurt. I'll confess to several middle-of-the-night calls full of tears and whispered s'agapo (Greek for "I love you"). Yet in a way, Alexi understood and appreciated the forces that were pulling me away even better than I did.

After graduation I moved home to Connecticut with my parents. The breakup had left me not only with a broken heart but also with

no idea what to pursue for a career. So I found a summer internship in Manhattan at a PR firm focused on travel—I knew for sure I loved to travel—and moved from there to a short stint as a lowly grunt at a prestigious PR firm that yielded only one good thing: Julie.

Julie worked upstairs and dealt with celebrities and socialites and club openings and such. I worked downstairs on real estate accounts. My favorite outfit of that period was a black miniskirt and a well-worn army green Sorbonne T-shirt that, I thought, went great with the army-green portion of the plaid in my unwrinkle-able plaid blazer. Julie, on the other hand, with her pretty face and perky haircut, would march down the spiral staircase looking like she was born wearing a suit and pumps. Suffice it to say our paths didn't cross much.

But one warm night in May, as a result of the rising tensions between the African American and Jewish communities after the Crown Heights riots, Julie and I found ourselves working side by side at an event in Harlem for the release of *The Liberators*, a book about an African American platoon liberating the last Jews from concentration camps at the end of World War II. The organizers had assembled the survivors of both groups to meet onstage, along with luminaries such as Jesse Jackson and Malcolm X's widow, Betty Shabazz. History was both healed and made that night as men from the 761st—the first African American tank battalion in World War II—met the Jewish men and women they had liberated from concentration camps in 1945, and Julie and I stood in the back of the dark auditorium holding hands and bawling like babies.

Most of my friendships up to that point had felt a bit like my early experiences in church: like I didn't belong when I was being myself. I'd comment on how beautiful the light was on the river and people would roll their eyes with a collective "whatever." I'd probe into the deeper emotions and questions of life and would get put down. But in Julie, I found a soul mate, someone with whom it was safe to see the beauty in things.


*A couple* of months later, Julie and I moved into a snug little apartment on the corner of Mott and Houston on the edge of SoHo and the East Village. On Saturday mornings, we'd throw on baseball caps, turn the collars of our fleeces up against the morning chill, and walk north on Broadway to the Union Square Greenmarket just as the city was waking up. My favorite days were on the cusp of summer and fall, when the light had shifted and the air was as crisp as a Granny Smith.

As we drew closer to the market, the faint scent of wood smoke would be replaced by that of mulled cider, and we'd see the pointed tops of the tented stalls that always made me think of Camelot. We'd sidle up to tables laden with plump New Jersey tomatoes, basil so fragrant that my shirt would smell like it all day, and first-of-the-season apples from the Hudson Valley. We'd always buy too much, and the handles of the plastic bags would cut into our fingers as we walked home.

Some nights, I'd cook in our minuscule kitchen. I still wasn't keen on many veggies but had broadened my repertoire beyond raw carrots and cucumbers to tomatoes (how could I not fall in love with tomatoes in Greece?) and zucchini. Sautéed zucchini with onions and thyme over rice was my specialty, and we'd eat at the little table we'd salvaged from the street and painted a merry Southwestern pattern of blue, red, yellow, and green. But truth be told, like all good New Yorkers, we ate out most nights.

We'd walk past the music clubs on Bleecker Street to John's Pizzeria, where coal-fired ovens made the chewy-crisp crust blistered and black in places. Or we'd head a block up Lafayette to Noho Star for its chicken in lettuce cups and awesome people-watching out the walls of funky pane glass. On warm nights, if we were feeling flush, we'd walk down Mulberry to the cheery red-linen tables on the sidewalk in front of Pellegrino's in Little Italy. We'd order penne with vodka sauce and a bottle of red wine from the real Italian waiters and feel grown up and sophisticated. And many nights, we'd stay out too late at Bleecker Street Bar, where Julie and I would win game after game of pool; there were nights when we wouldn't pay for a beer or a game ourselves all night. Most of my meals, though, consisted of fast food of some sort—Chinese takeout, McDonald's, deli buffets—or the fat-free snack foods I thought so virtuous that I'd often make meals out of them: pretzels, bagels, SnackWell's cookies.

Every couple of months Julie's dad, Ed, would come to town. Ed was a restaurateur in Denver with a wide, white smile who would sweep us up out of our entry-level-salary lives and into the world of glitzy, glamorous Manhattan. He'd take us to Broadway shows and then to swank restaurants like Frankie and Johnnie's or The Palm for dinners that would last well past midnight.

Ed wasn't a conversationalist. He was an observer. I loved watching him watch a room; he was always analyzing, always noticing, always learning. When we met him in the morning for breakfast, he often had tales of middle-of-the-night cab rides to the far reaches of the boroughs to seek out the best falafel, ribs, marinara sauce, whatever it might be that a bellhop or a bank teller or a checker at a drugstore had told him about.

Ed had an insatiable hunger for life that I related to. When I went to a street fair, I wanted to sample *everything*. When dinner was over, I wanted to go out for dessert. If we won a game of pool, I wanted to stay for one more. There was always something else just about to happen, if I stuck it out long enough.

This voraciousness for experience showed in the *way* I ate too. I know women who can polish off an entire three-course meal (with wine) and still have lipstick on (they tend also to be able to wear white pants in New York City without getting a smudge). I am not like that. I'm the one who leaves dots of tomato sauce and red wine on white tablecloths. I'm the one who leans on the table with her elbows when she's making a point. I'm the one who picks up the chicken thighs with her fingers and doesn't even attempt to be dainty as she tears the meat from the bones with her teeth. I simply have a hard time reining myself in at the table.

Later, much later, I was at a food conference at the Culinary Institute of America in California's Napa Valley where one of the food stations was serving suckling pig. I'd picked up the come-hither scent from across the room and made a beeline to the booth. I took the piece proffered to me and stood there biting through the crackly skin like a dog shaking a rabbit. I swooned over the savory juices (I really did); I licked my fingers. Someone walked by and I heard them say, "Now *that's* a woman who can eat." Ironically, my name tag read COOKING LIGHT CONTRIBUTOR.

*But the* most significant meal of my life during that time—in my whole life, really—didn't involve suckling pig or a fancy restaurant. In fact, it didn't even happen at a table. It was simply a cube of bread and a little cup of grape juice.

Throughout college, in addition to the growing physical pain and discomfort I was experiencing, I had battled panic attacks that felt like a gaping maw of chaos opening up inside me and threatening to erase my existence on the planet. They'd only gotten worse since I'd moved to New York. I tried journaling, I tried drinking, I tried staying up all night, but nothing really helped.

Then I began reading Shakti Gawain's book *Living in the Light*. For the first time, I was given a name for that "something deeper" I'd felt as a child: intuition. Gawain defines intuition as "a universal, intelligent life force that exists within everyone and everything. It resides within each one of us as a deep wisdom, an inner knowing."

I wholeheartedly embraced the quest to tune into my intuition, often reading my New Age books on one end of the couch while Julie did a Bible study on the other. We'd share insights. We'd talk about how we wanted to grow. We each respected the other's quest.

Julie had begun going to a church on the Upper East Side where the sanctuary had an Art-Deco-meets-Masonic-Temple-meets-ancient-Bethlehem feel to it. The pastor, Keith, was a friend's brother, and after we all joined a wine club together, I started going to church too, although I had no intention of actually becoming religious. At church, each time Keith broke the bread to serve communion, I would pass. He was clear that communion was just for those who believed, and I was clear that I didn't fall into that camp.

I didn't have an agenda when I started going to church with Julie. It was a diverse, quirky group of people (the woman who was Ariel's voice in *The Little Mermaid* used to sit next to us from time to time, and it was a *trip* hearing her sing), and Keith was an intelligent, engaging speaker and I simply liked being there. But I started to notice a calm when I was there that didn't exist in other parts of my life, a peace like I'd felt on that mountaintop in Greece. It was like the antithesis of the incessant, driving force of more, more, more that kept me in a state of perpetual, anxious motion.

One Sunday, when people started to rise and walk toward the front for communion, I suddenly felt a palpable nudge, and with it, a directive.

*Get up. Go to the front and be fed.*

I was shocked. Julie scooted toward the edge of the pew as people began moving out to the aisle, and this time, rather than staying put and having people work their way around me as I gave an awkward smile, I scooted too. It wasn't like a switch had flipped and I suddenly believed all that communion symbolized. It just felt more right to get up and take communion than it did to stay seated and pass.

I joined the line behind Julie in one of the two aisles that led to the front. But as the line moved toward the woman holding the basket of bread at the front of the church, I began to waver.

I got to the front, and the woman handed me a little cube of bread and a plastic thimble of grape juice. Behind her, flanged torchlike lights flanked the altar and made me think of Indiana Jones.

"This is the body and blood of Christ, take it in remembrance of Him."

Heavy doubts had crept in at the last moment, but there was a line behind me; there was no going back. I ate the bread. I drank the juice. And nothing could have prepared me for the feeling that followed.

I felt filled with light, like the bread and juice were leaving neon streaks of pure love in their wake as they worked their way through my body. I didn't know what to make of it in that moment, but something happened that day. The impermeable coating of skepticism that sheathed those early seeds of mystical faith was beginning to soften.

Little did I know how sustaining that simple meal would be. My path in life would lead me to other continents and across the country. It would have me cooking beside famous chefs and cooked for by famous chefs. Yet the bread and the wine (albeit grape juice) I was introduced to that morning would be the meal I would come back to again and again to nourish my soul and satiate the hunger.

❧

## SAUTÉED ZUCCHINI WITH ONIONS AND THYME

*This was my go-to "healthy" dish when Julie and I lived together in Manhattan. Back then, I was terrified of fat. I would heat the veggies in a pan with no oil so I would feel virtuous. But then I discovered the effect caramelization has on veggies (and the effect olive oil has on our bodies) and reengineered this dish to be not only virtuous but delicious. Serve this as a main course over quinoa or red rice, as a side dish, or any number of ways as a component . . . tossed with pasta, tucked into a taco, or folded into an omelet, for instance.*

3 tablespoons extra virgin olive oil

1$^1/_2$ pounds zucchini (or other summer
    squash), cut into 1-inch pieces

5 garlic cloves, thinly sliced

1 medium onion, chopped
3 thyme sprigs
Sea salt and freshly ground black pepper

Heat a large sauté pan with steep sides over medium heat and add the olive oil. When the oil is hot, add the zucchini, garlic, onion, and thyme to the pan, and toss to coat with the oil. Sprinkle with salt and pepper and toss to coat again. Cover and cook for 15 minutes, stirring occasionally, until the zucchini begins to soften.

Remove the cover, turn the heat up to medium-high, and continue cooking for another 10 to 15 minutes, scraping the bottom of the pan and turning the zucchini over on itself, folding the caramelized bits in, until the zucchini is almost completely broken down. Remove the thyme sprigs and serve.

SERVES 4

# CHAPTER 3

# HUNGRY FOR WHAT?

DECEMBER 1995

P oppy plain with a schmear, please," I said to the woman behind the Zaro's counter. "And a coffee, black." Spears of morning light hung suspended in the dust circling above the crowds at Grand Central Station and the air smelled of metal and humanity. I was in awe of that place; each time I walked through it—which was often—I felt like I had entered into a living, breathing piece of history.

I took the bag and cup from across the counter and threaded my way through the crowds to the platform and onto the train bound for Connecticut. I was headed to my family's house for New Year's Eve. We'd started a tradition the previous year of cooking a bunch of different homemade pastas, finishing with dessert at midnight. It had become a tradition because we'd all had so much fun planning, cooking, goading each other, and eating that we'd decided to make a tradition out of it.

I tore off a hunk of bagel, ripping it open like a book, and then folded the outsides into the middle; I liked tasting the soft innards and then having the resistance of the crust kick in. The train chugged through the dark tunnel, and the blackness outside the window was a canvas to my thoughts. I'd hopscotched from the PR firm Julie and I had met at, to a stint as a music publicist, to a job as a corporate proposal writer for a travel company (and I was cultivating a freelance writing career in my free time, in the wee hours of the night). A few nights earlier, I'd stayed late at the office to get a proposal done—which was not all that unusual. The next morning my boss grinned ear to ear as he squeezed my shoulder. "This girl is *hungry*," he'd said, clearly meaning it as a compliment. But it had planted a question in my head that stuck like the chorus of an '80s tune as the train rolled out of Manhattan.

*Hungry for what?*

Outside the window, graffiti-covered walls and a solid mass of brick and cement eventually gave way to more and more space. Green parks and bare trees that looked like charcoal drawings against the chalk-white sky blurred by, punctuated by church steeples. An hour later, the train slowed and the conductor called, "Westport, next stop." I grabbed my bag and stepped off, scanning the lot for Dad's blue Taurus under the dim streetlights.

Frozen snow crackled beneath my boots as I wove my way toward the car. Dad tucked my bag into the trunk and pulled me into a hug, smelling like flannel and fireplace and warmth.

"Hi, sweet pea," he said. "I'm glad you came."

"Are you kidding?" I said. "I wouldn't miss your fettuccine Bolognese for the world."

He chuckled as we climbed into the car. "What do you have in mind for yours?"

"I'm doing crab ravioli in a lemon butter sauce."

"That sounds fancy."

"I saw a recipe for ricotta ravioli in *Bon Appétit* and thought I'd add some crab to it to make it New Year's Eve–worthy."

"You're going for the win, aren't you?" Dad said.

"Always."

The next afternoon my brother, Russ, and I went out to provision and when we returned, there was a crackling fire in the kitchen fireplace and Louis Armstrong on the stereo. Dad had clamped the pasta maker to the kitchen counter, and Mom had the food processor and all the ingredients out and ready to go.

"It smells good," I said, dipping my finger into the pot of simmering Bolognese sauce. Dad smacked my hand away.

"No tastes for the competition."

"Fine," I said. "Russ and I will just start on the winning entry, then."

We started out by pulsing flour and eggs with a touch of oil in the food processor until it came together into a ball. Then we let the dough rest while we mixed together the filling.

"Do you think that's enough zest?" Russ asked.

I took a taste of the ricotta. "Let's add the full lemon."

We mixed the lemon zest with the ricotta and big hunks of crabmeat. Then we cut the pasta dough into small, tennis-ball-sized chunks and, one by one, fed them through the pasta maker, first several times on the widest setting to knead the dough a final time, and then gradually on thinner and thinner settings.

"I'll pull it through," Russ said, adjusting his hands to catch the flattened sheet as it came through the rollers. "You just keep feeding it."

"I'll help stuff," Mom said.

"Traitor," Dad mumbled under his breath.

"Honey, you do all the work yourself when you're making Bolognese," Mom said. "There's nothing left for me to do!"

"Fair enough," Dad conceded.

We sprinkled the counter with flour and set down a thin sheet of dough—I could just see the outline of my hand through it. Then I dotted the top with mounds of the filling and we draped another sheet over the top. Mom and Russ pressed around the filling mounds to seal the edges of the ravioli as I began on another sheet. Then we used a cookie cutter to cut out each of the ravioli and placed them on a floured piece of parchment.

By the time we rang in midnight we were as stuffed as the ravioli ourselves. The puffy ravioli in its lemony butter sauce—to which I'd added a bit of saffron—was at the opposite end of the flavor spectrum from Dad's Bolognese, which made it all too easy to go back and forth from one to the other, eating far too much of both.

Heading back on the train the next day, satiated and content from being with my family, I thought again about the question I'd come with.

I'd discovered something in the months since taking communion for the first time. Nothing—not Dad's Bolognese or my crab ravioli, not Ed's over-the-top outings or even getting my first article published—made me feel as satiated and complete as that simple "meal" of bread and wine a few months earlier. I wasn't ready to go all Billy Graham, but I did have some questions I wanted answered.

Which was what led me to Pastor Keith's office a few days later.

*"I've been* thinking," I said to Keith, unwinding my scarf and taking a seat.

"Uh-oh."

"No, really. I've been thinking. I definitely feel drawn toward something deeper. The whole intuition thing." I cocked my head to think. "But I feel like even though it's within me, it's also other than me, beyond me. Isn't that the same thing you're talking about with Christianity?"

We'd been around a lot of bushes over the course of several months, concerning the universe and God and such, but not that particular bush.

"In a way, yes. And in a way, no." Keith leaned forward and rested his elbows on his knees. "We all feel the pull of God, Lia—He designed us with a homing device in our souls—and some who hear Him seek Him. But only Christianity proposes that He loves us enough to seek *us* out."

"What do you mean, seek us out?"

"Let me start with what is not so special about Christianity: the concept of a sacrifice to bridge the gap between God's perfection and our imperfections. Every major religion addresses that divide with some sort of sacrifice, usually an animal or a fast, and the ritual has to be repeated over time to keep the slate clean, so to speak."

I was tracking with him so far.

"What's different about Christianity is that we believe God loves us so much that He sent *Himself* to be the sacrifice, so that anyone who believes could be with Him . . . in a living, present relationship with Him."

Keith sat back in his chair and tented his fingers. We were both silent for a long while.

"Would you say you believe in God, Lia?" Keith asked.

I paused only a moment; I knew the answer to that one. "Yes, I do. I believe God is at the other end of the intuition feedback loop. It feels too personal to me to be just a universal force."

"And what is God saying to you right now?"

I looked at my reflection in the pane of the window and let that question sink in, feeling the resistance mount. I knew the answer to the question, I just wasn't ready to admit it yet. I was a python cowboy boot kind of girl, not a patent leather Mary Jane kind. I was strong-willed, strong-minded, and I swore like a sailor; I liked who I was and didn't want to change.

But I'd had a dream just a few days earlier that had left a residual trace like incense leaves in a room. It evoked those deep, mystical experiences of my childhood in a way that hadn't happened since. My grandpa, who had passed away a year earlier, had a firm, quiet faith that I'd always admired yet never understood, and in the dream he told me that Jesus was the real deal. There with Keith, as I tuned in to that still, small voice, it was echoing the message of that dream.

I looked up and the words came out in a whisper. "God's telling me to believe."

A chorus of voices erupted in my head. *Your friends—and your father—are going to think you're nuts. . . . This is just a phase, you'll be over it in a week. . . . What are you thinking? . . . You never stick to anything, Lia. What makes you think this will be different?*

I didn't have answers to any of those objections. I only had the answer to what I sensed God was telling me to do—and had been leading me toward for some time. So I bowed my head and said yes.

*Just over* a month later, amid this maelstrom of shifting careers and budding faith, I met Christopher. Peter, a mutual friend of ours, had organized a group dinner—aka a thinly disguised blind date— while Christopher, who lived in California, was on a business trip in New York. The problem was, Peter had neglected to tell Christopher the setup part of the plan, so Christopher showed up with a date of his own.

My first impression was mixed. Christopher was tall and well built with thick, close-cropped brown hair, but I took his argyle cardigan vest as a sign of stuffiness until I noticed he was wearing purple Doc Martens. What got me from the get-go, though, were his eyes. I knew from Peter that Christopher had had a rough childhood, yet the eyes that came with that argyle vest and purple Doc Martens were lucid, intense, and *joyful*.

During a samba set at Lola's, Peter kept Christopher's date dancing while Christopher and I oohed and ahhed over the coconut-crusted shrimp and bantered about spirituality. He lived in California and was deep into all things New Age, and I was comfortable with the subject, having taken my circuitous route to Christianity through the same terrain.

But I was growing more and more restless with the conversation. As a new believer, I was bursting. Not with the fervor of recruiting new converts but with the desire to share what had been happening to me since saying yes. After a couple of glasses of wine, I squinted across the table. "I just became a Christian. What do you think of that?"

Christopher's eyes went wide. I was so surprised it had slipped out that I clapped my hands over my mouth. The samba drums throbbed in my ears and I felt dizzy with embarrassment. *He thinks I'm a freak*, I thought. *And he's going to tell Peter too.* But to my surprise, Christopher's gorgeous aquamarine eyes became blurry with tears.

He leaned toward me, and it felt like the whole world had been drawn into the flicker of candlelight that enveloped the two of us. "I've been going to church a lot lately," he said. "And all I can do is sit in the back and cry. Something is tugging at me, and I don't know what to do about it." I nodded wildly and reached across the table to take his hand.

"That's how I felt too. Intuition really made sense to me, but at some point I thought, 'It's not just me I'm hearing.' There's more there . . . and I'm pretty sure it's God."

"I totally agree." Christopher shook his head. "But I just can't buy into the whole Jesus thing."

"I didn't either. At first." I took a sip of wine and tried to formulate sentences out of the impressions and epiphanies I'd been storing up since that seed had burst open and I'd said yes. "I didn't really think it would stick when I said I believed, but now it—God and, and Jesus—feels like the most real part of my life."

"How?" Christopher looked at me like I was dangling a key to a treasure box in front of him.

"I don't know how to explain it," I said. How does one explain the experience of being rebuilt from the inside out?

The morning after I'd prayed with Keith—after I'd said my yes—I'd awoken to find that the screeching chaos that had kept me up every night and greeted me every morning was no longer there. Instead, there was peace. At work, I'd noticed how the "colorful language" that had peppered my speech for so many years—and that I'd defended so ardently as being a part of me—suddenly felt like a foreign body; like I was forcing words that just didn't belong. The big wow for me wasn't that I'd stopped swearing in the space of a few hours, it was that I didn't have any desire to curse. No one could have coerced me to do that; that was something supernatural.

A thought occurred to me and I poked a fork at Christopher. "Have you ever heard of Michelangelo's unfinished slaves?" He shook his head. "I learned about them when I studied art history in

Paris. They're these exquisite, writhing figures coming out of massive blocks of raw marble, but they're unfinished. They're trapped in the rock. Michelangelo didn't see sculpting as creating a figure so much as liberating what's already there."

"So how does that apply to you becoming a believer?"

I shook my head. "I don't really know how to explain, but it's the best analogy I can find. I used to think that becoming a Christian meant becoming a cookie-cutter cutout with good manners and a lot of cable-knit cardigans. But I had it totally wrong. I'm realizing that what God really wants is for me to hand *Him* the chisel and say, 'Have at it,' so He can liberate *me*."

I looked into the candle's flame and we sat in silence. "It's terrifying at times—like being made into an entirely new person—but it's also freeing." I chuckled. "And definitely humbling. I feel like I'm walking down Park Avenue in a bikini. And I know it's not me doing all that."

"You're feeling born again," Christopher said, without a trace of teasing.

I bristled at the phrase at first but then realized how well it fit. "Yes, I guess so."

Christopher dropped his head, and when he looked up his face was peaceful and his eyes sparkled in the candlelight. He squeezed my hand tight. "Would you believe that I prayed this morning for an angel to show me a church to go to in New York?"

With everything that had happened in the past six weeks or so, that didn't surprise me at all. So I took Christopher to church with me the following Sunday. And I married him, in that same church, the next year.

# CRAB RAVIOLI IN SAFFRON LEMON BUTTER SAUCE

*There's no question, making fresh pasta is an undertaking. But it's a fun activity for an event like New Year's Eve, where you can get multiple people involved. You get camaraderie and collaboration while cooking with the added payoff of a fantastic meal.*

### RICOTTA FILLING

1 cup fresh ricotta cheese

1 cup lump crabmeat

Zest of 1 lemon

Sea salt and freshly ground black pepper

### RAVIOLI DOUGH

$1\frac{1}{4}$ cups all-purpose flour

$\frac{1}{4}$ cup pastry flour

2 large eggs

1 tablespoon extra virgin olive oil

1 egg, beaten with 2 tablespoons water (for egg wash)

### SAFFRON LEMON BUTTER SAUCE

Pinch of saffron

2 tablespoons hot water

1 stick butter, cut into 1-tablespoon slices and chilled

2 tablespoons minced shallot

$\frac{1}{4}$ cup white wine

Zest and juice of 1 lemon

Sea salt and freshly ground black pepper

Make the ricotta filling by lining a strainer with 3 layers of paper towel. Spoon in the ricotta and add another triple layer of paper towels on top. Place a heavy bowl directly on top of the paper towels to weigh down the cheese for 20 minutes (you won't see much liquid actually draining, but a good amount will be absorbed into the paper towels).

While the cheese is draining, make the ravioli dough by pulsing together the flours, eggs, oil, and $\frac{1}{4}$ cup water in a food processor 10 to 12 times until it comes together into a ball. Transfer the dough to a floured surface and knead for 10 to 12 minutes, adding flour as necessary, until the dough takes on a sheen and is slightly tacky, but not sticky.

Cover the dough with plastic wrap and set aside to rest for 15 to 20 minutes. Mix the ricotta with the crabmeat, lemon zest, and salt and pepper to taste in a medium bowl and keep refrigerated until time to use.

Divide the dough into 6 portions and roll out one at a time with a pasta machine, keeping the rest covered with plastic wrap. Feed the dough through the largest setting eight times, folding it into thirds and rotating it 90 degrees each time. Then proceed to smaller and smaller settings (don't fold any more, and always feed the sheet through lengthwise), until you reach the second-thinnest setting.

Lay the sheet on a floured dish towel, dust with flour, and cover with another dish towel. Repeat with the remaining balls of dough. When each is finished, lay it on top of the previous sheet, dust with flour, and replace the dish towel over the top to keep the dough from drying out.

When all the pasta has been rolled out, lay three sheets of pasta (choose the smallest ones) on a floured surface. Mound rounded teaspoons of filling $1\frac{1}{2}$ inches from each other and $1\frac{1}{2}$ inches from the edge of the sheets.

Brush around the edges of the filling with the egg wash using a pastry brush.

Carefully lay the remaining sheets of dough over the top and gently press down around the filling, working from the inside out to force out any excess air. Make sure to press firmly enough to seal the pasta sheets together.

Use a 2-inch circular cookie cutter dusted with flour (or a knife or pizza cutter) to cut out the ravioli in 2-inch circles. Carefully transfer them to a floured kitchen towel in a single layer.

Heat a large pot of salted water to boil and reduce the heat to a gentle boil.

While the water is heating, make the sauce.

In a small bowl, place the saffron with the hot water and let it steep for 10 minutes.

In a medium skillet, heat 1 tablespoon of the butter over medium-high heat until just melted. Add the shallot and sauté for 2 minutes, until translucent. Stir in the wine and the saffron mixture and bring to a lively simmer for 5 to 8 minutes, until reduced to the consistency of syrup. Reduce the heat to low and add 1 tablespoon of the butter at a time, swirling the pan constantly to keep the sauce from separating. Season with salt and pepper and stir in the lemon zest and juice.

Carefully place the ravioli into the gently boiling water and cook for 2 to 3 minutes, just until they begin to bob to the surface. Remove the ravioli with a slotted spoon as they finish cooking and place in the pan with the sauce. Toss gently to coat and transfer to a warmed serving bowl.

SERVES 6

# CHAPTER 4

# NEW FLAVORS

OCTOBER 1996

T he way to a man's heart is through his stomach" may sound cliché, but in the case of Christopher and me, it was true. While Christopher and I loved eating out in whatever city we were in—we saw each other every few weeks on one coast or another during the months of our unconventional courtship—the meal that had won his heart was the birthday dinner I made him just a few months after we met.

I had moved into the garden apartment of a Brooklyn brownstone that March, just a few weeks after meeting Christopher. The kitchen had a tin tile ceiling and a tiny pantry closed off by old glass doors, and I'd painted the wall opposite the stove a pattern of white, yellow, and green that looked cheerful and sunny even when sunlight wasn't streaming in through the back windows.

One time, a couple of years earlier during a short stint as a music publicist (I had grown up playing guitar, writing songs, and playing in bands, so I thought being a music publicist would be the ideal job for me—it lasted a year), my boss had rented an old farmhouse in Nashville during a summer event and we stayed down there for a week. There wasn't a stitch of furniture in the place other than a big dining room table in the middle of the kitchen. I loved the way the light streamed through windows onto the whitewashed clapboard walls. I loved the big apron sink. I loved sitting on the stoop outside the kitchen topping beans with Alison Krauss one afternoon, as if that's what stoops and summers were meant for. I don't remember what else we cooked that night—or if I even cooked at all—but the overwhelming sensation of *home* stuck with me. My kitchen in Brooklyn felt like that.

I had spent three days and a small fortune gathering ingredients from all corners of the city for a birthday dinner I was making for Christopher in October, and was waiting for his flight to arrive. This was, by far, the fanciest meal I had ever made and I was somewhat shocked that it was actually *working*.

As I rubbed herbs onto the Dijon mustard I'd spread on the rack of lamb, I thought about how, from the get-go, a relationship between Christopher and me did not make sense. He'd brought another woman to our first date. He lived on the opposite coast. And another complication cropped up the day after he got home from New York City. Mere hours after he'd sought out a pastor and said his own yes to Jesus, Christopher got a phone call saying that his father had died. Decades of alcoholism had left a mess of an estate to work out, and since Christopher's mother and stepmother had already passed and his brother was in jail, Christopher was left to sort it out on his own.

The calls became more frequent, and when Christopher asked to stop in New York to see me on his way to Michigan to plan the funeral, I panicked. I'd been in too many relationships that had siphoned my energy and emotions into someone else's drama, and I worried I was repeating the pattern. Everything was moving so fast it was blurry, like I'd fallen while waterskiing but was still holding the rope. I wanted to let go. It made *sense* to let go. And yet, over the spray of water gurgling up my nose, I kept sensing that I should hold on. That I was right where I was meant to be.

So I did.

I dipped my finger into the veal reduction sauce I'd been working on for two days, and it was like poking melted chocolate. On my lips it was savory and complex and delicate all at the same time. Exactly as it should be.

Another, smaller pot held a truffle reduction sauce, which would be drizzled on the plate with the Scallops in Black Tie I was making—enormous sea scallops that I'd sliced and stacked with black truffle and wrapped in spinach and puff pastry, to be baked and finished with that reduction sauce. On the table was another indulgent addition, thanks to my new boss, Eric (I had recently made the move from publishing to marketing manager at a software company whose owner loved good wine as much as Christopher did): a bottle of 1992 Silver Oak Napa Valley Cabernet Sauvignon.

I was excited to see Christopher, but I was hesitant too. Both of us being brand-new Christians, and him having already been married once before, had made dating . . . interesting. Sometimes I felt like we were playing house in reverse, like adults feigning the innocence of kindergartners. But for the first time ever for me, spiritual matters usurped the physical as our relationship grew along with our faith. Someone once told me of a cool illustration. Picture each person in a couple as one of the bottom corners of a triangle. As each person seeks a closer relationship with God, sliding up the sides of the triangle, they also end up closer to one another. That's exactly how our months of courtship felt. We were growing closer in a way I'd never experienced before, and I soon realized—despite pesky challenges like distance and Christopher needing to crawl into his cave and my blinding bouts of jealousy—that I couldn't just replace Christopher when things got tough.

One time, just after I'd moved to Brooklyn, Christopher called me from a satellite phone in Honduras. He'd taken a leave after his father died and was traveling around Central America. "Meet me in Guanaja," he'd said. "It's an island off the Honduran mainland. I'll pay for your ticket, just call American and book it."

"I can't," I'd said. "I just moved. I'm nesting."

There was silence on the line and then Christopher said the words that sealed the deal. "And you call yourself an adventurer." I left to join him four days later.

This was a man who knew me. This was a man who loved me for my adventurous self rather than trying to put me in a box. I was supposed to stick with this one, for better or for worse, in sickness and in health. Little did I know how close I actually was to making those vows, or how gritty and real they would become.

That night of Christopher's birthday dinner, as Bernard Fowler crooned on the stereo and candlelight flickered off the tin roof tiles like a 1920s disco, Christopher asked, "What's next?"

"That's it," I said. "Dessert's all done, wine's all gone. That's it."

But he chuckled and redirected. "No, I mean, if you could do anything, live anywhere, what and where would it be?"

I shrugged. "I don't know exactly. But I think somewhere abroad. Maybe France again."

"I'd love to live in another country." He nodded, wearing a wistful look.

"Would you want it to be Europe, or Latin America?" I asked. Christopher had a profound curiosity about Latin American cultures. He even had a tattoo of Zotz, a Mayan zodiac sign, on his shoulder.

Christopher thought on that while he swirled the last of his Silver Oak. "Latin America, I think. Maybe Costa Rica. I've heard really good things about Costa Rica." Then he set down his glass and swiveled to face me. "What if we moved to Costa Rica?"

"What?"

"What if we move to Costa Rica together, and what if . . . what if we were married when we did it?"

I coughed so hard I had to plug my nose to keep wine from coming out. "Oh my goodness," I laughed. "You must have really loved that dinner."

A month later, we booked a weeklong trip to Costa Rica, leaving Christmas Day, and the night before, on Christmas Eve, Christopher proposed.

*Just weeks* before our wedding in April, I was in a rage that Christopher had gone on a dive trip to Bermuda instead of helping me pack up my place in Brooklyn to move to our new place in San Francisco. I was so livid I literally saw spots. But that night, I had a dream—a vision, really—that changed things. There was a blue figurine—kind of like a cocktail glass at a tiki bar—that I somehow knew represented Christopher or, more specifically, my relationship with Christopher. In this dream, God was asking me to give the blue figurine to Him, but I clung to it and turned away. He kept gently telling me to give it to Him, like telling a dog to drop a ball it had fetched. I slowly turned toward Him but felt enormous anguish at the thought of being parted from the figurine. At His gentle insistence, though, I eventually, with great strain to my heart, handed it to Him.

As soon as it was out of my hands, it was like an umbilical cord had been cut. I no longer pined and wrestled over the blue figurine; instead I observed it in God's hands as something beautiful and admirable. And then a most remarkable thing happened. He gave it back to me. Only that time, I held it differently. I held it with a grounding, peaceful love.

I hadn't been psyched about the prospect of a wedding ... or marriage for that matter. I harbored deep-seated beliefs that marriage did to couples what I had thought religion did to individuals— neutralize any trace of personality and passion. Every time we started talking about the wedding I felt claustrophobic; I even hyperventilated in the Denver Nordstrom's while looking at engagement rings. Weddings just weren't my thing.

But as it turned out, *this* wedding was. My parents told us over and over not to feel any pressure on their part, encouraging us to plan the wedding that *we* wanted. So I designed handmade invitations for eighteen people and asked them all to share words of wisdom at the ceremony, then designed an announcement that we sent to friends and family around the United States, saying we'd come to *them* to celebrate throughout the rest of the year. I introduced myself to the proprietor of a sweet two-story restaurant in an old brownstone a few blocks from church, and she gave us the whole ground floor and let us put together a three-course menu at no extra charge. It was perfect ... for *us*.

The next surprise came after the wedding, once we arrived in San Francisco. Instead of falling into a rut, each day with Christopher became an adventure. While Christopher traveled Monday through Thursday for work, I would explore my new city, taking in the scarlet and coral bougainvillea on the old stucco buildings throughout the Marina, hiking through the eucalyptus groves of the Presidio, and dog watching under the shadow of the Golden Gate Bridge on Crissy Field Beach. Salt air, foghorns, views of sea and uninhabited hills, all felt a world away from New York City.

*Most nights,* as in New York, we ate out. Back then, since we'd lived apart during our entire courtship, we'd treated every meal together as a special occasion. But that didn't fit the budget once we were married. So we made up an A-B-C system. A restaurants were special-occasion restaurants, like Farallon down off Union Square (even though we could still only afford the bar menu). B restaurants were once-a-month-type places, like PlumpJack on Fillmore or our favorite sushi place a couple of doors down—nothing fancy, yet still beyond our everyday budget. C restaurants were our staples. Thankfully, there were plenty where we lived in the Marina. Yukol Place had a chicken and eggplant in Thai basil sauce that I could happily eat every night, and Andalé had a lineup of burritos—carne asada, chipotle chicken, grilled shrimp—that we cycled through. But on Friday nights, we'd cook at home.

On Fridays, Christopher and I would pick a dish out of Anne Willan's *Look and Cook: Asian Cooking* and spend the afternoon combing Chinatown or Clement Street for ingredients and tools. Then we'd come home to our cozy apartment, with its 1920s stucco barrel ceilings and dark wooden doors, and cook for hours. We learned about things like fish sauce, shrimp paste, chile oil, and black cod. And we learned about each other too. As we sat cross-legged on the living room floor eating our pad Thai or larb or satay, details of our lives that had been left out in our unconventional courtship came spooling out like egg noodles bathed in peanut sauce.

But as we were settling into our new life, I was reaching the end of my rope with the pain and achiness and exhaustion I'd been feeling for years. What had begun in college had expanded to a nearly constant ache during my years in New York. It felt like my whole body was bruised, with occasional, localized flare-ups that felt like someone had skewered my shoulders or hips or knees with a dull sword. Along with the pain came chronic exhaustion and a low-grade fear that followed me everywhere. The fear said, If you feel like this in your twenties, how are you going to feel when you're thirty-eight or fifty-two?

Being in a new city, I went to see a new doctor and she ran me through yet another battery of tests and sent me to yet another specialist (I'd been there, done that numerous times in New York). Only this one finally gave it a name.

Systemic lupus.

Part of me was terrified to hear "This is a chronic disease that can be fatal if you don't manage it properly" directed at me. But part of me was relieved too: the part whose fingers ached too much to hold a pen and whose knees throbbed in her ears when she walked down the block.

I'd been hurting and exhausted for most of the eight or so years I'd been an adult, and the part of me in charge of putting on a happy face through it all felt vindicated. *I told you so*, it shouted at the doctors who had shunted me from office to office in New York for pill upon shot upon pill; at acquaintances whose faces betrayed that they thought I was being "oversensitive"; at me for always pushing the limits in nine different directions. There was something strangely gratifying about being sanctioned to be weak.

The doctor had made it clear how important "eating healthy" was to holding back the lupus. What he hadn't made clear was how to do it, and like so many people who face a grave diagnosis and are told to "eat better," all I could picture was a grim life of denial.

So I went on Plaquenil, stayed out of the sun (one of the side effects of the drug is extreme sun sensitivity), and tried to find "healthier" options at our A, B, and C restaurants, all the while nurturing a healthy dose of bitterness for having to do so.

But salvation came in the form of two books that gave me hope. One was Janet Fletcher's *Fresh from the Farmers' Market,* and the other was a big book by Sally Schneider with the unfortunate name of *The Art of Low-Calorie Cooking* that I'd found on a discount shelf.

In her introduction, Sally says, "Necessity set me on the path to find a way to cook and eat that would nurture my body as well as my soul and senses." In the dazed aftermath of the lupus diagnosis, those words hit me smack in the gut. Tears welled in my eyes. When I got to the sentence, "Most of the bleak 'diet' regimes address only the physical side of eating, ignoring the other hungers that good food satisfies: hungers for the connection it can forge to friends and nature, for its sensual beauty, its colors, aromas, flavors and textures; for the cultural and historical meaning it expresses; and, most important, for comfort and well-being," I did cry. Those words dripped down into some lost cavern of my soul. It felt to me like Sally was promising that idyllic marriage of joy and nourishment that I'd witnessed in Greece and been pining for ever since.

Fletcher's book was my bible for our Saturday farmers' market runs. As much as I'd loved Saturdays with Julie at the Union

Square Greenmarket, back then I would only buy what was familiar to me: lettuce, cucumbers, basil, tomatoes, zucchini—which were, at the time, a massive expansion to my vegetable repertoire. It never occurred to me to try vegetables I was unfamiliar with. Having Fletcher's book—and a lupus diagnosis like a gun against my back—changed things.

We tried her Warm Frisée and Fava Bean Salad; Cavatelli with Cranberry Beans; and Yard-Long Beans with Tomato, Ginger and Chile. I was open to trying new things. What I stubbornly refused to do was bring new eyes to old things. Like, for instance, peas, which I'd always known as mushy, brown orbs from a can that my mom would try to sneak me as a child.

That is, until one Saturday morning in spring when a farmer held out a pea to me and changed my world. "Try these," he said. I made a face and waved away the offer, but he wouldn't take no for an answer. The plump little orbs were almost bursting from the pod. "You have to. They're so sweet and delicate this time of year."

As I grudgingly brought the pea to my lips, I found that the farmer's pea was in no way related to the peas of my childhood. In fact, this pea tasted so fresh and bright that the word *spring!* pounced into my mind.

I bought a pound.

Soon after, my long-held prejudice against asparagus fell by the wayside when I experimented with charring them lightly on the grill. Beets were next, with Fletcher's Roasted Beets with Fennel Oil. My whole way of looking at vegetables started to shift . . . all because of that one little pea.

Cookbooks had taken us on adventures. They'd taught me how to heal and broadened my horizon with veggies. But eventually I reached a place where I itched to stretch my own wings.

I have a memory from when I was about seven years old. I was sitting beside my grandma, who was an artist, on a piano bench and had just played her a song that I'd written. Then I turned to her and said, "Grandma, teach me how to paint."

She paused and considered the request, then posed a question of her own. "How did you write that song, Lia?"

"It was just in my head," I answered, impatient to move on to painting. "And then I played around with it on the piano until it sounded like it did in my head."

A smile had grown on her face. "That's exactly how I paint pictures."

I formed a theory about creativity that day. I believe that creativity is less about the final manifestation and more about an invisible current that flows within all of us. For me, that current had manifested first as music, then in my early twenties as writing. Now I was discovering that cooking could be creative too.

So for Christopher's thirty-fourth birthday celebration, I combed my cookbooks for inspiration, then struck out on my own. One thing I'd discovered: I was a cook, not a baker. I liked tinkering with flavors rather than being bound by formulas. I started experimenting more and more with my own ways of mixing foods, flavors, colors, and textures, and quickly formed a sort of mental palette. Ginger and honey, cumin and coriander, pork and fennel. It was like a giant web was being woven in my mind connecting ingredients that complemented one another. When I was developing a recipe, as when I wrote a song or conceived an article, I knew how the flavors would work together before they got served up on the plate.

I set down menus as our friends Allan and Janis joined Christopher at the table: Ancho-Smoked Jumbo Prawns; Beet Risotto;

Braised and Seared Fennel. So much about that menu was different from the meat and potatoes I'd grown up with, from the meat
and potatoes I'd served just a year earlier. So much about *life* was
different.

"This is impressive, Lia," Janis said, scanning the menu. "You'd
give any of my chefs at the Marriott a run for the money with this."

I glanced at Christopher and saw the glint of adventure in his
eyes. "Actually, Christopher and I are thinking seriously about
opening a place of our own."

"Oh?" Allan said. "That's fantastic. Book us for opening night."

"Well," Christopher said, squeezing my hand. "You'll have to
book a room too."

"Why? Late night?"

"We're thinking of opening a place in Costa Rica," Christopher
said. We both laughed at the looks on their faces.

"Costa Rica?" Janis said. "Why?"

"Because we've talked since the beginning about living in another country, and Christopher has always been enamored with
Latin America," I said.

"But what about family?" Janis asked.

"We'll actually be almost as close to my family on the East Coast
in Costa Rica as we are here."

"But what about *family*?" Janis asked again, cocking her head.

I sat on Christopher's lap and looked him in the eye before an-
swering. "Kids aren't really in the cards for us," I said. "We've talked
about it and we're just not kid people." I could tell Janis was gearing
for a retort. "And on that note," I said, standing up and turning into
the kitchen, "I have to go stir my risotto."

I listened to them chew on the juicy bits of life we'd just served as I stirred the rice. The grains were beginning to plump up in the scarlet-hued liquid. I fanned the steam toward my nose and it smelled earthy and sweet all at the same time. I unscrewed the cap on a jar of coriander and shook some in; it would pick up the sweetness of the beets and prawns and be a bridge to the licorice notes of the fennel.

I spooned a mound of rice onto a plate—the risotto was the exact color of the bougainvillea climbing our wall outside—and laid a wedge of fennel in the middle. Then I arranged three prawns so their tails curled up into the air. A smile crept onto my face.

I wouldn't have chosen to have lupus. But I was grateful that, because of it, I'd been opened to a whole new way of eating. The plate in front of me felt totally unique to who I was, like the life Christopher and I were building together.

⤖

## ROASTED RACK OF LAMB WITH SAUTÉED SPRING PEAS

*This dish is sort of a combo of my old meat-and-potatoes days and the dawn of my new love of vegetables. Which is convenient, as lamb and peas are a natural pairing. I can't guarantee this meal will bring about marriage, but I can guarantee it will wow whomever you serve it to.*

5 garlic cloves
$^1/_4$ cup fresh rosemary needles
Sea salt

2 tablespoons extra virgin olive oil
2 racks of lamb (2 pounds each), frenched
Freshly ground black pepper
Sautéed Spring Peas (recipe follows)

Pound the garlic and rosemary together with a pinch of salt in a mortar and pestle (if you don't have a mortar and pestle, mince the garlic and rosemary on a cutting board, then sprinkle salt over the top and drag the blade of your knife horizontally over the top of everything) until it's a paste. Whisk the olive oil into the paste and rub the lamb all over with the mixture. Let the lamb marinate in the fridge for at least 1 hour or overnight.

Preheat the oven to 450°F. Set the racks fat side up in a large roasting pan, season with a good pinch of salt and pepper, and roast for 25 minutes, until a thermometer inserted into the center of the rack (without touching the bone) reads 125°F (for medium rare).

Remove the racks to a channeled cutting board, tent with foil, and let rest for 10 minutes before carving. Slice between each rib and serve with the spring peas.

SERVES 8

#### SAUTÉED SPRING PEAS

4 tablespoons unsalted butter
$1/_2$ cup sliced shallots

Sea salt and freshly ground black pepper
4 pounds fresh English peas in the pod, shelled
2 tablespoons chopped fresh mint
Flake sea salt (like Maldon)

In a large skillet, heat the butter over medium-high heat. Add the shallots and a pinch of sea salt and pepper and sauté for 3 to 5 minutes, or until softened. Add the peas and sauté for 5 to 7 minutes, or until tender. Add sea salt and pepper to taste. Remove from the heat and stir in the mint. Finish with a sprinkling of flake sea salt.

SERVES 8

# CHAPTER 5

# I AM ALIVE

DECEMBER 1997

I had vivid memories of my first impression of Paris, on an exchange my senior year in high school, walking up the steps of the Saint-Michel Metro station as the façade of Notre Dame Cathedral came into view against a brilliant blue sky. I had stood in awed silence at the top of the stairs watching the Seine River flow past. I'd never seen anything so beautiful in my life.

Later, when I studied in Paris during college before living on Corfu, I took classes all over the city, and my routes often took me past neighborhood markets where I saw and smelled things I never had before: the vacant stares of whole pigs' heads; hanging carcasses, both furry and feathery; and the sharp, pungent tang floating from the cheesemongers' booths. At first I was repulsed. But after months of being exposed to these sights and smells, I became more curious than disgusted. Only I didn't have a kitchen, so I never had the chance to cook with any of it. Truth be told, I ate terribly while I lived in Paris, vacillating between mushy steamed green beans in the cafeteria, which I would virtuously dip in mustard (a fat-free meal!), and the pizza or steak frites (*quelle horreur!*) I would inevitably go overboard on when I got tired of eating steamed green beans.

Which is why I had rented an apartment for the vacation Christopher and I had planned to Paris just after Christmas. It was Christopher's first trip to France and I couldn't wait to take him to my old haunts and cook with the foods I could only look at before. Only the trip had turned out much differently than the one I planned. The day before leaving, I'd gotten a call from my doctor saying that my Pap test had tested positive for high-grade dysplasia—which sounded terrifying to me, despite her reassurances that it was a fairly common and predictable cell abnormality of the cervix. I already had a bad habit of playing worst-case scenarios over and over in my head, and I didn't do well with this one.

*If you* looked at the photos from our trip, you'd guess we had a marvelous time.

There we were with the seared prawns the fishmonger had talked us into at the market and the scalloped potatoes that had never really set but were rich and creamy anyway. There were Christopher's pink cheeks and giant smile peeking over his scarf during a picnic of stinky cheeses and a bottle of young Bordeaux at the Luxembourg Gardens. There we were all dolled up at the Hotel Lutetia, where we'd enjoyed a lavish, nine-course feast for New Year's Eve.

But when I looked in my eyes in those photographs, I saw another story too, one that Christopher, even though he was beside me in each and every one of the photos, didn't see. Up and down the streets of Paris I toted a gripping, clenching terror that this would be the first and last time I'd see Paris with my husband.

On our last day there, Christopher ate a croque monsieur at Ma Bourgogne on the Place des Vosges, and oohed and ahhed through five courses at a restaurant by the new Opera. But by that time my stomach was knotted with anxiety and I had no interest in eating. My fear was eating me from the inside out.

*The next* eleven months were torture, with monthly visits to the gynecologist for painful tests to try to find signs of the dysplasia. Each time I walked out from an appointment, I'd climb into Rex—the name we'd given the Ford Explorer we'd bought—and let him roll down the hills of Pacific Heights toward home while I bawled so hard I could barely see. Ironically, nearly every time I turned Rex's key in the UCSF parking garage, Shawn Mullins's song "Lullaby," with its chorus of "Everything is gonna be all right," would be playing. I took this as both a sign and a promise from God, like getting the same fortune in a fortune cookie three times in a row.

Not everything about that year was doom, though. My freelance writing was shifting from travel toward food. I'd even gotten bold enough with my own creations to start developing recipes for publications. Whether at home or exploring someplace totally unknown, food had become the lens through which I viewed the world.

*That November* I was in the gynecologist's office for tests again. In the waiting room, I was surrounded by pregnant mothers with that bright-eyed look of expectancy on their faces. Some had partners beside them holding their hands, gazing at them in adoration. Other moms bounced babies while everyone oohed and ahhed. A sea of magazines surrounded us: pregnancy magazines, baby magazines, parenting magazines.

I was there to make sure I didn't have cancer.

Let me be clear, I had no desire to be there as an expectant mother. Our new Rhodesian ridgeback puppy, Talisker, was all the baby I needed. But the cancer part sucked. After umpteen visits looking for any trace of what the original Pap had found, though, the doctors still hadn't seen anything, which I was taking for good news; Christopher and I had just booked another trip to France for the New Year, this time a home exchange in Nice, and I was hoping to have a better go of it than our trip to Paris.

Dr. Subak called me into her office and sat me down. I couldn't help but stare at the photo collage of the babies she'd delivered. I felt guilty for being such a downer in that world of joy. I wondered, did she dread our visits as much as I did?

"Well," she said, looking bright, "I'm ready to close the books on this. We've done several thorough exams over the course of the year and can't find a trace of what had shown up in the Pap. It must have been eliminated with the original test."

She sat with her hands folded over the file looking very pleased. I was confident in her abilities and attention to detail, yet something was bugging me.

"You know," I said, "since that original pathology report is the only place this dysplasia ever showed up, and since that test was done by my primary care doctor and not here, would you mind taking one more look at that first test before closing the books?"

She considered my request and nodded. "I don't see why not. I'm doubtful we'll see anything we haven't already seen, but if it'll make you feel better about it, then OK."

I'm not sure it made me feel better, but it did feel like the right thing to do. I was buoyed by Dr. Subak's optimism and even managed to make it down the hill without shedding tears. I thought about Nice and felt light little bubbles of joy. Maybe everything really *would* be all right.

Two days later, I was finishing up a surprise project I'd started when Christopher left for Marriott headquarters in Maryland earlier in the week. We'd painted the underside of the arches above our dining room window a rich blue, the color of a clear evening when the sky slips past dusk and seems to glow; it's a time of night we call "our sky." I was adding a smattering of gold stars for fun.

I'd called Christopher after my appointment with Dr. Subak, and he was thrilled with the news. I was thrilled he'd be home in two days. I smiled, thinking of the saying we'd thought up—*tomorrow's tomorrow*—to make it not seem so long.

The phone rang, and I walked to the living room to answer it, thinking it would be Christopher. It was Dr. Subak. "I hate to make this call, but we have to talk." I'd never heard a chord of tension in her voice before. It made my throat tighten.

Before I could say anything, she continued. "It turns out the first lab misdiagnosed your original pathology. It's not dysplasia."

"Well, thank God for that," I said, wondering why she sounded so stressed.

"Unfortunately, it's something much more serious."

I steadied myself with a hand on my desk and eased myself to the ground as Dr. Subak told me they'd found an extremely rare glandular level irregularity called adenocarcinoma in situ that moved in an erratic pattern.

"I would highly advise an immediate hysterectomy, but I'd like you and Christopher to get a second opinion from an oncologist first." She was quiet for a beat; I had my hand over my mouth so she couldn't hear me sobbing. "We have to move quickly on this, Lia. I'm so sorry."

*When Christopher* and I met with the oncologist on Monday, I still felt like I was living in an alternate universe. We walked up to the building and I thought, *I can't believe I'm walking into an oncologist's office.* During the appointment, I felt as if I were listening to him talk about someone else.

Christopher squeezed my hand as the doctor told that other person that adenocarcinoma in situ is extremely rare, extremely hard to catch, extremely unpredictable, and often deadly. He told that other person he wouldn't risk waiting to do the hysterectomy to have kids, saying, "This isn't a wait-and-see kind of cancer."

Christopher and I looked at each other. I closed my eyes and sent up a pleading, desperate "What should we do?" to God. But we already knew the answer. I'd known it all along. God had never intended me to be a mom.

The oncologist scheduled not one but three surgeries. The first would test how extensive the adenocarcinoma was, with the results dictating whether I'd need a simple or radical hysterectomy later in the week.

A few days later we had The World's Worst Day. It started with three awful pre-op appointments during which we were told of all the horrible, awful things that could happen during surgery. Fun things like they might accidentally snip a nerve and paralyze me, or find that the cancer had spread too far and just give up.

When the meetings were finally over, we pointed Rex down the hill to pick up Tally from the vet (ironically, we'd taken him in to be neutered that day) and were longing for all of us to be together, safe, as a family. I was so numb I didn't even cry as Rex rolled down Divisadero Street.

But when we walked into the vet's office, we could see on people's faces that something was wrong.

"What is it?" I said. "What's wrong with Tally?" None of them knew that I was holding it together by a thread finer than dental floss.

The vet came out and told us that we wouldn't be able to take Tally home for at least three days; Tally, it turned out, had Von Willebrand disease—a blood-clotting disorder—and had nearly bled out on the operating table.

My floss broke.

So we went home. Alone. But the day wasn't over yet.

Christopher was checking voice mail messages in the dining room when I heard the phone drop on the glass table. I hurried in and saw him with his head on folded arms, heaving silent sobs. "What's wrong?" I panicked. "Did something happen with Tally?"

He shook his head only slightly and looked up at me with an exhaustion that seemed to span three lifetimes. "That was my brother's roommate," he said. "Todd's in the hospital. He tried to kill himself."

We sat on the couch and clung to one another in silence, unable to speak, unable to even cry. It was like after a really loud bang where there's a constant ringing and all voices are faint and distant. The only thing I could really feel was the full-breath calm that was slowly filling me. A calm I knew was not of me. In the weeks and months and years to come, Christopher and I would grow familiar with that feeling, that gift from the Spirit during unthinkable hardships. We dubbed it the "irrational calm" of God.

The next day, as I prepped for the first surgery, Christopher looked up all the scriptures he could find on hope and laid them beside me like an offering. One in particular stood out to me: "Suffering produces perseverance; perseverance, character; and character, hope. And hope does not disappoint, because God's love has been poured out into our hearts through the Holy Spirit, who has been given to us."

That sounded a lot like irrational calm to me.

Other verses all seemed to whisper another promise: that, while God obviously did not intend me to bear *children,* He very much intended me to bear things of beauty and worth. I just had no idea what, exactly.

Mom came out the day before the surgery and slept with Tally on the pull-out couch. She held my hand the next day when they gave me, as Mom put it, "the three-martini shot" that makes you woozy enough not to freak out when they stick an IV needle into your hand.

It was a year, almost to the day, after receiving that first call from my doctor that I went into the operating room at age twenty-six a whole woman and came out unable to bear children.

I suffered through two surgeries that week, and in the days of waiting for the post-op lab results I battled a constant assault of fear. Yet despite the fact that I viscerally dreaded the phone ringing and felt pierced through the stomach each time it did, I eventually came to a tectonic-plate-shifting realization: no matter what Dr. Subak said on the other end of the phone, God would be there. And somehow, as Mom and Christopher held turf wars over meals and coddling and keeping Tally from jumping on me, I felt an undeniable ember of hope that something greater lay ahead, whether here in this world or ahead in the next. And, shockingly, during those miniature moments of understanding that seemed to expand like the universe, it didn't matter to me which it would be.

Still, when Dr. Subak's call came with the news that all was clear, I felt like I drew my first full breath in a month.

*Christopher and* I decided, against admonitions from family and friends, to take the trip to Nice. Whereas they saw the trip as an energy output that would impede recovery, I—we—looked on the trip as respite. Christopher and I were most alive when immersed in other cultures and cuisines. And I needed to feel alive.

Christopher pampered me on the way to the airport, carrying bags and holding my hand. What surprised me was how tender I was with myself. In the mightiest of all ironies, I caught myself looking pensively out the plane window with hands crossed protectively over my belly, like pregnant women do. What they're thinking, I cannot say—just as I couldn't say what they were thinking in the waiting room with me at the gynecologist's office. Yet I've always suspected it had to do with a natural instinct to protect. My thoughts had roots in a fearsome protectiveness too. My body had just taken me through something profound, like a loyal steed who leaps through a burning building to bring its master to safety. I couldn't put words to it yet, but I knew that I'd taken my body for granted, taken my health for granted—even with the wake-up call of lupus—and I was ready for that to change.

By the third day in Nice I was feeling strong enough to take a walk. We headed down to the boardwalk on the beach and walked east toward the Cours Saleya, Nice's main market. The sky was a dove gray, with enough white underbelly to mark the line of silvery sea. We strolled slowly, with Christopher's arm around me and my hand tucked in his back pocket, my head leaning against his shoulder.

I was acutely aware of the silence. The peaceful, unfettered silence between Christopher and me, and the internal silence within me. The gremlins and fearmongers that were ever present a year ago in Paris and throughout the ensuing year were gone. But it wasn't from a naïve root of thinking nothing "bad" or hard would ever happen again. It was from having gone through something so painful and being carried through by the "peace that surpasses all understanding," as if by a supernatural balm that shows up only in the moment.

"I'm excited to cook tonight," I said to Christopher. It had been weeks since I'd spent much time in the kitchen. "Anything you're leaning toward?"

"Let's just see what we find at the market," he said, just as we turned the corner into the Cours Saleya.

What a second earlier had been the peaceful hum of a breeze turned to a cacophony of shouts echoing around the large, flagstone square. My nose took in the scent of a thousand spices, and aromas of roasting meats and fried seafood and coffee. I was stupefied. I saw a vendor with just olives, in all sizes and shades of black and green, and another with spices the colors of a Matisse painting. Fishmongers were selling tiny smelt beside slabs of dried cod, and women were hawking all sorts of tapenades and pestos in little baskets lined in colorful Provençal fabrics.

I stood there for a long moment, dizzy with a gratitude so strong it made my eyes water. *I am alive,* I thought as I breathed in the abundance around me. *I am alive. I am alive.*

⤜⧽⧼⤛

# SCALLOPED POTATOES

*So this is how I wish those potatoes in France had turned out. It's a perfect example of how a few simple ingredients can bring about sublime results, which the French have known—and practiced—for centuries. Use a mandoline or food processor to make quick work of the potatoes. I highly recommend pairing these with the Roasted Rack of Lamb with Sautéed Spring Peas from the previous chapter.*

2 pounds Yukon gold potatoes, peeled and thinly
    sliced (about $1/_{10}$ inch; don't rinse)
2 cups whole milk
Sea salt and freshly ground black pepper
2 thyme sprigs
1 bay leaf
1 garlic clove, halved
$1/_4$ cup heavy cream

In a medium saucepan, place the potatoes, milk, a generous pinch of salt and pepper, the thyme sprigs, and the bay leaf, and bring to a simmer over medium heat. Adjust the heat to maintain a low simmer for 6 minutes, until the milk has thickened to the consistency of heavy cream, scraping along the bottom of the pot with a spatula to make sure the potatoes don't stick.

While the potatoes are cooking, preheat the oven to 425°F. Rub the bottom and sides of a 2-quart baking dish with the cut side of the garlic.

Remove the thyme sprigs and bay leaf and spoon the potatoes and milk into the pan in an even layer. Pour any remaining milk over the top and drizzle with the cream. Bake for 40 to 45 minutes, uncovered, until golden brown on top and bubbly around the edges. Remove from the oven and let rest for 10 to 15 minutes before serving.

SERVES 8

## CHAPTER 6

# THE GRINGO MOBILE

MARCH 1999

Mud sucked at our tires as we climbed a ridge in the Marin Headlands, the wind screaming past Christopher and me so loudly it was pointless to even try to speak. Not that we would have anyway. In the three months since we'd come back from Nice—since we'd come out of that year of worry and grief—Christopher's eyes had become empty and lifeless, and conversations had dwindled to single syllables.

As we'd tried to put our life back together, we spoke longingly of simplifying. For Christopher, to step off the corporate ladder at Marriott and find another, more fulfilling path ahead. For me, time and space to find myself so I could be a whole person again.

The problem was, we didn't know how. We'd tried to move to the country but kept getting beat out by the twenty-three other renters there before us. We'd tried to buy a restaurant in Healdsburg, a little town in wine country north of San Francisco, but Julie's dad, Ed, had talked us out of it ("You've got no capital, kids").

Both of us felt stuck. Which was why we'd come to the headlands for a bike ride. It had been raining for days and the sky was that silvery white that looked threatening or promising depending on the way you cocked your head. It felt so good to move, to breathe.

We rounded a turn and my nostrils filled with the spicy scent of wet sage. Eucalyptus branches cracked in the distance and I could just detect their musty mint underlying the salt of the sea. It wasn't foggy, yet sea and sky were opalescent mirrors of one another and I couldn't tell where one began and the other ended.

The bubble of a memory worked its way up to the surface. Two years and a few months earlier, the day after Christopher had proposed to me on Christmas Eve, we'd flown to Costa Rica for a vacation to take a first taste and see if we might want to live there. On the third day, we'd driven west from the capital over the 11,000-foot Cerro de la Muerte mountain range. The road was windy and ill-maintained, with eighteen-wheelers barreling down on us from ahead and behind.

But the day had been glorious. The sky had been as blue as an exotic butterfly, and puffy clouds pirouetted below us. We'd felt like we were in heaven. Three hours later, we'd begun the descent toward the Pacific and saw the bright sun setting directly in front of us.

"Um, honey," Christopher had said, his eyes growing brighter and brighter. "That's not the sky. . . . That's the ocean." It had been our first glimpse of the Pacific in Costa Rica.

Now I stared at our slice of the Pacific in California as we coasted down the mountain toward the estuary, remembering how we'd dreamed of living—and even opening a restaurant—in Costa Rica someday. It had even factored into our decision to buy Rex—the Ford Explorer was the only SUV with a solid carriage, which we were told was important for rough roads.

Why had we forgotten it all when it seemed like the perfect

solution? But before the question was even fully formed I knew the answer. Because that was Before Everything Happened. *Remember, you're weak now,* the little gremlin inside me whispered.

*To hell with that,* I whispered back. What if I wasn't weak? What if the dream didn't die? What if Costa Rica was our answer to finding the life we both felt drawn toward?

"What if we drove to Costa Rica?" I called out over the wind to Christopher.

"What?" he called back over his shoulder, and cruised to a stop beside the estuary.

I put my foot down and pulled alongside him. "Let's just drive to Costa Rica," I said. He looked at me, startled, but I was unfazed. "It's simplicity itself, and you've always wanted to live abroad. ... And we can do reconnaissance to see if we want to live there permanently."

A flock of brown pelicans stretched their legs out for a landing, and we got off our bikes and walked to a bench. Christopher was shaking his head while the pelicans flapped and spluttered to a halt, but I could tell it was more of a "did I really hear you right?" than a no.

I reached over and laid my hand on his arm feeling a surety that seemed, quite frankly, totally out of context. "Let's do it," I said. "Let's drive to Costa Rica."

"When?"

"I don't know." I shrugged my shoulders. "How about the new year? The new millennium seems like an appropriate time for new beginnings." I smiled. Christopher did too. And I knew then that the crazy idea was actually going to happen.

When we got home, Christopher pulled out a yellow lined notepad and wrote *Salva Vida Trip* at the top (Salva Vida meant "life saver" in Spanish ... it was also the name of our favorite Honduran beer) and then, *We will leave for Costa Rica by December 31, 1999*. We signed and dated it, feeling every bit as fizzy as the bubbles we toasted with, and the next day, we kicked into gear. Something fundamental had shifted for both of us, and what had appeared to be legitimate obstacles to any of our attempts to pull up stakes—money, safety, security—now were simply logistical boulders to be climbed over or worked around.

Just a few months later, everything was falling into place. We had our visas. We had our income through a long-term project I was working on with British Airways. We even had our house, paid in full: a lovely-sounding two-bedroom set in the jungle-covered hills above Dominical, the stretch of mountainous southwestern Pacific Coast that had stolen our hearts two years earlier. The irony was, as we wound down our lives in San Francisco, my food writing career began to take off.

One day in early fall, Christopher and I were on our usual Saturday pilgrimage to the farmers' market. It was one of those September days in San Francisco that rival the best of summer elsewhere; the air was as clear and brilliant as crystal, the sun warmed my cheeks, and a lilting breeze off the bay tasted like salt on the tip of my tongue.

We made our rounds among the tents, filling up bags of greens from Dirty Girl Farms, finding figs wherever we could, and stashing giant, end-of-summer tomatoes carefully in the bottom of our market bag. When we were done, we succumbed to the siren call of spicy, garlic-laden smoke coming from the Aidells Sausage stand, as we did practically every week.

This time, though, as we made our way through the crowds, I spotted the grizzled gray beard of Bruce Aidells himself. I knew that face not only because it was on every package of sausage I bought, but also because I had seen Bruce speak on a panel about cookbook collaborations at the International Association of Culinary Professionals (IACP) conference in April. It was a dream of mine to work on a cookbook with a brilliant chef—I'd even had preliminary talks with Charles Phan of Slanted Door—so I had hung on Bruce's every word.

I seized Christopher's elbow. "That's Bruce Aidells," I scream-whispered, fighting hard against the urge to point. My heart sped up. "Should I say hello? He won't remember me. I probably shouldn't even bother, right?"

"Why not?" Christopher said as he maneuvered me toward the table. "You've got nothing to lose."

I stepped up and ordered two fennel sausages. Nothing happened. My heart had not burst forth from my rib cage, and Bruce had not read my mind, waved a magic wand, and made me a food writer. I took a breath and forged ahead, pushing past all the gremlins telling me I was being silly for wasting his time.

"Hi, Bruce," I said. "I was at the IACP conference in April." He smiled and nodded as he tucked the sausages into their buns. "I'm trying to break into food writing and really enjoyed your panel."

He squinted as he handed me the sausages across the table. "Tell me your name again."

"Lia," I said, holding his gaze. "Lia Huber."

He held up a finger—it, too, resembled a sausage—while he fished in his pocket. He pulled out a wrinkled card and pointed at the bottom. "That's my office number," he said. "Give me a call, I may be able to help you out."

.  .  .

*Sunday came* and went. Monday morning came and went. By 1:00 on Monday afternoon I figured it was safe to call without seeming too eager.

I sat at my desk in the corner of our apartment. The soft sunlight filled the room and gave the old stucco walls a luster like fresh cream.

I picked up the phone and dialed, tapping my fingers on the amber wood of the table with each ring. And then, a click.

"Hello," Bruce said, his voice rich and thick like a well-marbled rib eye.

"Hi, Bruce. We met at the farmers' market on Saturday. I'm Lia Huber." My words tumbled out in a rush, and then there was dead silence. "I'm the one who wants to be a food writer." I wanted to hang up. I wanted to melt under the table.

"Oh," Bruce said. "How did you get my number?"

"You gave me your card and told me to call you." Sweat was beading at my temples, and my armpits felt clammy.

He sighed. "Do you have any formal training?"

"No, I don't. I'm just starting out," I said. "Any advice?" I asked, cringing.

There was another pause, but the tenor had shifted; I could tell he was thinking.

"Recipe testing, for cookbooks and such, is probably one of the best ways to break into food writing." He picked up speed and I picked up a pen. Several minutes passed before he paused again. "Let me poke around and see what else I can turn up. What's your number?"

I hung up and sat with my hand resting on the phone, shaking from excitement and relief. I felt like I'd just run a marathon.

Not a minute later, the phone rang again. I picked it up eagerly, thinking the conversation must have jogged a thought for Bruce, but a woman's voice was on the other line.

"Is this Lia?"

"Yes," I said, deflated.

"I'm Lisa Weiss," she said. "I'm working on a cookbook for Farallon Restaurant with the chef, Mark Franz. Bruce Aidells just gave me your name and said you might be interested in recipe testing for us."

My hand fluttered up to my mouth. She was talking about *the* Farallon Restaurant. The one a block off Union Square. Our number-one A restaurant.

"I can't really pay you anything," she said while I focused on trying to catch my breath.

"That's fine," I squeaked. "I'd love to."

"Terrific," she said. "We'll start Wednesday. If you could be at my house in Tiburon by nine o'clock, we'll plan on testing throughout the morning with Mark."

*On Wednesday* morning, I drove across the Golden Gate Bridge and wound through the streets of Tiburon out toward the tip of the peninsula, where Lisa's house was perched. When I walked in I was equally struck by the stunning views of San Francisco encased in a rosy morning mist, and the casual atmosphere in the kitchen. Everything about that day felt epic and life-changing for me, yet Lisa was in sweats, finishing up breakfast with her family. Like it was any other day.

"Take a seat," Lisa said, pulling out a chair at the rustic dining room table at the side of the kitchen. She sat down beside me with a laptop. "Here are the recipes we'll be testing," she said, pointing to a spreadsheet.

I skimmed the list and saw things like Black Bass and Sea Urchin Tartare in a Crisp Nori Sandwich with Shiso Dressing, and Duck Breast Prosciutto with Summer Melon, Fig Compote and Lemon Verbena Granita. Many of the entries to me read as if written in a foreign language.

"We'll be testing the recipes in three rounds. First, we'll just be writing them down—you'll be working on that with Mark as he cooks the dishes. Then we'll test what we've written. Then we'll edit those recipes, test again, and then send the recipes out to others for one last test."

Lisa poured coffee while we talked through the recipes we'd be testing that week. I marveled at the fact that I was witnessing the inception of an actual cookbook and was struck by how at ease I felt. An hour or so later, Mark arrived with several bags, which he unloaded onto the giant island in the middle of the kitchen.

My job was to follow Mark around and record what he did—in essence capturing the bones of the recipes. My naïveté turned out to be a forte. His patient answers to my constant barrage of questions—"What is duxelles?," "What is yuzu?," "What does it mean to 'sweat' onions?"—helped Mark capture the information that would be helpful for home cooks.

One day, he sliced firm, pumpkin-orange Fuyu persimmons— which I'd never known existed—paper thin on a mandoline and arranged them on a tangle of bitter greens with crunchy-sweet candied walnuts, pomegranate seeds, and a tangy vinaigrette he'd emulsified in the blender with sherry vinegar and walnut oil. I'd never seen or tasted a salad so sublime.

Another day Mark fried prawns as large as my hand in a rice-flour batter, which he explained made the coating extra crisp. He poached tuna in olive oil over heat so low I could barely even tell it was on for fish that became as tender and unctuous as foie gras . . . which was another ingredient that showed up frequently in many of the dishes we made. Each time, while I tasted in a reverie of contentment, Lisa and Mark would break down each bite to identify things that were missing or needed to be tweaked to get the dish exactly right.

The dish that stands out most in my memory, though, was one that was never intended for the book. Mark had just prepped a lobster sauce for the Braised Veal Cheeks with Lobster Tails and Cauliflower Purée we'd be making in the afternoon when we broke for lunch. He'd roasted the shells of the steamed lobster and then beaten them for a half an hour in a mixer to release their collagen and color (yes, I did ask, "Why are you beating those shells in a mixer?"), upon which he mixed in a few cups of aromatic fish stock for an intense, coral-colored broth that tasted like eating lobster in a forest. For lunch, he whipped up a quick bisque by sweating (which, I'd learned, meant sautéing in butter until they're translucent) perfectly diced onions and adding them with some cream to that elixir-like lobster broth. He ladled it into bowls and we ate on stools pulled up to the island. The dish tasted like lying on silk sheets beneath a down comforter while eating lobster in a forest.

As much as I learned over the weeks, though, I discovered something else too.

Whenever I pulled into Lisa's driveway, I would self-consciously turn down the Christian music playing in Rex and stash away any thoughts of Jesus, like tucking a compact back into a makeup case.

Whether innate or self-imposed, my two worlds were divided, and I was becoming more aware of the differences between them. I was noticing that anything that brought me deeper into the conversation *about* God or into the conversation *with* God resonated with a thrum deep within me like a crackling, sustaining fire. The pleasures I got elsewhere—from the amazing food we surrounded ourselves with, from good wine, from the occasional pampering indulgence—were more like a fireworks display; lovely and brilliant, but fleeting. I began to wonder, would there ever be a way to bridge the two?

A few weeks into the Farallon testing, I got my second break into the world of food writing, which also stemmed from the IACP conference. This one came from a panel with the editors from *Cooking Light, Bon Appétit,* and *Food & Wine*—magazines I knew as intimately as my apartment—where they each talked about what they were looking for and how to make an effective pitch. A few weeks after the conference, I sent a pitch to *Cooking Light* for quesadilla salads, and the editor liked the idea. I'd once spent days crafting recipes for a *Cooking Light* contest, hoping to have one show up in print; now *Cooking Light* was paying *me* to write recipes for the magazine.

Life had done a one-eighty in the past six months. I'd gone from feeling stuck and aimless to building a career with an adventure ahead.

We'd laid out a giant patchwork of maps on our living room floor and plotted our course, with the help of the Sanborn's Guide that Christopher had found. We'd enter Mexico at Juarez, head south and west through Chihuahua to explore the Copper Canyon, then back southeast to trace a vertical line down the center of Mexico through the colonial towns. We'd cross the border into Guatemala and hug the Pacific Coast, jogging inland as the road did, through Honduras, El Salvador, and Nicaragua, all the way to Costa Rica.

Much of our trip would be on the historic Pan-American Highway, a road system conceived in the 1920s to connect the Americas from Alaska to the southern tip of Chile. The section we'd be on was called the Inter-American Highway, which runs down Mexico's spine and then connects each Central American capital on CA-1.

You know how, when you first look at a map it's just lines and dots, but once you've been to a place it's like looking through holographic glasses when you look at the map? Like you can *see* it? I marveled at the fact that, within months, all those squiggles and lines and dots would become three-dimensional like that for us.

*On the* day of our departure, the sky was luminous, the air crisp, and the sidewalks bustling with the young Marina crowd enjoying the day after Christmas. As if everything were normal. As if life weren't about to take a hard right. I was shocked when the movers announced they were finished; did it really only take a few hours to pack up a life?

Christopher pulled up in Rex. He'd gone all out, with little curtains for the back windows made out of chile pepper fabric. He'd gotten wind flanges so we could drive more comfortably with the windows down, changed out the hubcaps, and swapped the license plate holder from our Silver Oak "Life's a Cabernet" to a thick chain link. He even hung his grandmother's rosary and a pair of fuzzy dice from the rearview mirror.

"No one will ever guess we're gringos!" he'd said, beaming, when he first showed me his handiwork.

We drove up the slope of Divisadero as I wept into Tally's fur, clinging to his neck for as long as I could before having to relinquish him to our dog sitter. Our friends Kelly and Albert would be flying him down once we arrived in Costa Rica, but that was still over six weeks away.

And then, with just the two of us and Rex, we were on the road.

*Just outside* Reno, we decided to peel off of I-80 and take Highway 50, which was dubbed the Loneliest Road in America. A large portion of Highway 50 parallels the route of the original Pony Express. As I looked out my window and watched the landscape whizzing past, in my mind's eye I could see a man bent to a forty-five-degree angle on the back of a galloping horse, mane flying wildly in the wind. *That* was what I wanted to feel like on this trip. Tethered only to the scribble of road that lay before us, I felt buoyant and light and free . . . the way I was meant to be.

On our fourth day out we pulled into Denver, which felt odd right from the get-go; Denver was a place where we flew to visit Julie, my best friend and old roommate from New York, and her husband, Steve. Arriving on four wheels seemed like we were shouting "This is not normal!" Arriving with snow-covered beach chairs strapped to the roof, as we were, just seemed absurd.

We concocted a ridiculously elaborate New Year's Eve feast—it *was* the millennium, after all—based on a black-and-white truffle theme: the Scallops in Black Tie I'd made for Christopher's birthday three years earlier, a creamy mushroom risotto perfumed with white truffle oil, a beef Wellington with truffle pâté mixed into the duxelles and *2000* in puff pastry on top, and a flourless chocolate truffle cake for dessert.

The morning of our departure, the four of us gathered in the frigid underground garage of Julie and Steve's apartment building. Steve clapped his gloved hands to warm them, and the echo thudded against the low concrete ceiling. Something about this final gathering felt momentous to me as we stomped our feet for warmth, like a primitive ceremony among cave dwellers. In just a few minutes, Christopher and I would be emerging into a life none of us could envision, but there was still one thing left to do.

"I think it should go here," said Christopher, pointing to the metal part of the bumper as he positioned the fish-shaped sticker. Truth be told, I was a little fidgety. During the days of the early church, the ichthys was a secret symbol for Jesus's followers. Nowadays, it's a not-so-secret declaration of being a Christian. As someone whose father was an atheist and mother's main thoughts of Jesus revolved around the Christmas crèche, I was still more comfortable portraying Darwinian tadpoles to the world than Christian ichthyses.

But when Christopher hovered it in place and looked at me, I knew we were making yet another vow to one another—and to God—by pasting a fish to Rex's backside: that no matter what lay ahead, we'd trust that God had the steering wheel. And *that* I could get behind.

We pulled out of the garage a few minutes later with Julie and Steve waving in our rearview mirror. I felt peaceful and present and draped in that irrational calm. So what if people thought I was a Jesus-Freak-Born-Again-Christian? One thing I knew without a doubt: I was moving toward who I was meant to be.

❧

# FRISÉE SALAD WITH PERSIMMONS AND WALNUT-CRUSTED GOAT CHEESE

*This is a perfect holiday salad—the gem-colored pomegranates and warm orange persimmons bring color and a sense of something special. Mark served his salad with candied walnuts, but I've taken to serving this salad with a couple of disks of goat cheese coated in toasted walnuts instead. Either way, it's the perfect play of bitter greens, sweet fruit, and an earthy bass note from the nuts.*

1 tablespoon minced shallot

$1/_4$ cup champagne vinegar

2 tablespoons extra virgin olive oil

2 tablespoons toasted walnut oil

1 tablespoon pomegranate molasses or honey

Sea salt and freshly ground black pepper

$1/_2$ cup walnut halves, toasted

4-ounce log goat cheese

1 pound frisée (about 6 cups), cleaned and
    torn into bite-sized pieces

1 Fuyu persimmon (or a ripe-but-firm pear),
    sliced in half and then into thin wedges

$1/_4$ cup thinly sliced red onion

Seeds from 1 pomegranate

Preheat the oven or toaster oven to 350°F.

In a tightly sealed jar, shake together the shallot, vinegar, olive oil, walnut oil, pomegranate molasses, and a pinch of salt and pepper. Set aside.

Place the walnuts in a zip-top plastic bag and gently crush them with a rolling pin until they're the texture of coarse sand. Cut the goat cheese log into 8 pieces and shape each into a fat disk. Press into the walnuts to coat both sides and place on a foil-lined baking sheet. Bake for 5 minutes, until the cheese is warmed through.

In a salad bowl, toss together the frisée, persimmon wedges, and red onion. Give the dressing one more shake and pour it over the top. Toss to mix and portion out onto 4 salad plates. Top each serving with 2 goat cheese rounds and sprinkle evenly with pomegranate seeds.

SERVES 4

CHAPTER 7

# PEELING BACK THE LAYERS

JANUARY 2000

W e had a problem.

The bleak sunlight, already diffused by a scrim of winter clouds, was fading fast, so that Christopher's face in the driver's seat looked gray and monotone. And with the impending darkness, the temperature had plunged below freezing.

This was a problem because, while Christopher and I were cozy warm in Rex at the moment, we were parked outside El Tejabán, a remote resort—which, it appeared, was closed—perched on the rim of Mexico's Copper Canyon, and the only other being around was a growling Rottweiler behind a chain-link fence.

Creel, the mining town on the outskirts of the canyon where we'd stayed the night before, had felt too populated. We wanted to find some place relaxing, away from the crowds. So when we read the one-sentence description of El Tejabán in Sanborn's, we decided it would be a great place to decompress for a few days. What we didn't know then is that calling the Copper Canyon "remote" is sort of like using the word "kitty" to describe a lion.

The Copper Canyon is actually a system of five canyons that

plunge to a depth of seven thousand feet in places—far more massive than the Grand Canyon. They were formed over the course of 100 million years or so by an uplifting of volcanic rock, which was then etched into canyons by rivers. Aside from intermittent mining activity over the years, the area's sole inhabitants are Tarahumara Indians, who were driven into the wilderness during the Spanish conquest in the seventeenth century and who still largely live in caves or small, primitive dwellings.

We had aborted an attempt at lunch along the way to El Tejabán when some Mexican men outside the only restaurant between El Tejabán and Creel gave Christopher the runaround. I had wanted him to push harder, to let me negotiate, but he'd insisted we just forge on. So an hour or so later we'd turned off the road onto a granite slab that had EL TEJABÁN and an arrow etched into it and driven—well, Christopher had driven—for three hours on dirt roads strewn with boulders and webbed with ravines and rivers. We'd passed through one canyon that was indeed the color of copper, and another that was as lush as Jurassic Park. It was stunning, but man, was it hairy; as we zigzagged across the crests our mantra became "Hug the mountain, hug the mountain." After passing dozens of Tarahumara Indians in colorful garb herding animals, it became apparent that we weren't actually driving on *roads,* per se, as much as goat paths.

Navigating back down in the dark was out of the question, and we didn't have enough gas to run Rex all night. And while we had a tent buried somewhere in the back, we had no way to keep ourselves warm through the twenty-degree night.

I was panicking—and I was hungry—and because I am not at my finest when I am panicked and hungry, I had begun pointing fingers too.

"Why didn't you get out at that restaurant this afternoon to even *ask* if they would serve us? Why didn't you just let me get that freeze-dried stuff from REI? I *told* you we'd use it!"

Christopher looked away, and I sat and fumed.

"Forget it," I said. "If you're not going to do anything, I will." I opened the door and was met with a chilly blast of pine-scented air that would have been pleasant had we not been about to perish on a remote mountaintop in Mexico.

"Don't get out of the truck!" Christopher said. "That Rottweiler will tear you apart!"

"I'm getting out of the truck," I retorted. "If I don't, how else are we going to know if anyone's there?"

But I already knew no one was there. Even as I hugged my arms against the cold, what chilled me most was the lack of smoke coming from the chimney. During our first two days of driving through northern Mexico, nearly every village we drove through was marked by a hazy halo of wood fires. During the cold winter months, smoke meant warmth. Smoke meant life. And there was no smoke coming from this one and only refuge for miles around. I stood at the gates, craning my neck to find some sign of life beyond the Rottweiler's foaming mouth.

And then I heard it. The *ka-ka-ka-ka-ka* firing of a small engine that sounded to me like wings of angels flapping down from heaven. I walked back to Rex with my head cocked and opened the door.

"I hear something," I said. Was it a generator coming from the next town? *Was* there a next town? I trained my ears on the sound like a sailor does the wind. No, it was coming toward us.

Over the crest appeared our deliverance. A little green ATV was carrying a small brown man and woman with broad features and

worn clothes. The rubber band that had been holding my question-
able composure in place snapped, and I ran toward them.

By the looks on their faces, they were as surprised to see us as
we were to see them. Jose, clearly the man in charge, ushered us
through the gates, and the killer Rottweiler covered us with slob-
bery kisses.

Jose led us into a grand marble rotunda walled in glass that
was perched on the precipice of two canyons. Christopher and I
watched the last wisps of day turn mauve and periwinkle as darkness crept up the sides of the canyon. Jose brought us cold beers
and explained that there were precious few provisions to be had,
as it was off-off-off-season at El Tejabán, and that we were the first
ever—and probably the last ever—to drop in by automobile; it
turns out the hotel had a landing strip and was primarily used by
groups that fly in. In the summer.

He lit a fire in a grand central pit that brought light, warmth,
and comfort to the room, as it did to me. Ramona, the woman who
had been on the ATV with Jose, brought out a crude salsa made
of pounded onions and jalapeños with a squeeze of lime. The beer
and salsa and fire felt almost elemental, becoming a part of us just
as we were becoming a part of the night and the canyon as darkness
descended. I found Christopher's hand and he gave mine a squeeze;
all was forgiven.

We stayed at El Tejabán for three days. One day, we hiked along
burro paths for seven hours three thousand feet down to the Urique
River and back up. Ramona's brother Octavio was our guide, and
Perro (which means "dog" in Spanish), the formerly fearsome Rottweiler, was our companion. Christopher and I were decked out
in our finest adventure gear: wicking tops, pants with zip-off legs,
shiny new Tevas, weatherproof hats, and walking sticks. Octavio

had a tattered button-down shirt, too-large pants cinched by a too-large belt, and tennis shoes whose soles flopped like cows' tongues when he walked. He also had such a bad cold that a perpetual pendulum of snot hung suspended just beyond his seven yellowed teeth. I'll give you one guess as to who kept up the greater speed without stopping or breaking a sweat.

Octavio lived in a tiny cluster of crude wooden homes built into the side of the mountain on the other side of the river. He walked this path twice a day. The air smelled of smoke and scrub brush and pines. As Christopher and I stumbled on the slippery gravel that crunched underfoot like pistachio shells, Octavio exhibited a sure-footed grace and saintly patience when Perro quit a hundred feet into the ascent. Octavio simply fashioned a leash from palm fronds—the climate is more balmy and tropical at the bottom of the canyons—and half dragged, half carried Perro back up the mountain.

*The next* morning we drove southeast through foothills and wheat fields and onto the vast high plateau, which is hemmed in by the Sierra Madre Occidental mountain range to the west—of which the Copper Canyon is part—and the Sierra Nevada Oriental to the east, both of which run almost due southeast paralleling the coasts.

While we had left the physical, geological layering of the Copper Canyon, we found a different sort of layering to be evident as we explored the colonial cities of central Mexico over the next couple of weeks.

We were taken completely by surprise by Zacatecas, a silver-mining town and colonial outpost set among scrubby hills at eight thousand feet. We were charmed by the dizzying baroque façade of its early-eighteenth-century cathedral and lush gardens bordered by wrought-iron fences, by the charming cafés, cobblestoned streets and rosy-hued stone buildings lining Avenida Hidalgo. I felt like I was in Paris, only Paris with a posh hotel built into a nineteenth-century bullring and aqueduct, and exotic things that I had no idea how to cook with—like cactus paddles and dried hibiscus leaves—for sale at the open market. The fact that these colonial cities would have such a strong European influence had somehow escaped me. In fact, my whole paradigm of Mexico was being rocked. All my life, I'd absorbed the subterranean implication that Mexico was a dirty, dangerous place full of bandits and outlaws, yet we were finding it to be a beautiful, multifaceted country with friendly, proud, hospitable people welcoming us at every turn.

We rolled on to Guanajuato as pastureland fanned out on either side of the road, punctuated by striated mesas. Roadkill was different here. In addition to the occasional squirrel or rabbit, we often saw larger carcasses of steer or dogs in varying states of decay; vultures were a constant of the landscape.

Death loomed in the abundant crosses that lined the sides of the road too, taking a toll on my overactive imagination. Each time we passed a cross or shrine—always impeccably maintained with frilly flowers or decorative painting—I imagined what sort of scenario had led to the accident, and how painful it must have been for the families left behind. But I eventually started to see that Mexicans don't hold death the same way I do. We passed decaying towns that felt barren and lifeless with a cemetery on a hill above that was pristinely whitewashed and decked with fresh flowers. Rather than getting mired in mourning and melancholy, Mexicans celebrate life through honoring the dead.

When we arrived in Mexico City, Christopher's colleague from

Marriott, Ben, put us up in a luxe suite at the J. W. Marriott, where he was general manager, in the swank Polanco district. Over the next few days we toured the ancient city of Teotihuacan, visited the pre-Columbian Aztec ruins of the Plaza Mayor—which were across the street from the enormous cathedral—and marveled at Diego Rivera's murals in the Palacio Nacional, which captured layer upon layer of history.

This mélange of culture seemed to come alive in the bustling markets on the streets tucked off the zocalo. Women with long gray braids were selling bundles of herbs, and pushcart vendors hawked colorful nuts and seeds. Men in T-shirts sold fragrant grilled meat marinated in an orange paste, and women in intricate woven tops hawked giant blue corn tortillas topped with mashed beans, shards of snowy white cheese, and salsa that we learned were a Oaxacan dish called *tlayudas*.

We had been blown away by the food in Mexico in general—from the eggs with dried beef *machaca* we'd had at a truck stop in Chihuahua, to the rich, tangy *asado de boda* stew in Zacatecas, to the brothy *frijoles charro* studded with bacon and peppers at a nondescript rotisserie restaurant we frequented in Guanajuato. Nothing in Mexico was as we'd expected.

The next afternoon we drove due south to Cuernavaca, where I had booked a weeklong cooking class. We pulled through the scrolled wrought-iron gates of the ranch and up a long drive past lush gardens, parking under a yolk-colored portico trimmed in white. We were shown to a suite so big I had to ask our porter if it was all ours (it was), and then we struck out to explore the grounds.

We wandered down hidden paths through gardens exploding with torch flowers and multicolored bougainvillea, past benches and gazebos, and through the grand stables with gorgeous palominos whose coats and manes echoed the colors of the buildings themselves. We found cotton-candy-colored flamingos—like, real ones, and they really do stand with one leg bent—and colorful birds in cages that talked sass when you spoke to them. We met Vaughn, the owner of the property, and his girlfriend, Bambi—both from Atlanta—who would be joining us for the cooking class.

The next morning, class began. Rhonda, whom I had been in touch with and booked the class through, was a plump, jovial Aussie whose stature and voice made her a commanding presence. Her counterpart, Vanessa, was the exact opposite—a petite, reserved Mexican woman who looked to be not long out of high school; the top of her tall toque reached the height of Rhonda's eyebrows.

Between the two of them, all the disparate threads we had learned about the many layers of Mexican culture over the previous weeks were stitched together through the common language of food. The first thing that Rhonda taught us is that there is no such thing as Mexican food. The food that Americans think of as Mexican is actually a remnant of the food common to the northern region of Mexico that is now Texas, characterized by a lot of beef, wheat tortillas, melted cheese, and spicy beans. Known as *Norteña* cuisine, it was rustic, with few vegetables, and was ubiquitous to both rich and poor. As one moves south through the country, highly differentiated cuisines unfold with, not surprisingly, various cultural influences layering one upon the other in their formation.

Rhonda divided Mexican culinary history into not two periods, but four: the pre-Columbian era (which encompasses thousands of years of regionalization in and of itself) that centered on the trifecta of corn, chiles, and beans and used primitive tools like the metate to grind maize into masa flour, and a mortar and pestle called a *molcajete* to pound chiles, seeds, and nuts into sauces; the arrival of the Spanish introduced fats and oils, wheat, garlic, and spices like cinnamon and nutmeg; the French intervention in the 1880s brought increased refinement to pastries, along with cream, soft cheeses, and the like; and then there was what Rhonda called the "post-blam" era from the 1950s on, when the blender transformed traditional cooking techniques, and the advent of air-conditioning opened up the balmy, disease-infested coasts to the well-heeled, who brought with them influences from around the globe.

That afternoon Vanessa showed us how to make a variety of *antojitos*—little finger foods—using techniques from throughout the four eras. We roasted chiles, garlic, onions, and tomatoes on a flat, steel *comal,* and then pounded them all together in a big, rough, stone *molcajete* to make a rustic, tangy salsa. We made masa from scratch, and then pulled off little balls and pressed them into boats that we fried and filled with refried beans, cream, cheese, and our *molcajete* sauce.

My favorite *antojito* was a multistepped affair called *chilorio.* First, pork shoulder is boiled and shredded. Then the sauce is made from toasted spices and chiles blended with vinegar, which is then "fried" in oil to thicken. Finally, the pork and sauce are mixed together with a squeeze of orange juice and set to simmer until the sauce has thickened even further and the pork is succulent and shot through with flavor. We let it cool while we pressed and toasted flour tortillas, and then we rolled spoonfuls of *chilorio* into the tortillas, so they were shaped like little cigars, and deep-fried them.

When we were done cooking, we found that kitchen helpers had magically transported everything to a sun-splashed tiled verandah where we gave our aching feet a rest, and Rhonda surprised us with tamarind mezcal margaritas (as further evidence of the "post-blam" era, of course), which went beautifully with the smoky notes of the *chilorio*; I couldn't stop eating those little rolls. The tortilla would shatter in your mouth to reveal a bite of savory, tart, smoky meat rounded out by creamy, homemade guacamole. In the course of one afternoon, we had time-traveled across thousands of years in both technique and ingredients.

The next two days Rhonda took us on field trips. The first was to the Cuernavaca Market, where pyramids of tomatoes and avocados and onions and cabbages all seemed to outdo one another in their perfect form. Rhonda started us off at a counter across from pigs' heads hung on spiked hooks and snow-white honeycomb tripe draped like streamers. She ordered a thick, milky drink made from cornmeal called *atole*, which reminded me a bit of Malt-O-Meal. Then she walked us through an aisle lined with white buckets mounded with pastes that ranged from golden brown to deep brick red to the color of dark chocolate: all moles. She had us take a pinch of each one and report on what we tasted and how it ranked (I preferred the golden peanut mole; Christopher leaned toward the darker, more complex mole Especial). The next stop was a stand where a woman coaxed the flame of a grill with a fan woven out of palm fronds for a barbecued goat taco with peanut salsa (out of this world). Across the way a woman patted black beans into a thick tortilla, then dropped it into hot oil where it puffed like a balloon. Then she punched it down and added mushrooms, cheese, and salsa. I would have eaten all day, had I had room. Christopher and I bought a *comal*, a tortilla press, and a lime press for $10 total before heading back to the kitchen with bags and bags of produce.

That afternoon, Vanessa taught us how to cook with all the ingredients that had stumped me when I'd seen them at earlier markets. We made a salad with strips of jicama mixed with pineapple chunks, cashews, and pomegranates, with a smoky vinaigrette made from dried chile morita and hibiscus petals. We made black bean soup with minty epazote leaves, strips of nopales—the cactus paddles we'd first seen in Zacatecas—and creamy *panela* cheese. We even sautéed zucchini flowers, which we stuffed into poblano chiles with strips of cheese before wrapping it all in puff pastry and topping the packets with a creamy cilantro sauce and garnet-colored pomegranate seeds.

The next morning, Rhonda took us to visit a cheesemaker, Señor Cuevas, a debonair man with thick, black hair and a manicured handlebar mustache. He had been a structural engineer making cubicles in Mexico City before he and his wife decided to try their hands at farm life. He led us through an idyllic scene of cows grazing on undulating green hills, past frolicking bunnies and a wobbly legged filly, into a chilly, sterile white building with two metal vats and several racks.

We watched the alchemy of milk curdling, thickening, and shrinking away from the sides of the troughs. Señor Cuevas scooped some of the curds into molds and topped them with chopped epazote before setting them on racks. Then he continued to work the milk mixture with a giant, serrated spatula until the mixture came together like a ball of dough. He reached in with his hands and pulled it into long ribbons, like pulling taffy. The rope would come out thick and return to the vat thinner, until it was one giant loop turning into a smaller and smaller rope. He cut the cheese rope into sections and twisted each into balls about the size of softballs and handed one to each of us. We pulled off strands, like string cheese; it was creamy and delightfully chewy with just the right amount of salt. We couldn't stop nibbling it. That, he told us, was cheese made in the style of Oaxaca. Apropos, since Oaxaca was our next destination.

Bambi's expat friends had come with us to Señor Cuevas's, and while they'd taught us some helpful things (for instance, making an OK sign in Mexico didn't mean everything's OK, it meant you were calling someone an asshole ... good to know if, like me, you talk with your hands, although I cringed to think of how many checkpoint officials I'd accidentally called assholes), Christopher and I began to feel like we were at a nineteenth-century plantation instead of a twenty-first-century hacienda. The women referred to the cooks and domestic help as "their girls" and "the help" and made comments like "You just have to treat them that way, they have no initiative." The whole idea of colonialism made me feel uncomfortable enough, and the last thing I wanted was to feel separated from—or even worse, artificially elevated above—the very people we wanted to get to know.

Mexico and its people were teaching us that everything is evolving. Mountains are evolving into canyons, lives are evolving into memories, cultures are evolving with the changing influences and influx of other cultures, and traditional cuisines are evolving as a result. I was evolving too—already I felt like a different person than when we left—and it made me wonder, what would the next layer reveal in me?

❧

## ROASTED TOMATO AND CHILE SALSA

*We made a version of this in Cuernavaca with the pre-Columbian basalt molcajete. In this one, I skip into what Rhonda calls the "post-blam" era for less fuss and a smoother texture.*

2 guajillo chiles, stemmed, halved, seeded, and deveined

1 ancho chile, stemmed, halved, seeded, and deveined

$^1/_2$ jalapeño pepper, stemmed, seeded, and deveined

$^1/_2$ medium onion, cut into 3 wedges

3 garlic cloves

2 plum tomatoes

Sea salt

1 teaspoon freshly squeezed lime juice

On a *comal* or in a large cast-iron skillet, toast the guajillo and ancho chiles over medium heat for 20 to 30 seconds per side, just until they develop a sheen, and transfer to a blender.

Place the jalapeño, onion, garlic, and tomatoes on the *comal* or skillet and roast for 10 to 12 minutes, turning often, until they are semicharred and softened.

While the vegetables are roasting, blend the chiles until they're pulverized. Add the jalapeño, onion, and garlic to the blender. Slip the skins off the tomatoes, cut off the tops, and add to the blender with any accumulated juice. Add a generous pinch of salt and the lime juice and pulse until just smooth (add water by tablespoons if needed to blend smoothly). Let the salsa sit for 20 minutes to allow the flavors to come together, and season with salt if needed.

MAKES 1 CUP AND WILL KEEP IN THE
REFRIGERATOR FOR UP TO A WEEK.

# CHAPTER 8

# TREASURE HUNTS

JANUARY 2000

I cracked my window to get some air as we descended into the Oaxaca Valley and it smelled of a thousand chimneys. Shawn Mullins sang "Everything is gonna be all right" on the stereo, and a surge of emotion welled through me with memories of all the times I'd drifted down Divisadero Street after doctor's visits, crying so hard I could barely see. I wiped my cheek with the back of my hand and watched the mountains smear past in a million shades of taupe.

Christopher took my hand and squeezed it, and for a moment we were perfectly enveloped in the present tense. From the outside, it would be easy to reach the verdict that everything did *not* turn out alright—I did still have lupus, and I was down a uterus. But I was learning that if God were to take my prayers as marching orders—please, please, please, God, take this danger, this discomfort, this unknown from me—my life would be a lot less rich and I would be a lot less me.

If the colonial cities had whetted our appetite for our Cuernavaca cooking course, the course itself had prepared us well for the renowned culinary scene in Oaxaca.

We started our Saturday at the sprawling Abastos Market, following Rhonda's lead with bowls of thick, steamy chocolate *atole* that we sipped while sitting on rickety square stools, watching vendors arrive for the day. Men carried huge, door-sized boards on their heads piled high with breads and sweets. Women swathed in brightly patterned *huipiles* hawked fried grasshoppers dusted with brick-red chile powder. Other women were clustered together with baskets between their legs like snake charmers, pulling back a woven napkin to reveal the huge tortillas inside, called *tlayudas,* that we'd seen in Mexico City.

We were on a quest at the market to find a *molcajete,* the giant stone mortar and pestle that we'd grown enamored with in Cuernavaca. We bought a bag of piping hot, slightly scorched peanuts, whose smell reminded me of New York in wintertime, and walked up and down the aisles of Abastos for over an hour. We passed ladies selling every kind of salad you could imagine; women with long braids carrying platters on their heads piled high with bowls of food; chiles of all sizes, shapes, and hues of red; black pottery, garlic, corn, grains . . . but no *molcajetes.*

Over the next few days we ventured out into the *pueblas* surrounding Oaxaca. We explored the impressive ruins and treasures of Monte Albán before picnicking on Señor Cuevas's cheese and smoked pork chops we'd bought at the Abastos Market that morning. We bought black pottery in San Bartolo Coyotepec and a charming painted wooden jewelry box for our goddaughter, Kate, in San Martín Tilcajete. We met a weaver at the market and he invited us to his home in Teotitlán del Valle, where we bought three beautiful rugs before having the best mole ever at a local restaurant. It was like a Willy Wonka Gobstopper. One bite tasted like chocolate, the next like cinnamon, the next tobacco. Yet it was lighter and thinner in consistency than any other mole I'd had.

Oaxaca was growing on us. We liked it so much, in fact, that we overstayed our thirty-day visa for Mexico. So we went from official to official seeking counsel on how to extend our visa and were eventually shuttled to a man in a bureaucratic-looking office painted the same lemon-chiffon-meets-mint-sherbet hue as every other government office in Mexico. He sent us on a mission that had us hopscotching through the city from official to official for the better part of a day, in search of the elusive Form 5a.

When we returned to him that afternoon with sheaves of paper bearing various official-looking stamps expecting to get the final, essential stamp to our form, he looked up from his paperwork and, without emotion, flatly refused, saying it was impossible to grant us our request.

We were so aghast and deflated after so many hours of such weighty bureaucracy that we didn't really flinch when, without further ado, he stood up, plucked his suit jacket off the back of his chair, and said, "You must be famished. Let me take you to the best market in the city."

Truth be told, we *were* famished. So we followed him up the street, around the corner, and into what looked like a smoky train station set up with a rustic food court, although this smoke was a luscious, savory, meat-laden smoke that made me drool. Our friend—because in the space of three blocks he had indeed become a friend—left us with a friendly nod and an "enjoy Oaxaca" before exiting through the haze.

We felt all eyes on us as we, the only gringos in the place, gaped at the strips of meat sizzling on mini grills. I walked up to one smiling woman and bought raw, spice-tinted pork and beef. She put it on the grill and nodded toward an old woman sitting next to it with a basket of tortillas. Christopher asked for some and the woman put two tortillas on the grill grate and fanned the coals with a reed fan. I gravitated toward another smiling face, this one of a sweet, young woman, and was handed a bunch of *cebollitas*—bulbous onions that looked like scallions on steroids—and given a large wicker tray. She shooed us back to the old lady with the fan, who shoved the onions into the coals. By this point, most of the people in the area realized we had no idea what we were doing, and were giggling and offering direction at will—"Yes, the *quesilla* (the local term for Oaxaca cheese) is over there," "No, you get the guacamole and salsa from Clara when you bring the onions back to her."

We gathered our meat and onions and tortillas and headed back toward Clara, who was practically guiding us in for a landing with her wide smile. She squirted lime and sprinkled a touch of salt on the onions, and then produced a plate of guacamole and salsa. She called a little boy over to lead us to a seat in the neighboring building, who fetched us Frescas and napkins. Everyone was so effervescent and encouraging, I felt like the whole place was going to break into applause that we'd made it through the maze.

We layered shreds of pork with Oaxaca cheese, guacamole, and salsa in a chewy flour tortilla that was perfectly scorched and crispy just along the rim. I alternated between bites of my makeshift taco and the charred onions, whose smoky skins would slip off to reveal sweet, almost creamy onions beneath. Meaty juices dripped down my forearm and I licked them off, not willing to let one drop go to waste.

On our last morning in Oaxaca we arrived at the Abastos market, sat on our usual rickety stools for *pan dulces* and *atole,* and forged off on a last-ditch effort to find a *molcajete.* We had asked several people on earlier trips where to find *molcajetes,* and had homed in on one area of the market that we thought was promising. As

I turned a corner, my heart skipped a beat when I saw piles and piles of *molcajetes* silhouetted against the harsh slant of the morning light through the aisles. But on closer inspection, they were all mass produced and buffed smooth. We went up and down several more aisles until I turned to see a woman with a face as wrinkled as a bunched-up linen jacket, who came up to just below my shoulders. There was a small pile of rough-hewn *molcajetes* beside her, although still too smooth for my taste. I waded farther into the stall and pointed to a large, irregular one made from porous stone, with a yellow *Recuerdo de Oaxaca,* which means "Souvenir of Oaxaca," painted on the side. "That one," I said with conviction. She smiled widely and her blue eyes twinkled.

"That one is much better than the others," she said.

Our final discovery on our Oaxaca treasure hunt.

The next morning, we traveled southeast again toward Mexico's isthmus, the Oaxaca Mountains a deep midnight blue against an azure sky, with green hills and spiky agave fields in the foreground. We descended five thousand feet into hot, flat, windblown, tropical forest, pausing for a night in Juchitán, and then paralleled the Pacific Coast to Tapachula, near the Guatemalan border. Our plan was to stay in Tapachula Sunday night and cross over to Guatemala first thing Monday. But both of us were curious to see what the border was like, so we drove up to check it out.

A throng of boys besieged Rex as soon as we rolled to a stop. Thanks to Sanborn's, we were somewhat prepared—we knew this troop were called *transmitadores,* boys who hired themselves out to ferry paperwork through the borders. Christopher picked out a *transmitadore* named Victor and stepped out of the car. I leaned across the seat and held the door open.

"What are you doing?" I asked, my voice higher than usual.

"I'm just going to check everything out so we'll be ready to go tomorrow," he said. He shut the door, sealing me in, and walked into the border building with Victor. Minutes passed. An hour passed. Had the officials arrested him because we didn't have Form 5a stamped? Had bandits from Chiapas overrun the border patrol and shot him? My heart pounded as I tried to block out all I'd heard about the mountains that surrounded us. In Chiapas, to the north, the Zapatista revolt had been raging, with hundreds of people being tortured and executed. In Guatemala to the east, a thirty-six-year civil war that had claimed more than 200,000 lives was just winding down, and in its place, vigilante lynchings had become a not-uncommon occurrence. I sat in the cool, air-conditioned cocoon of Rex while cold sweat dripped down my neck.

Over an hour later, Christopher came back with a smile on his face. "We've got our paperwork," he said. "Victor says we can go over the border tonight, and then come back and stay here like we planned. It'll make crossing easier in the morning."

Red flags deployed in every corner of my mind. "Are you sure?" I asked, finding it hard to believe that border officials would let us hop back and forth.

"I'm sure," Christopher said sternly. "Move over, Victor is going to ride with us." I scooted onto Rex's center console, my neck bent nearly ninety degrees to accommodate.

"Are you sure?" I asked, again, because I was absolutely, 100 percent *not* sure.

"Honey," Christopher growled. "Trust me."

We crossed the border, all 100 meters of it, and then parked again. The two went into yet another building and I was left alone again. I had been sitting for what seemed like hours when a drunkard on a dilapidated three-wheeled bike crashed into Rex and slid down the window as if he were melting, staring through the glass directly into my eyes. I wanted to help him, but I was terrified of what was on the other side of that glass.

Where the hell was my husband?

When Christopher did come out again, over an hour later, he was not wearing a smile.

"So now we go back to Mexico?" I asked. Compared to Guatemala, Mexico felt as benign as Wichita, Kansas.

"Um," Christopher said. "It doesn't look like we can do that after all. But it's OK," he assured me. "Victor is going to take us to a hotel. He lives in Malacatán."

"What do you mean, we're staying in Malacatán?" I asked, trying to keep the edge of accusation out of my voice. "It's dark, it's Sunday night, we don't know where we're going, and it's *Guatemala*." I was scooted yet again up onto the console. I had to push my palms against Rex's roof to alleviate the pressure against the side of my head. Guatemala was a place where people went missing, and I didn't want to become one of them.

But what choice did I have? Once we were in the town, we dropped Victor off, checked in at a tidy hotel not far from the central plaza, and walked to the local *parilla,* a rustic, thatch-roofed building that served simple grilled meats and *cebollitas.*

After the day at the border, the tension between us was more gristly than the meat, something you had to saw through to get to anything tender. I swallowed my silent I-told-you-so's with a couple of beers and was feeling pleasantly numb by the time we passed through the plaza on our way back to the hotel.

For a border town, the Malacatán plaza was quite pleasant. There was a canary-yellow gazebo and cement benches painted hibiscus red. Strings of lightbulbs draped from tree to tree gave it a festive atmosphere, and we heard music coming from what looked like a storefront.

"It must be a concert," Christopher said. "Let's go check it out."

I gingerly tucked my hand into his. As we got closer, we realized it was indeed a concert of sorts; it was an evangelical worship gathering. We drew closer and two men with welcoming smiles rustled up chairs and added them to the overflow on the sidewalk.

"*Por favor, por favor,*" they said. "*Bienvenidos.*"

We sat down while children craned their necks for a view of us gringos. Three bold ones flanked us—Milton, Milton, and Karen, we learned—and peppered us with questions. "*Con permiso,*" they'd ask, "how do you say 'Milton' in English?" "*Con permiso,* how do you say 'God' in English?" We answered each one and couldn't help but giggle along with them. They couldn't have made us feel more welcome.

At the end of one song, a lone woman stood and wailed at God for the pain she'd suffered—one of the many people at the gathering who were living with the enormous void of a loved one who *had* gone missing. She stood with her arms outstretched in the middle of the room and repeated "*Porque?*"—"Why?"—at the end of each petition. The intimacy of that question—posed to an almighty God—gave me chills. As others held their hands toward her in respectful support and the band fell silent, I felt that I was in a very ancient, very sacred space.

Karen nestled beneath my arm and began playing with my buttons, and a man tapped us on the shoulder and held out a basket of bread and a cup of wine.

"*Comen,*" he said. "Eat. Join us. *Tomen el cuerpo y la sangre de Cristo.*"

# GRILLED PORK EN ADOBADA
# WITH CEBOLLITAS

*This recipe takes me right back to the Mercado 20 de Noviembre in Oaxaca—I can almost picture Clara holding out the cebollitas. In Oaxaca, the meat is cut accordion-fashion into long strips. I've simplified that technique here by cutting the loin into thin slices with the grain, which keeps the texture authentic to what you'd find in Oaxaca.*

3 ancho chiles, stemmed, halved, seeded, and deveined
2 guajillo chiles, stemmed, halved, seeded, and deveined
$^1/_4$ cup chicken broth
3 garlic cloves
$^1/_4$ small onion
$^1/_4$ teaspoon dried oregano
$^1/_4$ teaspoon freshly ground black pepper
$^1/_8$ teaspoon ground cumin
$^1/_4$ teaspoon ground cinnamon
Sea salt
2 tablespoons canola oil
2 tablespoons cider vinegar
1 pound boneless pork loin, trimmed of the fat cap
2 pounds scallions (white and green parts)
1 lime

On a *comal* or in a large cast-iron skillet, toast the guajillo and ancho chiles over medium heat for 20 to 30 seconds per side, just until they develop a sheen, and transfer to a medium saucepan with the broth. Bring to a boil, then turn off the heat and let the chiles soak for 10 minutes.

While the chiles are soaking, add the garlic and onion to the *comal* and sear for 5 minutes, turning occasionally, until slightly charred. Transfer the garlic and onion to a blender with the oregano, pepper, cumin, cinnamon, and a generous pinch of salt. Add the chiles and broth to the blender and pulse until smooth.

In a large skillet, heat 1 tablespoon of the oil over medium-high heat. Add the chile mixture (careful, it will splatter) and cook for 5 minutes, stirring constantly, until the mixture darkens to a sort of brick color. Remove from the heat, season with salt if necessary, and let cool completely.

In a wide glass container, combine the chile mixture and vinegar. Slice the pork loin horizontally into $1/4$-inch-thick slices, as if it were a deck of cards. Add the pork to the glass dish and rub the marinade over both sides of each slice. Cover the pork and refrigerate for 8 hours or overnight.

When ready to cook, heat a grill or grill pan to medium-high heat.

Grill the pork for 2 to 3 minutes on each side, until just cooked through. Transfer to a serving platter when done.

Toss the whole scallions with the remaining 1 tablespoon oil and a generous pinch of salt and grill for 5 to 8 minutes, turning often, until pliable. They should be slightly charred on all sides, but not burned. Transfer to the platter beside the pork chops and squirt lime juice over the top.

SERVES 4

# CHAPTER 9

# THE JUNGLE HOUSE

FEBRUARY 2000

I was already on edge when we arrived in Dominical. On the long slog through four countries (and eight border crossings) to Costa Rica, we'd been fording rivers because of washed-out bridges and barreling down twisting, mountainous, two-lane roads, hemmed in by eighteen-wheelers. And now we were facing our biggest challenge yet, just when we thought we'd reached our destination.

"Pull the mirrors in," Christopher said.

"What? Why?" I chirped.

"Pull the mirrors in so they don't hit the support cables," Christopher said. His voice sounded unreasonably calm, given the circumstances.

Our new landlady, Robin—who was leading us up to our house—had driven her SUV across what appeared to be a wooden footbridge that crossed over a river fifty feet below. I had watched as Robin drove over. The slats of the bridge sank below the weight, as if the truck were plowing the bridge forward and ironing it out. *Rickety* didn't begin to describe that bridge.

Now she was waiting on the other side, expecting me to follow.

I wiped clammy hands on my thighs. "But we've got Rex loaded!" I said, trying to keep the panic from my voice. "Do you really think we should do this? Maybe you should drive."

"Honey." Christopher laid his hand over mine on the gearshift. "You can do this."

Just imagine how you'd feel driving four thousand miles only to find that the yellow brick road—or the Pan-American Highway, in our case—led to a ramshackle bridge and certain death. (And that you'd spend eternity listening to your husband saying, *I told you to stay in the middle!*)

"Screw it," I whispered to myself, and threw Rex into drive.

I could see the slats rising in front of me like a tidal wave in reverse. My heart was beating so hard my throat ached. Board by board, foot by foot, I slowly caught up to Robin's taillights on the other side. Miracle of miracles, the bridge held.

She led us up steep, scrim-covered inclines over boulders so sharp I was sure they would puncture a tire, and through mini waterfalls cascading down steep embankments. Ten minutes later, we made a broad, slow turn around a steep drop-off through a tangle of palm fronds and pulled into a fairly nondescript-looking carport. Nondescript except for the spiders the size of my hand clinging to webs as large as Rex's wheels.

Christopher climbed out. Robin was already reeling off details while her two dogs—a sweet Rhodesian ridgeback named Lina who made me miss Tally, and a giant teddy bear of a Great Dane–mastiff mix named Sam—romped around the yard. I just sat there holding the steering wheel, trying to stop shaking.

I unfastened my eyes from the spiderwebs and stepped out of Rex. My knees, my whole body, felt like Jell-O. I walked into the side yard while Robin and Christopher spoke and saw a riot of color around me: flaming yellow hibiscus the size of a cornet's horn, fuchsia bougainvillea, and waxy red torchlike plants. The sun was sinking low on the horizon through a cleft between two overlapping mountain slopes with a sliver of sea just visible at the base, like a blue kerchief tucked into the bosom of a wrap blouse. I closed my eyes and breathed in a scent that was so green and lush it seemed the scent itself was a living, sentient thing. The shadow of a smile snuck into me; maybe I would survive this after all. Maybe this *would* turn out to be the simpler life Christopher and I had been seeking.

I walked past the spiderwebs in the carport and joined Christopher and Robin inside, liking what I saw. The bulk of the house was one big room with Saltillo tile floors and a two-story cathedral ceiling. A long, narrow butcher block island divided kitchen and dining area, with the living space on the far end. On either side of the room, tall French doors opened onto a tiled terrace that wrapped around the whole house. Stairs behind the kitchen ran up to the second-story bedroom with dark teak floors, windows on three sides looking out onto the jungle canopy, and a door on either side leading to the upper balcony.

Except there was no TV, no phone, no Internet, no hot water, and our closest neighbor was at the entrance to the road at the base of the mountain across the bridge.

I had never felt so isolated, so alone, in my life.

Robin lingered a little too long and the sun had set when she pulled away. The receding crunch of stones under her tires sounded like the end of civilization to me.

"Oh my God," I said, clamping trembling hands over my mouth with the effort to hold it together. "What have we done? We're stuck in this house for three months because I am *never* going down that mountain and across that bridge again!"

Christopher hugged me, and it felt so good to set aside all the reasons I was angry with him from the borders and just feel the reassurance of his chest beneath my cheek. "We'll get used to it," he said. "It may not seem like it right now, but we will."

That evening we unpacked the groceries we'd bought on our way through San Jose and put our clothes away for the first time in six weeks. A few hours later, exhausted and sweaty—there was no light and no hot water in our shower, and we'd had enough adventure for the day—we dug a bottle of wine out of a box and carried a bench upstairs to the balcony. The evening breeze felt soft and sultry, and we could hear the waves crashing in the distance.

"We're not driving to Costa Rica anymore," Christopher said pensively. "We're here."

"We did it," I said, holding my glass up to Christopher. His face glowed with accomplishment in the flickering yellow light of the citronella candle and he touched his glass to mine. But there was something about the way the jungle swallowed up the clink that gave me chills despite the heat. What *had* we done?

*In the* middle of the night, I awoke to something rapping on the door leading from the bedroom to the deck.

"Christopher!" I said, shaking him awake. "There's someone out there!" I pointed toward the door to the balcony and the sound came again. Christopher's eyes were still closed, but as the knocking continued, his eyebrows arched up and a smile formed on his face.

"That's not a some*one*," he said, "that's a some*thing*." My eyes went as wide as saucers. He threw his legs over the side of the bed, took my hand, and led me to the door. When we peeked through the glass, we saw a rare coatimundi swinging from a rope hanging from the beams holding on to a bunch of bananas. A loose, hysterical laugh unspooled from the very center of me, and I tried to reassure myself that I had nothing to be afraid of as I looked into the white-rimmed eyes of the cute, fuzzy creature.

The next morning brought more discoveries: grasshoppers larger than the span of my hand that we dubbed flying Cadillacs, poisonous frogs the color of fire engines, and giant blue morpho butterflies that looked as if fairies had painted oak leaves Caribbean blue and set them aflight with a slow, sultry animation.

We quickly had to learn to adapt everyday routines for our new circumstances. How to make toast without a toaster? Answer: char it on the steel *comal* we'd bought from the market in Cuernavaca. How to make coffee without a coffeemaker? Answer: strain it through as clean a sock as you can find.

We unpacked Rex box by box, eager to get settled after nearly eight weeks on the road. I wanted to believe that material things didn't matter to me—simplifying was one of the main reasons we'd made the trip after all. But I won't lie, as we unpacked towels and bowls and pots and knives, I began to feel like the ground was steadying beneath my feet once again. The only problem was, I found that the kitchen was only stocked with two of everything—forks, knives, spoons, and plates—which meant we needed to provision before our friends arrived with Tally the following week. So we planned a trip to San Isidro de El General, a hilltop town of forty-five thousand tucked in a bowl atop the mountains forty-five minutes away.

The stress of the borders and the activity of unpacking coupled with the heat and humidity had taken a toll on me. I wanted to feel radiant and energetic, like the adventurer I envisioned myself being. We'd come here on reconnaissance to see if Costa Rica was where we were meant to sink our roots and open a restaurant, after all. But the truth was, just climbing the stairs left me winded and wincing in pain. In my weakness I'd become clingy, needing constant assurance that Christopher still loved me even if I felt like a sloth. This, of course, sent Christopher into his cave, which made me feel shut out and even more desperate; you can see where that spiral leads, and it ain't pretty.

As we wound up, up, up the steep jungle road toward San Isidro, Christopher—deeply ensconced in his cave—felt like a black hole next to me; dark, opaque, and volatile, with the power to crush anything within reach.

"Can you believe Tally's going to be here tomorrow?" I said to break the silence.

He looked at me like I'd just smeared a dead bug on his arm. "I know we don't have everything we need. Why do you think I said we need to go to San Isidro before they come?"

I turned my head away and squinted into the sun. The landscape looked like an Impressionist's canvas, the forest's mottled green smudged with golden *corteza amarilla* and lavender jacaranda. I felt dizzy and thought it must be from the altitude but realized that I'd barely been breathing for the last several minutes.

We turned left at the zocalo as we came into town, then right onto one of the many semipaved streets that all looked alike. Christopher pulled up onto the shoulder in front of a nondescript catchall store that Robin had told us about. A cloud of chalky dust snaked around us as we stepped out.

Inside, the store was excruciatingly dim and void of any sort of ambiance. There were simply rows and rows of hip-high bins full of everything: mouse traps, spoons, paper towels, inner tubes.

Christopher turned right toward the napkins. I walked toward the plates. I picked out six and added them to the cart, then wheeled to the silverware bin.

"What are you doing?" Christopher's voice jolted me. I turned to him and held up a fist full of forks.

"I'm getting forks," I said.

"Why six?"

I shrugged. "In case we have people over. Or if we don't want to wash forks in between every meal." I began to set them in the basket, but he grabbed them from me.

"We don't need six forks," he rumbled. "We can't afford to just buy whatever we want."

I grabbed them back and pointed to the white piece of cardboard above the bin with bold, black handwriting. "I know we can't buy whatever we want. But at fourteen cents apiece, I think we can afford to buy six forks."

Christopher put his fingertips to his temples. "You just don't get it."

"I do get it!" I said, throwing all but two forks back into the bin. "Fine, you can do the dishes in between courses!" I shoved the cart into him. "You pay, I'll be out in Rex."

I stomped out of the store and climbed into the comfort of Rex, combing through the conversation not for vengeance, but to make sense of it. *Was I out of line?* I wondered. Christopher's admonition had hit a tender spot; I'd gotten myself into debt more than once and knew I could have blinders when it came to money. "Fourteen cents a fork?" I said out loud. I shook my head and agreed with my-self that I had not, in fact, been out of line.

Christopher opened the door and threw the bag in my lap. He slammed the door and started the engine and I held my breath, waiting for it. Christopher's knuckles were white where he gripped the steering wheel, the corners of his mouth turned down in what looked like a snarl. We made it a block, and then he opened his mouth and out it came. A full-throttle tirade about how I don't lis-ten. How I don't trust him to know what's right.

Midsentence, I opened the door and jumped out of Rex.

Rex's brakes squealed and the window rolled down. "Get in the truck, Lia," Christopher yelled.

"No!"

"Get. In. The. Truck," he said. Each syllable felt as sharp as a meat hook.

"No. I can't listen to this anymore." I turned away down the street and heard gravel spewing under Rex's tires as Christopher sped away in the opposite direction.

I walked aimlessly, feeling the hot sun beating on my bare head and through the SPF 50 shirt I was wearing. As I neared the zocalo three blocks away, reality sank in and did nothing to calm me. I had no identification, no money, no phone, and no way of reaching Christopher. I didn't even have an address or phone number. My heart was pounding so hard a white corona rimmed my vision with every beat.

I started to walk in a long rectangle, pausing five, ten, fifteen minutes at each corner of the zocalo, then three blocks to the curb where we parted and down the block to the store, then retracing my steps again. My pulse quickened each time I turned a corner, hoping I'd see Rex's bulky black form before me. But each time, there was nothing.

I tried to pray, but my emotions were so jumbled I couldn't hold a straight thought. I was furious with Christopher—"He left me!" the tape screamed over and over in my head. But I was also peeved at myself. What kind of a woman jumps out of her truck, abandons her husband, and takes to the streets of a remote town in a third-world country . . . without her purse?

The sun was dipping beneath the treetops as I walked past the zocalo a final time, having decided to go to the gas station at the edge of town to beg a call to Robin. How I, or they, would find her number I had no idea. At that point, I was beyond caring.

Two blocks past the zocalo the gas station came into view, along with a masculine silhouette that melted my heart. Rex. I saw Christopher climb in and start to pull away and I tried to cry out, but my throat seized up. I jammed my fingers into my mouth and let rip a high-pitched whistle that had stopped many a cab from two blocks away in New York City. It worked. I saw Rex's brake lights. Then his white reverse lights. I ran toward him and the passenger door opened as if by an invisible force.

I was sobbing, hard, when I climbed in and didn't have a clue what to say. As we ascended up and out of the mountains, the low hum of Rex's motor and soft curve of his bucket seat offered some comfort, but I was nauseated with anger and embarrassment and desperation. Everything had shifted. I felt unsure and terrified, like when you don't trust the very ground you're standing on after an earthquake. The sky turned mauve as we wound back down the mountain, and I was still crying forty-five minutes later when we pulled off onto our dirt road.

"That was stupid what you did, Lia," Christopher said.

I sank further into my seat. He was right. It was.

"I don't want to be here anymore," I said, barely able to get the words out. "I just want to go home."

"Where do you want to go, Lia?" Christopher barked. "Because this is home now. This is all we have."

When we pulled up to our jungle house my body was throbbing so palpably it felt as if someone were beating my sinews like a drum from the inside. I went straight upstairs and lay on the bed, too shocked and depleted to muster up more tears.

Quite a bit later, after I'd slept and awoken and dozed and awoken again, Christopher came in and lay down beside me, both of us curled like quotation marks with the space in between. "It's just us, you know." His voice was soft. "You can't run home, because there is no home right now. We are all the home we've got, and we'll work this out."

I could still feel Christopher's body imprinted on the mattress after he got up. I closed my eyes and pined for those easy, early days of snuggling under a warm comforter listening to the foghorns in the marina while mist swept by the window. When we were we, and I was whole. But the leaves outside rustled and the jungle breathed, hot and sticky on my skin. Christopher was right. For better or for worse, we were here now, with nowhere else to go.

*The arrival* of the Costas didn't help my situation. From the get-go, a biting insecurity rose like bile in me at Kelly's abundant wit and effortless charm. I tried to hide it—I tried not to feel it—but that, too, was an effort. I could feel my energy seeping out like a wrung-out dish towel.

Our first night, Christopher made "jungle rum" cocktails and we sat up on the balcony trying to harness an evening breeze. Cicadas hummed, the crash of the ocean kept beat, and the jungle leaves whished and swished.

"How are you doing?" Kelly squeezed my knee. To our friends who had been there for us through the lupus diagnosis and hysterectomy, I was someone to be coddled and considered frail. I could see it in their eyes, hear it in their voices.

But that wasn't who I wanted to be.

I could feel the exhaustion stalking me, looming in the shadows like a wildcat readying to pounce. I thought about the disaster the day before, and how ruptured and distant I felt from Christopher.

"I'm good," I lied, nodding. "We're settling in."

The one arena where I felt confident and at ease was in the kitchen. Christopher popped open frosty Imperial beers and put Bob Marley on, and I assigned tasks for the evening's dinner, a mash-up of our favorite dishes from our class in Cuernavaca.

Christopher and I recounted stories of our wild-goose chases and treasure hunts in Oaxaca as Kelly pounded guacamole and salsa cruda in the *molcajete,* which we ended up blending together and dubbing "salsamole." I boiled pork for the *chilorio* while Christopher and Albert set up an assembly line to press and toast tortillas, perfecting the size of the masa ball, the tension of how hard to push on the press, and the gentle pat of the tortilla on the *comal* to cause it to puff in the middle. Then Kelly and I shredded the pork and simmered it in the vinegary sauce until it turned a deep brick red.

"Ready to make the *pastel imposible*?" I said to Kelly.

"So what's so impossible about this cake?" Kelly asked.

"You mix up two batters, one for chocolate cake and one for flan, then pour them in a pan. When it starts out, the chocolate cake batter settles to the bottom and the flan on top, but by the time you pull it out of the oven, the two layers have flipped."

"Stop."

"Seriously. And it's not even a marbly thing, it's like perfect layer flip."

Kelly made the flan batter while I made the chocolate cake batter, and we prevailed in making a perfect *pastel imposible* despite it being even more impossible without a blender, buttermilk, or the right pan.

I sat back in my chair at the end of the meal relishing the lingering hum of the chiles on my tongue under the sweet creaminess of the cake. Yes, I was in pain. Yes, I was exhausted. But I'd been able to bring a meal to the table that we would all talk about for years to come, and that brought a momentary truce to the gremlins battling it out within my psyche to convince me how wretched and unlovable I was.

Which was good, because the war began again the next day and I went downhill fast—battling blinding fits of jealousy and self-loathing so strong it almost made me gag.

"You guys go to the beach without me," I said as we left the café we'd gone to for breakfast. "I've got to go home and lie down."

Christopher seemed to brighten. But maybe not. They drove Tally and me up to the turnoff to our house and I got out and slammed the door. Tally and I crossed the rickety bridge and walked the boulder-strewn flat as I stewed on how Christopher seemed so uninterested in anything I had to say. How could we have traveled four thousand miles together and be so disconnected from one another? Were we going to be one of those couples you see in restaurants who stare vacantly across the table at each other? I groaned. Seeing Christopher react so animatedly to Kelly and Albert made me feel like a worn wool sweater, something that's comfortable and there but isn't really something you spend time thinking about. He would deny it, of course, and cite all the times he'd asked how I was doing, and when he said he liked a meal, yadda, yadda, yadda. But that was exactly the point. I didn't want our marriage to be about compliments to a meal or checking up on how his sick wife was doing. I wanted it to be full of soul-baring truth and provoking conversations, talks where we looked each other square in the eyes and listened with our whole being. I thought that was one of the reasons we'd come here. To learn to savor those simple moments and grow closer in the little realities of who we were.

Tally and I turned the corner and started the steep trudge up the mountain. *I am an adventurer,* I thought. It was how I'd defined myself before getting sick, it was why Christopher fell in love with me, and it was what prompted this harebrained idea of driving to Costa Rica. I pushed the boundaries, I said yes when others said no, I didn't stop. In my book, there were no limits for an adventurer, and that was who I was.

Or was it? As Tally and I walked into the house and I marched up the stairs and into the shower, I had a sobering thought. *What if I've taken it too far this time?* What if the gremlins were right and I *was* just weak? If I wasn't an adventurer, what did that make me? And what would be left for Christopher to love?

I was exhausted. Exhausted from the incessant heat. Exhausted from being baked in the sun too many times. Exhausted from grappling with my weakness, and exhausted from beating myself up for my weakness. I was exhausted from second-guessing situations and the effort it took to do the simplest things. I was exhausted from feeling completely disconnected from Christopher, and exhausted from struggling to find God in any of it.

I stepped out of the shower without drying off and dropped onto the bed. When I turned my head and looked out the window, I saw a smudge of yellow and thought it was one of the canary-yellow birds that were so ubiquitous. But it was the breast of a much larger bird. The yellow splotch was rimmed in bright red that matched the undersides of his wings, which he scratched every now and then with his large, curved bill.

It was a toucan, and he was magnificent.

We watched each other and I felt myself grow calm. I watched him follow other birds with his gaze in a way that wasn't predatory so much as patient. I'd always thought of toucans as silly, cartoon-like creatures, but this one had a wise stillness to him. After ten minutes or so, he gracefully flew over to another tree—it looked more like a giant hop than actual flying—where he was joined by another toucan. They hopped from branch to branch, cooing softly, and were joined by yet another. Then they flew into the dense, dark green of the forest. I dressed and went out to the balcony and lay in the hammock, listening to their calls, feeling more serene than I had in days.

I wanted to be like that toucan, alert, strong, and confident. He wasn't in the tree freaking out about whether he was good enough. He was content to simply be.

Hours later, I heard Rex pull up and gingerly made my way downstairs, feeling like an octogenarian. I tried to smile and act carefree, but I could tell Kelly wasn't buying it, and I felt bad that she felt bad. We planned a dinner of tortillas stuffed with cheese, a couple of salsas, fried plantains, and a big salad. But when I tried to cook the plantains, sweat started pouring down my face and I had to go lie down. Christopher came up a few minutes later and laid his hand on my forehead. "You OK?" he asked.

"I'll be fine," I said. "I'll be down in a few." The truth was, I wasn't sure I'd be able to get back out of bed. I wasn't sure at all that I'd be fine. His kiss felt cool on my forehead and he walked out the door and down the stairs.

"Is she OK?" I heard Kelly whisper to Christopher. The tone of pity and concern in everyone's voices made me want to scream.

No, it made me want to disappear. I closed my eyes and warm tears trickled out their corners. I already had disappeared, though. Where had the me that I knew gone?

꒰ ᜊ꒱

## PASTEL IMPOSIBLE (IMPOSSIBLE CAKE)

*This recipe is adapted from our Rancho Cuernavaca cooking class. It's a fun one to assemble as guests arrive so they can see the transformation— how the layers flip neatly as it bakes—when the cake comes out of the oven. Cajeta is a sort of Mexican caramel made from goat's milk; you can find it at Mexican markets.*

Butter for greasing the pan
1 cup *cajeta* (or dulce de leche)

CHOCOLATE CAKE BATTER
$1^3/_4$ cups all-purpose flour
$^2/_3$ cup unsweetened baking cocoa
$1^1/_2$ teaspoons baking soda
$^1/_4$ teaspoon salt
1 stick unsalted butter, softened

$^3/_4$ cup granulated sugar

$^1/_2$ cup packed dark brown sugar

2 large eggs

1 teaspoon vanilla extract

$1^1/_3$ cups buttermilk

FLAN BATTER

6 large eggs

1 12-ounce can evaporated milk

1 14-ounce can sweetened condensed milk

1 teaspoon vanilla extract

Grease a 10-inch round 3-inch deep cake pan with butter, all the way up the sides. Spread *cajeta* evenly on the bottom of the pan. Preheat the oven to 350°F.

Start by making the chocolate cake batter. In a medium bowl, whisk together the flour, cocoa, baking soda, and salt. In a large bowl with an electric mixer, beat together the butter and sugars for 2 to 3 minutes, until fluffy and light. Add the eggs one at a time, beating well after each addition. Beat in the vanilla.

Reduce the speed to low and add one third of the flour mixture, then half of the buttermilk, just until combined. Scrape down the sides of the bowl, then beat in half of the remaining flour mixture, followed by the buttermilk and the rest of the flour mixture, just until combined. Scrape the batter into the prepared pan and smooth the top with a spatula.

Next make the flan batter. In a blender, combine the eggs, evaporated milk, sweetened condensed milk, and vanilla and blend until smooth.

Pour the flan batter on top of the chocolate cake batter. Place the pan in a large roasting pan and fill the roasting pan with enough hot water to reach halfway up the cake pan. Bake for 60 to 90 minutes, or until a toothpick inserted in the center comes out clean.

Remove the cake from the oven, run a sharp knife around the edge, and let cool completely on a cake rack. Refrigerate until set and cold. To serve, place the cake pan on the stove for a few seconds to melt the *cajeta* slightly. Run a knife around the edge once more, then invert the cake onto a platter. Serve with *cajeta* spooned over the top.

SERVES 12

# PART II
## *ROOTS*

*After a tomato seed softens, it sends out roots to anchor it to the earth, and shoots erupt above ground to search for light.*

THE NEW SEED-STARTERS HANDBOOK

*Maybe you are searching among the branches, for what only appears in the roots.*

MEWLANA JALALUDDIN RUMI

# Chapter 10

# ANOTHER KIND OF COMMUNION

FEBRUARY 2000

Two days later, I awoke out of a sluggish sleep alone in bed. Christopher had taken the Costas back to San Jose to catch their flight and stayed over to find a Ford dealer to fix Rex's spare tire, which was currently stuck to his underbelly. I was feeling too weak to go anywhere or do anything, so I opted to stay back at the house. I lay there for a long while, already feeling the grip of the heat as if my body were a balloon that the air around me was trying to pop.

The prospect of a good, strong cup of coffee from the French press Kelly had brought buoyed my energy. Tucking my sundress into my underwear to maximize any hint of breeze, I padded downstairs and sat on a stool to wait for the water to boil on our wimpy propane burner. I was alone, and yet I felt a presence beckoning me as subtly and tangibly as the rustle of leaves through the forest.

God wanted me to sit with Him, be with Him.

But how could I? The last few days had surfaced the very worst in me, like a pimple red and ripe for popping. I was an insecure, self-centered, manipulating, jealous . . . bitch. What the hell would God want with *me*?

I poured hot water into the coffee grounds and a thick, chocolaty scent swirled up. I picked up a broom and tried sweeping the kitchen floor while waiting for the coffee—the jungle delivered never-ending detritus—but tired out after three swipes and had to sit back down.

"Stop," I heard. "Slow down. Listen. Be still." So I surrendered, clomping upstairs with my coffee mug and tucking my legs underneath me on the bench on the balcony. The heat made it feel like noon even though it was just past ten. I opened the Bible in my lap to the book of Hosea, a story of God's enduring love for his people.

*Therefore, I am now going to allure her. I will lead her into the wilderness and speak tenderly to her.*

Let me just say right here that I came to the Bible warily, even after I became a Christian. In the beginning I viewed it as a collection of poems and wisdom and stories to help me live my life the way I was designed to and point me toward the one who designed me. But the more time I spent in its pages, the more I discovered that there was something else too: that the Spirit seemed to be almost curating what verse or snippet reached me on any given day, and clarifying—or amplifying—its meaning. It was uncanny how often I was fed exactly what I needed to hear, exactly when I needed to hear it. As was the case in the jungle that day.

I don't know how to explain what happened next except to say that it felt like God's presence up and sat right there beside me on that bench. I looked out at the jungle and felt like He was looking out at the jungle too, my breath in rhythm with His breath. *My God,* I thought. He did allure me. He did bring me into the wilderness. He orchestrated every little thing in my life to bring me here—to this steaming hillside in Costa Rica—listening to these tender words, here and now.

I looked back down at the page—*There I will give her back her vineyards and make the Valley of Trouble a door of hope*—and for the first time since being broken by the hysterectomy and the lupus, I felt hope that I would be whole again. I'd thought getting my food writing career off the ground would make me whole. I'd thought being on a great adventure would make me whole. But they didn't.

Those words did.

Or at least they gave me palpable hope that wholeness was on the horizon.

If I hadn't been so broken, I think the immense, unwarranted love and tenderness that flowed out of those sentences would have bounced right off me. Instead, it knocked me to my knees. It was as if I were reading a personal love letter sent directly from God, like I could feel His palm against my back.

There's a *Star Trek* movie in which the *Enterprise* crashes onto a planet where the natives were such masters at mindfulness that they could slow down time and be so present in each moment that they could see the flap of a hummingbird's wings. That's how it felt at that moment.

I drank in scriptures and the world around me through every pore and synapse in my body.

As the rough boards scratched my already throbbing knees, I sobbed. I cried out of shame for the wreck that I was, and I cried out of overflowing gratitude. God did indeed call Christopher and me into the wilderness, but not to abandon us and leave us in splinters. He brought us there into the wilderness to strip us bare so He could redefine our concepts of home and life and love. He brought us there into the wilderness with a tender promise to give me hope again, to give me *me* again. And in that moment, I trusted with every bit of me that He would.

I lay there bowed over my knees on that balcony, as if praying to the jungle, until my sides hurt from sobbing, then walked in a daze downstairs, marveling that Tally was still lazing on the tile verandah as if nothing had changed. But God was there. God had brought me there. And that changed everything.

I opened the refrigerator, lingering in its chill, and found two passion fruits I had bought earlier at the market. I took them out to the verandah and pricked one open with my thumbnail, forcing the fissure open to reveal a cobwebby mass of opalescent seeds. With great care, I tore off a section of peel, using it as a scoop, and gingerly sucked its gelatinous meat from the shell. Little by little I teased the flesh out of its casing, recklessly tossing the carcass into the jungle as I finished each piece, licking the juice where it trickled down my arm. Flavors of orange and lime and pineapple tumbled around my mouth while the texture and mystery brought to mind a pomegranate. If I had to pin down the moment in time when my culinary odyssey began, when food began to have meaning and make sense to me, it was Mama's fried egg in Greece. Then, the simple pleasure of *everything* had been mysterious and new.

I'd grown a lot since then. I'd learned about exotic ingredients like yuzu and persimmons, and luxe foods like foie gras and caviar. I'd broken into the magazine world, writing recipes of my own, and was now on the road to becoming a restaurateur with Christopher.

But there in Costa Rica we were starting from scratch. Nothing looked the same. Not the produce, not the cooking circumstances, not myself. And after that morning I was more ready than ever to face—to be—a blank slate.

So I decided to make a pot of beans. That may not sound remarkable, but that morning the act of making beans felt no less than an act of communion with God Himself. The only way I'd known beans growing up was from a can. Yet in Latin America beans were the heartbeat of a meal, a constant staple that could be relied on for nourishment. *Those* were the kind of beans I wanted to make.

I decided to hedge my bets by referencing both of the cookbooks I'd brought—Diana Kennedy's *Cuisines of Mexico* and Rick Bayless's *Authentic Mexican.* I followed Diana's advice to start the beans in hot water, only I had to wait about an hour for the ten cups of water to come to a boil on our sputtering stove. When it finally did, I added the beans, lard, and garlic (per Rick's instructions; sorry, Diana, no onion), and let it simmer for three hours.

Later in the afternoon I started to think about dinner. Provisions were slim; we'd gone through almost all the fresh food we'd bought for Kelly and Albert's visit. But the beans were so meaty and flavorful, they were a meal unto themselves. I mixed some masa with water and worked it until the sandy flour became like clay, then let it sit to make tortillas with when Christopher arrived . . . if he arrived.

But instead of my usual anxious mode (*Where is he? Is he safe? It's almost dark!*), I calmly charred the last of our vegetables—two tomatoes, three serranos, two cloves of garlic, and a *cebollita* with its greens—on the *comal*, then chopped them, pounded them all in the *molcajete*, and added everything to the last of the mangoes, which I'd diced super fine. I stirred in some chopped cilantro, olive oil, and juice from a lime. I took a bite, then added a touch of cider vinegar and salt.

I was grateful for the basics—tomatoes, onion, garlic, chile—but I was missing the variety of vegetables I'd grown used to at home and in Mexico. It was like going from Bach to "Row, Row, Row Your Boat."

I heard a low hum in the distance, and Tally and I both cocked our heads. The unmistakable sound of stones crushing beneath tires heralded that Christopher and Rex were home. I smiled. And then my smile grew wider as I realized how foreign it felt to smile a genuine, from-the-gut smile. I felt like my whole being had been scrubbed clean by a strong rainstorm. I could think more clearly, feel more clearly, *love* more clearly.

I turned the burner on to heat the *comal* and walked to the door to greet Christopher. His eyes drooped and his hair was matted with sweat.

"You look spent," I said, holding out my arms. He draped himself over me and set his chin on my shoulder.

"I am."

"Thank you for taking them without me. And thank you for getting Rex fixed."

"I'm just so glad it all worked out." He sniffed the air and straightened, looking brighter. "It smells good, you've been cooking."

"I have. We didn't have much left, but I did the best I could." I led him to the kitchen and sat him down at a stool, then took a spoon from the drawer and dipped it into the pot. "I made beans," I said, holding the spoon out to Christopher. "Try."

He took a bite and closed his eyes, chewing slowly and making a low hum. "Who needs meat when you've got these?"

"That's what I thought." I smiled and scooped some of the mango salsa onto a tortilla chip. "Try this too."

He took a bite and this time his eyes went wide. He dipped another chip into the salsa while I pulled two Imperials from the refrigerator. "You really need to write these things down," he said.

I clinked my beer against his and marveled at how radically different I felt from just twenty-four hours earlier. Calm instead of angst, trust instead of anger, strength and confidence instead of insecurity. Like night and day.

*The next* week, Christopher and I were swinging in our hammocks on the deck reading our respective books and trying to catch a nonexistent breeze.

I'd been reading Richard Foster's *Freedom of Simplicity,* and it was rocking my world. Foster's whole premise is that the more detached we become from finding joy through money, power, sex, recognition from others, and so on, the freer we become to find pure joy through the Spirit. Through it, I was beginning to redefine freedom, not as a reckless joyride focused on my own pleasure, but as the relinquishing of the things—physical and emotional—that drove the go, go, go, do, do, do in me. To find that elusive stillness that allowed me to hear what God was saying to the deepest parts of my soul. In the presence of *that* kind of freedom—like I'd gotten a taste of that morning on the balcony—all other illusions seemed as shallow as a singles bar on ladies' night.

So many thoughts were stirring up, and I ached to talk to Christopher about them. But talking to him was no easy task. I wanted to toss my thoughts on the table like Yahtzee dice and hash out together what they all meant. But Christopher required more structure. He had very defined rules on when we should and should not talk, and how much should be said. He just wasn't sharing the rulebook with me.

As it was, most of our communication revolved around food.

One day, Minor, the young man who took care of the grounds,

told me about *flor de itabo*. He'd pointed to a stalk of white flowers that had erupted out of a giant yucca. "*Puede concinar con ellos,*" he said. You could cook with them.

"I've got a challenge for you," I said to Christopher a few days later. "Minor told me about this yucca flower you can cook with, and I've been thinking about what to do with them. I think I'm going to sauté them with shrimp and garlic for a pasta sauce."

"Awesome," Christopher said. "What's the challenge? As long as it doesn't involve peeling the shrimp."

"I've been sussing out the yuccas and the only one I can find with flowers still on it is hanging off the cliff on the edge of the driveway."

Christopher thought for a moment before marching toward the door. "Follow me," he said. "I've got an idea." He grabbed the machete and told me to climb into Rex.

"Why Rex? It's just a hundred feet or so down the driveway."

"Trust me," Christopher said, holding Rex's door open. "Climb in."

We drove all of five seconds, to the bend in the drive that was carved out of the mountain with a steep slope up one side and down the other. A super-sized yucca poked off the side of the dropoff like an oversized pricker.

"Hold the door open," Christopher said, coming around to the passenger side. He used the seat as a step to climb onto Rex's roof. "And hand me the machete."

"What?" I asked. "What are you going to do?"

"Hand me the machete. I'm going to lean over and chop down the stalk."

I lifted the hilt of the machete up to Christopher with wide eyes. "But, babe, if you fall off you'll fall all the way down the mountain."

He grinned. "Then I'd better not fall off." He whacked at the stalk, while leaning precariously into it. "Besides, I'm not missing this dinner."

I groaned, but the stalk eventually gave way and Christopher handed it to me as he climbed down. It was heavy, loaded with star-shaped white flowers about the size of a silver dollar with a lustrous, matte sheen. "I'd say you earned your dinner." I grinned.

We drove back up to the house and I brought the stalk into the kitchen and plucked the flowers off, swishing them around in a bowl of water to get rid of dust and crawly critters.

I flavored butter and olive oil with crushed garlic in a warm pan, then chopped the *flor de itabo* and added it to the pan. While the flowers were cooking, I boiled spaghetti, then added shrimp to the *flor de itabo* with a touch of pasta water and a sprinkle of chile flakes, and tossed everything with the spaghetti. The combination was outstanding. The *flor de itabo* had an unusual flavor that was somewhere between artichoke hearts and asparagus and had a texture that was both meaty and delicate, all of which went beautifully with the shrimp.

*One night* we were over at our friends Max and Vittoria's house. Vittoria was an Italian hotelier and Max was a Dutch sailor. They owned the casitas we'd stayed at the first time we visited Dominical. I was sipping wine watching Vittoria make pasta with broccoli sauce.

"Where do you get your vegetables?" I asked. "They're always so beautiful." We'd been disappointed by the food we had encountered in Costa Rica. There were no buckets of moles, or dozens of dried chile varieties to choose from. There were half-rotten tomatoes, and brown heads of broccoli, and spoiled fish, and a lot of men in white hazmat suits spraying chemicals everywhere, which had made me feel wary of food—and protective of my body—in a way I never had before.

She looked at me with a bright smile, her wild, brown hair a halo around her head. "You must go to Finca Ipe, darling," she said. "Tell Greg I sent you."

So we did, and found a bucolic, fertile farm in a sunny bowl between two valleys, where we negotiated a deal for Christopher to help out twice a week on the organic co-op farm in return for some of the harvest.

Inspired by the goods coming from Finca Ipe—taut purple eggplant, a rainbow of tomatoes, broccoli rabe, and much, much more—I began to experiment. One night, I grilled beets and onions and sliced them over romaine, sprinkling it all with a feta-like cheese we'd bought from a nearby Mennonite community. Another night I pounded garlic and olive oil in the *molcajete* and tossed it with boiled broccoli rabe and rigatoni, squeezing lime all over it. I even tried chayote, a semihard-shelled, teardrop-shaped squash with an oblong seed in the center like a mango. Guided by Rick Bayless, I peeled it and cut it into chunks, boiled it, drained it, and stir-fried it in olive oil and garlic, adding tomatoes and olives at the end. It was both beautiful—a lovely translucent green, like sea glass—and delicious, like an artichoke meets zucchini.

*But I* was beginning to realize it wasn't just quality food I was missing. M. F. K. Fisher opens her memoir, *The Gastronomical Me* (another one of my hammock reads), with the line *There is communion of more than our bodies when bread is broken and wine is drunk,* meaning that when we tend to physical hunger with attention and care, deeper hungers are satiated too.

As much as we longed to share that communion with the locals, as I had in Greece and France and we both had throughout Mexico, they simply weren't meeting us there. So we sought it elsewhere. We heard of a Frenchman who made baguettes, so we took weekly pilgrimages an hour down the coast to buy a dozen at a time, which we'd cut into thirds and freeze. Our favorite café in town, Pow Wow, was owned by a Dutchman, Paul, who was committed to sourcing his coffee from small farmers. There was also a rustic restaurant in town called La Capanna that served incredible Italian food, although Rosanna, the chef's wife, gave us the cold shoulder every time we went.

We were deliberate about the food we were putting in our bodies, and I was feeling more creative and unfettered in the kitchen. We'd also begun doing yoga, and I found that the moves, while deceptively simple—the inverted V of a down dog, the tiny upward curve of an up dog, the hands-up lunges of warriors—added up to an effect I'd never experienced before. I'd leave class feeling energized yet calm, elongated yet strong. I felt like I was finally inhabiting my body and becoming more intimate, more loving, with myself than I'd ever been.

But I still had a lot of growing to do. In *Freedom of Simplicity,* Foster says that living simply doesn't just mean renouncing material possessions or turning away from the lures of the modern world. In fact, that's really just the first step out of three stages identified by François Fénelon, a seventeenth-century theologian and poet. The next is where we are immensely aware of our shortcomings and faults and constantly trying to rid ourselves of them. I felt caught between those first and second stages, analyzing my every thought and action, and wondering if I could have done better.

It reminded me of making stock. I'd taken a class on soups,

stocks, and sauces at the Culinary Institute of America in Napa when we lived in San Francisco, and we learned that you have to continually skim off the impurities that float to the surface as the stock simmers if you want a clean broth.

The same was true with faith. As we become more concentrated in our faith, our impurities—in my case, jealousy, insecurity, and judgment, to name a few—bubble to the surface and need to be dealt with before breaking through to the next level.

According to Foster, the good news was that that process in and of itself is an integral part of the growth, just as the releasing of impurities from bones and scraps is an integral part of extracting flavor. The bad news was, it could last quite some time.

The third stage Fénelon identified is where we don't even think of ourselves; we're completely unself-conscious. Movements, thoughts, being, are all simple, focused, and centered in the Spirit and everything radiates from that center. *That* was where I desperately wanted to be, although it seemed quite impossible. But I felt hopeful. Maybe, if I persevered through the burbling and skimming long enough, I too would become less clouded by fears and insecurities and gain clarity on what really mattered.

꧁᯽꧂

## FRIJOLES DE LIA

Frijoles de olla *are a traditional dish of brothy beans cooked in an earthenware pot (an* olla) *that are hearty enough to be a meal in and of themselves. The recipes I followed in Costa Rica—from Diana Kennedy and Rick Bayless—followed a simple equation of beans, lard, an onion or garlic, and*

*epazote. I've taken the liberty of adding a few more goodies that I've ap-*
*pended on over the years.*

1 tablespoon canola oil

1 medium onion, chopped

2 large poblano chiles, seeded and chopped into $\frac{1}{2}$-inch pieces

4 garlic cloves, smashed

2 teaspoons ground cumin

2 teaspoons ground coriander

2 teaspoons oregano

2 teaspoons ground ancho chile

$1\frac{1}{2}$ cups dried black beans, rinsed and soaked
    overnight (or fast-soaked in a pressure cooker)

Sea salt

In a large, heavy-bottomed pot, heat the oil over medium-high heat. Add the onion, poblano chiles, and garlic and sauté for 15 minutes, stirring frequently, until the onion is golden brown. Add the cumin, coriander, oregano, and ancho chile and sauté for 1 minute, until fragrant.

Add the beans, a generous pinch of salt, and 6 cups cold water and bring to a boil. Reduce the heat to low and simmer, uncovered, for $1\frac{1}{2}$ to 2 hours, until the beans are tender.

Using a potato masher, mash the beans until there's a mix of whole beans and creamy mashed beans.

SERVES 10 TO 12

# CHAPTER 11

# "WHEN SOMEONE ASK, I GIVE"

APRIL 2000

Rosanna placed her hand on my shoulder. This was a big deal because, as I mentioned earlier, for the first month we lived in Dominical, Rosanna—one of the three owners of the Italian restaurant in town called La Capanna—wouldn't even look me in the eye. Two months in, though, we'd become buds and La Capanna became our home away from home. Which was appropriate, since *capanna* means "shelter" in Italian. Shelter in the sense of a lean-to, but shelter also in the sense of comfort and warmth. And La Capanna served as both. It was more like a pop-up *palapa* than an actual restaurant, with a thatched roof (no walls), candles on each of the eight or so tables, and strings of glittered cardboard stars and moons made by local kids hanging from rafter to rafter. The whole vibe was one of bohemian nomads just off a caravan.

Rosanna and Fausto had met as professional ballet dancers on tour before joining the circus. But most important, they were from Bologna, Italy's most epic food city—the city that gave the world Bolognese sauce and tortellini and is surrounded by the towns that gave their names to Parma prosciutto, Parmigiano-Reggiano cheese, and balsamic vinegar from Modena.

Bolognese men in the kitchen are a good thing.

Through Rosanna's gentle tutelage we learned about *burrata* ("like cream wrapped in buffalo mozzarella, darling") and fried zucchini flowers ("stuffed with ricotta and light as air") and were offered any of the soups "wit or wit'out pasta" as Rosanna buzzed between the tables. We feasted on fried calamari, puffy pillows of gnocchi in Gorgonzola sauce, and spaghetti with seafood in a garlicky, pungent olive oil sauce spiked with chiles. But all were like little cousins to the crowning glory, the lasagna.

Now, I had grown up with the kind of lasagna that came from the freezer section in a foil pan. In contrast, Fausto's lasagna was like silk sheets sandwiching a filling that was simultaneously fluffy and lush, bathed in the best Bolognese sauce I'd ever tasted in my life (sorry, Dad); hand-cut veal and beef simmered with milk and wine and aromatics for several hours while everything—meat, wine, garlic, onions, herbs—became one, like a choral ensemble whose solos were captivating, yet whose whole was transcendent. All I could do was sit with my eyes closed and hum as I tried to take it all in.

The night I felt Rosanna's hand on my shoulder, we'd come down late, after our weekly massage session with Omar and Marie in the open-air rooms above the restaurant. We'd lain there surrounded by soft candlelight and gentle breezes that rustled the white drapes. Fausto belted Bocelli below while wafts of Bolognese sauce crept up through the rafters. As Christopher and I were kneaded into a sweet bliss, we'd silently, individually, been plotting our dinner before promising Omar and Marie that we wouldn't eat any heavy food or drink wine while our bodies worked out the toxins from the massage. Then we'd made a beeline for La Capanna.

By the time we finished dinner—it was lasagna for both of us that night, along with a bottle of Montepulciano—everyone was gone, and Rosanna set down three glass bowls filled with scoops of chocolate ice cream. "The last of the ice cream," Rosanna said as she dropped into a chair. "On me."

At 11:00 p.m., the air was sticky-hot and still. "Mmm," I answered, feeling the tiniest bit guilty for breaking my promise to Omar for the fourth time that evening. "Thank you." The ice cream was cold and creamy. Rosanna fanned her sweaty cleavage with a menu. "How did you guys start La Capanna?" I asked, curious about what it would take for Christopher and me to open a restaurant of our own there in Dominical.

She lit a cigarette and took a long drag. "We build all the chairs and tables ourselves while we live on the beach," she said. "It took us so long time to gather the wood and raise the money." Then she let loose a big, lusty laugh. "And then someone stole them all."

"What?" I asked, aghast. "What did you do?"

Rosanna shrugged and swatted a mosquito. "We build again. We have lots of help. One person build that chair, someone else build that one. And we help when we can too. Like when one of our friends want a TV and we give him money to buy."

This stopped me midbite, which was saying something. "Wait.... You had no money yourselves. You were living on a beach. And you gave someone money to buy a TV?" The concept went against everything I had been brought up to believe. First, that one must be financially secure oneself before one even considered giving to others. Second, that giving away something as high-ticket as a TV would foster sloth and moral decay, or something like that. I mean, I could understand money for a roof or food. But a TV? "Why?" I asked. "Why did you do that?"

Rosanna shrugged again and closed her eyes to savor the last bite of ice cream. "Because they ask," she said. "When someone ask, I give."

As part of our quest for simplicity, Christopher and I had been thinking a lot about radical giving. The whole idea of giving based on someone's need—or simply someone's want—rather than what *we* felt comfortable with giving felt as out of control to me as a roller coaster with no rails. In Costa Rica, we were surrounded by plenty of expats who were giving souls. There was Paul and his Pow Wow café; he put a portion of his profits toward things like after-school programs for kids. Vittoria had set up a center for street kids in San Isidro. Seeing so many people concoct ways to give and contribute and help gave me hope that we too could become giving people.

But Maarten, another Dutchman, had a different opinion. We had been taken by some paintings at another local restaurant and were introduced to Maarten, the artist, when we asked if we could buy one. Maarten had said that he'd consider selling to us, but he'd have to interview us first.

So one uncharacteristically windy afternoon we were standing on the edge of the beach looking at Maarten's canvases in the back of his truck.

"I love that one of the lifeguard stand," I said, pointing to a large painting in Maarten's signature style of splashy color and bold brushstrokes.

Maarten grunted. "That one is a statement about what happens when expats come down here and try to do good." He swept his hand contemptuously at the tawny sand and churning surf. "This beach is dangerous, with lots of undertows and riptides. A couple of people die off this beach every year. And one do-gooder group got the idea to build a lifeguard stand." He pointed at the dingy white chair on the beach, which was rendered in all the colors of the rainbow in his painting.

"But isn't that a good thing?" I asked, thinking him morbidly cynical.

"For what it was, yes, I suppose." He waved us toward the painting and pointed out shadowy figures along the edges of the structure. "But like everything, it has a consequence. For every action, a reaction."

"What are those?" Christopher asked, pointing to shadows around the base of the structure.

"Those are the drug dealers who started hanging around by the lifeguard stand. It became a sort of meeting place. So, you see, the good was outdone by the bad." He lifted the painting to reveal another below, of three giant pineapples splashed in Technicolor on a four-foot-square canvas.

"That's our favorite," Christopher said. "That's the one we'd like to buy—the whole pineapple hospitality thing."

Maarten shook his head vehemently and my heart sank. "Don't you get it? The pineapples don't stand for welcome. They stand for deception and decay." At that point, I really wished he'd just stop talking, because he was totally ruining the juju for me. "The pineapples are like Costa Rica—they entice you with their exotic sweetness, but then you get to the core and it's bitter, rotten."

As depressing as that talk with Maarten was, his paintings *were* beautiful, and we'd passed whatever test he'd needed us to pass to let us walk away with the pineapples.

And then the rains began.

The first night it rained, Christopher and I thought it quaint. We lay in bed and listened to the patter of raindrops on the jungle leaves outside and it felt like we were in a scene from *Robinson Crusoe*. But unease had been building in me for weeks that I'd been struggling to put into words and, as much as I hated to admit it, the conversation with Maarten had helped some of those thoughts congeal.

"I didn't expect it to be like this," I said.

"What?" Christopher asked. "The rain?"

"No," I said. "I just ... It's just what Maarten said about expats and do-gooders and consequences. Maybe he's right. You can never know for sure that an action you want to be taken as positive will be seen or used in that way."

Christopher sighed deeply, a long, windy tone against the staccato of the raindrops. "I hear you. I mean, how many stories have we heard about a foreigner coming down here and buying land from a poor farmer, and rather than it being a good thing for the family, it tears them apart when the father goes off and spends all the money on booze and women and cars."

"I just feel so separate from the people here," I said. "I feel like because we drive a truck and are wearing shoes and living in a house like this that we'll never be seen on equal ground. We'll only be seen as expats who want to come here and either take or give ... but never as equals." With the exception of David, from whom we rented horses, and Jose, who taught us Spanish in San Isidro, almost no Costa Ricans had engaged us in real conversation. It was the exact opposite of the embrace I'd received in Greece. "I just want the people here to see us as human beings, interested in them as human beings, regardless of how little or much either of us have."

*The rains* soon became relentless. Drops pinged so hard against the tin roof that Christopher and I would go hours without talking, since we would have had to yell to hear each other. Within a week, there was a stubbly fuzz of green mold growing on our clothes, the bucolic Baru River had turned into a torrent the color of chocolate milk, and the bug life had transformed into a whole new ecosystem. But it wasn't just external things that were becoming spoiled. As Maarten had predicted, we began seeing a kind of rot in people too.

One night, we met Max and Vittoria for dinner at La Capanna. "How are you?" I asked, hugging them hello.

But instead of a benign "We're good," or "Fine, fine," Max answered with, "Well, I don't think he's trying to kill me anymore." A shocking response, obviously. Suffice it to say it involved stealing, drug runners, the DEA, and death threats from a gun-wielding meth addict all colliding on Max and Vittoria's property.

Near the end of our meal, the perpetually drunk Spanish teacher in Dominical came up and leaned on Max's shoulder. "There are squatters on my land." With fumy breath, Julian told the tale of how squatters with guns had taken up on his land and were selling beer and charging rent. "I'm just gonna buy a bunch of shotguns and go take 'em out," he declared.

When we got home, Christopher and I agreed. Costa Rica was not the place for us. It was time for us to leave.

We packed up the following week and rolled out of Dominical on a cold, dreary day, spending our final night in Costa Rica just south of the border at Peñas Blancas. I decided to buy a bag of chocolates for the kids at the border. So this time, rather than remain hermetically sealed inside Rex while Christopher was busy with the *transmitadore,* I rolled the window down and beckoned a boy toward me. He looked a bit startled but warmed up instantly when I held out a candy. "*Quieres* chocolate?" I asked. His eyes lit up. His friends gathered around. As I doled out chocolate I shook each of their hands—caked with dust and grime—and asked their

names. To each one I said, and meant, "*Mucho gusto.*" (It's a pleasure to meet you.)

We stopped for the night in Granada, a port town on Lake Nicaragua with cobblestoned streets and squat colonial houses with wrought-iron railings and terra-cotta roofs that looked like what I imagined Cuba would look like—whether that's because Cuba really does look like that or because we had Buena Vista Social Club playing in Rex, I don't know. We found a cheap hotel, took a stroll, and, as night fell, we could see through the tall barred windows of people's homes to the high ceilings and immaculate tile floors. The flip side of this well-kept city-on-the-rise, though, was the large contingency of young street urchins working the square and surrounding hotels, like Hotel Almedra, where we went for dinner. Most wouldn't look us in the eyes or leave us alone, but one boy wore a smile as he held out a bag of nuts. "*Anacardos?*" he said.

"Are those peanuts?" I asked, and was met with a pained look of hurt pride as the boy shook his head.

"They not peanuts. They *cashews.*"

We bought two bags and found out his name was Ivan. We talked a bit about Granada, and about Tally—with the kids it was always about Tally—and then Ivan told us he was hungry.

"Can I buy you a bag of cashews?" I asked.

He shook his head and pointed to his tooth. "I have a toothache. I can only eat soft things like hamburgers or pizza." He grinned devilishly. "They have huge pizzas right next door for fifty córdobas." Rosanna's words echoed in my head: *When someone ask, I give.* I looked at Christopher to see if he was thinking the same thing; he already had his wallet out.

"Go get yourself some dinner," Christopher said, pulling out fifty córdobas. Ivan took the bill with a thank-you and scurried off while

Christopher and I sipped beers on the balcony. "That felt good," he said with a smile.

I squeezed Christopher's hand. "It did."

Ten minutes later, Ivan came back covered in JESUS LOVES YOU stickers.

"Thank you for dinner!" he said, holding out two stickers to us. "Pizza was good." He rubbed his tummy and laughed.

"You're welcome," I said, patting the sticker on my shirt. "It's true, you know," I said, pointing to the one Ivan had stuck to his nose. "Jesus *does* love you."

Ivan lingered, and we sipped our beers with contented smiles and JESUS LOVES YOU stickers on us.

Then Ivan turned to us and his twinkly eyes became imploring. "You give me twenty dollars for bike?"

"What?" Christopher put his beer down and his smile faded.

"I already save up fifteen," Ivan said. "But I need another twenty to buy bike."

I raised my eyebrows and Christopher shook his head. "We can't do that, Ivan," he said.

"Why?" Ivan asked.

"Because we already gave you five dollars, and if we give you everything we won't have anything to give anyone else."

"OK," Ivan said. He shrugged in an *I didn't think it would work, but thought I'd try anyway* way and was lost from sight among the other kids within moments.

Everything changed. Instead of laid back and relaxed, Christopher and I were both stick straight and tense. I felt like my lips were pursed. The waitress brought our meals—overpriced, fishy-tasting pasta—and I broke the silence.

"That was the lamest thing we just did. I mean, here we are wearing JESUS LOVES YOU stickers saying, 'No, we're sorry, we already gave, we can't give to you *again*.' We could've gotten street food and bought that bike for Ivan with what we'd saved on dinner."

I felt as foul as the shrimp smelled on my plate. The truth was, I didn't really like either of the characters who had been sitting in my seat just a few moments before. Not the smug, finger-wagging "Jesus loves you" (even if he does) benefactor, nor the pinch-faced tightwad she'd suddenly morphed into. *Real* radical giving had no place for either of these characters. Why was it so hard to respond in Rosanna's compassionate-yet-detached *when someone ask, I give* way?

"Let's see if we can find him," Christopher said.

"What?" I said, watching Christopher peel off córdobas and flag down a waiter.

"Let's see if we can find Ivan and give him the money."

So Christopher and I left our fishy pasta and threaded our way through the sea of children in the Central Park of Granada at well past 10:00 p.m. to try to find Ivan. Not the safest or smartest thing to do, but we felt driven to make amends. After three sweeps of the park, though, we gave up. We weren't going to find Ivan again. We weren't going to get a second chance. It was a lesson we would not forget.

❦

## FAUSTO'S LASAGNA

*I've been attempting to imitate Fausto's lasagna ever since our time in Costa Rica. This is the closest version I've come to yet. You may be taken aback by the lack of tomato sauce and ricotta in this recipe, but this is a true Bolognese-style lasagna. Trust me, once you try it, you'll never go back.*

BOLOGNESE SAUCE

2 tablespoons extra virgin olive oil

2 tablespoons butter

4 ounces pancetta, diced

1 large yellow onion, finely diced

1 large carrot, finely diced

1 celery stalk, finely diced

2 garlic cloves, minced

Sea salt and freshly ground black pepper

1 pound ground beef

1 pound ground veal

1 cup dry white wine

1 cup milk

3 tablespoons tomato paste

In a Dutch oven or large saucepan, heat the oil, butter, and pancetta over medium heat until the butter has melted. Add the onion, carrot, celery, and garlic to the pan with a generous pinch of salt and pepper and toss to coat the vegetables. Sauté for 10 to 12 minutes, until the onion becomes translucent.

Increase the heat to medium-high and add the beef and veal. Break up the meat as it browns, and add the wine to the pot as soon as the meat is cooked through. Scrape up anything stuck to the bottom of the pan and bring the wine up to a simmer. Reduce the heat to medium-low and stir in the milk and tomato paste. Simmer for 2 hours, stirring occasionally to make sure the sauce doesn't stick to the bottom of the pan.

PASTA DOUGH

$1^1/_4$ cups all-purpose flour

$^1/_4$ cup pastry flour

2 large eggs

1 tablespoon extra virgin olive oil

In a food processor, make the pasta dough by pulsing together the flours, eggs, oil, and $^1/_4$ cup water 10 to 12 times until it comes together into a ball. Transfer the dough to a floured surface and knead for 10 to 12 minutes, adding flour as necessary, until the dough takes on a sheen and is slightly tacky, but not sticky.

Cover the dough with plastic wrap and set aside to rest for 15 to 20 minutes.

BÉCHAMEL SAUCE

$2^1/_2$ cups milk

$^1/_4$ cup butter

$^1/_4$ cup all-purpose flour

Dash of nutmeg

Sea salt

In a medium saucepan, heat the milk to a low boil over medium heat.

In another saucepan, melt the butter over medium heat. Sprinkle the flour over the top and cook, stirring, until the mixture just starts to color and smell slightly nutty, 1 to 2 minutes. Add the nutmeg, a pinch of salt, and half of the hot milk, whisking constantly to incorporate. When smooth, whisk in the remaining milk. Bring the mixture back up to a vigorous simmer and continue to cook for about 10 minutes more, whisking constantly, until just thick enough to coat the back of a spoon.

FOR ASSEMBLING

Sea salt

1 cup grated Parmesan cheese

Divide the pasta dough into 6 portions and roll out one at a time with a pasta machine, keeping the rest covered with plastic wrap. Feed the dough through the largest setting eight times, folding it into thirds and rotating it 90 degrees each time. Then proceed to smaller and smaller settings (don't fold any more, and always feed the sheet through lengthwise), until you reach the second-thinnest setting.

Lay the sheet on a floured dish towel laid over the back of a chair. Repeat with the remaining balls of dough, laying each over a dish towel laid over the back of a chair.

Bring a large pot of salted water to a boil and lay enough dish towels on the counter to accommodate all the pasta sheets in a single layer. One at a time, gently lower a pasta sheet into the pot for 30 seconds. Then remove with tongs and a slotted spoon (or whatever utensils you have on hand that work for you . . . those pasta sheets are slippery suckers) and lay flat on a dish towel. Repeat with the remaining pasta sheets.

Preheat the oven to 375°F. In the bottom of a 9 × 13-inch glass, stainless steel, or enameled baking pan, spread $^1/_4$ cup of the Bolognese sauce. Use two sheets of pasta to cover the bottom of the pan. Then top with a third of the Bolognese sauce, a third of the béchamel sauce, and a third of the Parmesan cheese. Repeat with two more layers of pasta, Bolognese, béchamel, and Parmesan.

Bake uncovered for 30 to 40 minutes, until the top is browned and the sauce is bubbling around the edges.

Let cool for 10 minutes before slicing into squares.

SERVES 8

# CHAPTER 12

## *YO, LO CREO*

JUNE 2000

Four days after leaving Grenada, we pulled into Antigua, Guatemala. Carnival-colored buses lumbered along the cobblestone streets with a *bum-bum-bum-bum*. Stocky, gumball-colored stucco buildings lined the streets. In the center of town, we passed wrought-iron workshops and furniture stores selling the rustic, hand-hewn chairs and tables we'd fallen in love with throughout Mexico.

We found a cheap hotel two blocks from the plaza, then spent the rest of the morning on a walking tour. Antigua is fairly compact, built on a grid pattern from the sixteenth century inspired by the Italian Renaissance, with nine latitudinal and nine longitudinal streets crisscrossing around a central plaza, where we parked for the better part of the afternoon to soak it all in.

Life in the plaza was vibrant, colorful, animated. A three-tiered fountain with Circe-like figures shooting water through their nipples stood at the center, surrounded by strolling couples, children scampering about with playthings on a wire, bands of boys with shoe-polishing kits tucked under their arms and smudges on their faces, and women in colorful native blouses called *huipiles* and long skirts called *trajes* hawking bracelets and weavings and trinkets. Dogs with nipples larger than the fountain's scavenged like rats, and children's giggles melded with the call of the ice cream vendor. Lacy lavender jacaranda blossoms draped over the far end of the square, framing the façade of a creamy-white cathedral against a cerulean sky.

Three volcanic peaks soared over the whole scene. One, Agua, was a gentle, fertile rise with patches of coffee and other crops making a mottled green color along her slopes. The other two, Acatenango and Fuego, were sharper, just as their names were: dull gray cinder cones puffing clouds of volcanic gas like chain smokers.

Everywhere we went there was a sense of irrepressibility. We'd learned from our tour guide that Guatemala's economy was in shambles and its political system corrupt after the thirty-six-year civil war that had left hundreds of thousands dead. Yet the people we passed radiated joy. Even the ruins teemed with new life. Jungle-esque tufts of bougainvillea sprouted from the cracks of crumbling seventeenth-century buildings; boutique hotels were built into centuries-old rubble; and decks were built atop old walls to make bars and cafés with gorgeous views of the city and surrounding hills.

That evening, we found a Chinese restaurant with a gorgeous punched-tin sign—Beijing—and stucco walls that looked as if they'd been rubbed with blood. After months of meals consisting mainly of rice and beans, our plate of noodles in a thick peanut sauce flecked with earthy cilantro was a meal from heaven. Kung pao chicken, with big wedges of bell pepper and lofty notes of ginger spiked with whole dried chiles, made us gaga. We strolled back to our hotel that evening hand in hand, feeling like we'd stumbled upon a jewel of a town.

Just a few steps from our hotel entrance sat a hunched woman with gapped teeth and a weary look. She could have been twenty or eighty. Three small children sat beside her covered in a layer of dust so thick they nearly matched the sidewalk. As we passed them, Christopher paused and let go of my hand. *"Buenos noches,"* he said as he knelt. *"Soy Cristobal. Cual es su nombre?"*

The woman's face became animated as she answered, morphing from beggar to human being.

Christopher poked his hand out to tickle one of the little boys, who recoiled in a fit of giggles. And then they all pounced, laughing. They climbed onto Christopher's back and dodged under his arms. A few minutes later, we hugged them all good night and left them with our leftovers from Beijing.

*"Gracias, amigos,"* the woman said as we disappeared into our hotel. *"Y vayan con Dios."*

*At four* o'clock that morning, I was deep in a dream. There was a drummer, whose incessant drumming was pulling me reluctantly out of sleep until I realized it wasn't a dream at all, but someone pounding on our door.

"Your truck has been broken into!" the voice on the other side yelled. "Come, quick!"

"Oh my God." I panicked. "Did they take everything?"

Christopher and I scrambled out of bed and into the cool night. Even at that late hour, a growing group of people stood around watching the commotion. Rex's alarm was deafening, and for the first time, I was thankful for it. His right rear window had been shattered, but on inspection, almost everything was intact. The one thing that had been taken was a large duffel bag that we'd used as a sort of catchall place for flip-flops, towels, and a slew of other things we considered nonessential.

We were both strangely calm all morning as we waited for the police station to open. Later, as we sat in the sparse, gray room—such a contrast to the riot of color in the plaza just outside the windows—tallying up what had been in that bag for the official police report, we both noticed it.

Neither of us felt any anger at all. In fact, it was just the opposite.

The total value of the stolen goods—random things that we wouldn't even miss—came to roughly $1,000, which led to a question that night over dinner.

*What would it be like if we gave back to Antigua the amount that was taken from us?*

Let me just pause a moment and elaborate on how foreign a reaction that was for either of us. We're talking about a man who has a conniption when someone is going too slow in the left lane, and a woman who totes along a dossier of entitlements with her wherever she goes.

Our first natural reaction, absolutely, without a doubt, should have been anger and outrage. The fact that it didn't show up—not there on the street, not at the police station, not at the Guatemala City Marriott, where we were staying while Rex's window was fixed—was so disconcerting it felt like an arm had been amputated. We kept looking for it, wanting to lean into its familiar comfort. The fact that it simply was not present for *either* of us felt entirely new.

"It's just so wrong." I scooped up a bite of rice—the ever-present rice—and shook my head, trying to comprehend how radically my idea of "wrong" had shifted in twelve hours. "I mean, a thousand dollars would feed a family for three months here," I said.

"I know," Christopher said, spearing a tomato. "And we didn't even really need anything in that bag."

We sat in the dark-paneled restaurant among tables of gringo parents with mocha-skinned babies—we'd quickly learned that the Guatemala City Marriott was like the maternity ward of adoptions in Guatemala, spawning dozens of new families among its walls every day—trying to figure out what giving back might look like. Because we were, quite frankly, bushwhacking.

"What about that organization our guide mentioned?" Christopher asked. "The one just outside Antigua? I think it's called Common Hope."

"Yeah," I said. "She said something about sponsoring kids for school. Do you want to check it out?"

The yes we said that night may have sounded wary and hesitant at the time, but it would resound within our beings for years to come, until we—and everything in our lives—were transformed by it.

*The next* day, we drove right by Common Hope on our first attempt to find it, then doubled back to the long, nondescript cement wall, only noticing the small gated entrance because a woman in a beautiful blue *huipile* with a baby strapped to her back happened to step through at the same time. We followed her and, like everything we found in Antigua, there was a whole world beyond that wall.

Men and women in traditional garb bustled about, some with children appended directly to them with pieces of fabric, some with children frolicking around them. There was no trace of pity or shame, two elements that tended to be ever present on the periodical chart of charity. Instead there was an atmosphere of congeniality and welcome. As we walked down the corridor toward the office, people met our eyes with a smile and a *"Buenos días."*

"Common Hope is based on a foundation of respect and accountability," the young woman, Jenny, told us as she took us on a tour of the compound. It was rimmed with no-frills cement buildings that acted as administrative offices, a medical clinic, a cafeteria, a library, classrooms for tutoring and adult workshops, and dormitories for groups of visiting volunteers that they called Vision Teams.

"When a child is matched with a sponsor, all of the child's school expenses are paid for, and the entire family receives medical care, guidance from one of our social workers, emergency food help, access to any of our programs to learn new skills, and the opportunity to earn sweat equity hours working here on campus toward things like a clean-burning stove or even a new home."

"They get all that from one sponsor?" Christopher asked, echoing my surprise.

Jenny nodded. "It's not about handouts here. It's about partnering with people who are fully committed to breaking the cycle of poverty by working hard and taking full advantage of what we have to offer."

One look around the place and we could clearly see that the premise was working.

"How can we get involved?" I asked, watching a group of young teenage boys come through the gate in school uniforms with satchels over their backs. They wore wide smiles and were elbowing each other with shy, self-conscious giggles the way all teenage boys do.

Jenny smiled. "Funny enough, we happen to be assigning sponsors today. Would you like to pick out your godchild?"

Christopher and I went mute. We had no idea, really, what our financial situation would be like when we got back, let alone a year or two later. The idea of a long-term financial commitment was daunting. I thought of Foster's *Freedom of Simplicity*. I thought of Rosanna. I thought of Ivan.

"I don't know," I said, deflecting the real source of discomfort. "How would we be able to choose?"

"Well, we know we want to help someone whose need is the greatest," Christopher said. "So maybe a single mother, who's supporting her family on her own. And maybe a god*son*, since we've already got Kate."

I nodded in agreement. Allan and Janis had asked us to be godparents to their daughter Kate, who had been born prematurely just two months before we left. "That sounds good," I said. "That sounds really good."

"Then how about I match you with a godson who has a single mother, and you can check in with me tomorrow to find out who he is."

"That sounds perfect," I said. And, shockingly, it did.

*The next* day, I was squished onto Rex's console, as I had been so many months before with Victor, the *transmitadore*. Only this time Gina, the social worker from Common Hope, was in the passenger seat. She was pointing us up a long, tree-lined drive.

"Rene-Antonio's mom is the caretaker of an estate," she said. "The family lives in Guatemala City and isn't here that often, but they only allow her to live with one son, Rene-Antonio. Rene has an older brother who lives with his grandmother in the highlands."

"So the family can't be together?" I asked, stunned by that thought.

Gina shook her head. "It's a pretty common situation here in Guatemala."

We pulled up to the whitewashed hacienda set amid a carpet of emerald grass. Standing outside by a fountain was a tiny woman with black hair in a long plait down her back. A smaller replica, with white hair, stood beside her. A little boy in jeans and a soccer T-shirt broke free from his mom's grasp like a thoroughbred out of the gate and threw his arms around my waist, giggling into my belly. *"Padrina!"* he said, calling me *godmother*. And before I could even react, he latched on to Christopher. *"Padrino!"*

Without missing a beat, Christopher picked Rene-Antonio up and threw him over his shoulder like a potato sack, and all six of us broke into a fit of laughter. Rene-Antonio's mother and I hugged each other tightly for a good long while, and I felt a brand-new well of love boring itself down toward my belly. I don't know what I had expected. Something more somber, maybe? More serious? A formal round of hellos and thank-yous and you're-welcomes? What I hadn't expected was to feel an instant bond miles deep.

Rene-Antonio's mom led us through a back door into a small room, sparsely furnished, with whitewashed cement walls. There were two beds, no bigger than cots. Christopher, Rene-Antonio, and I sat on one of them, and Gina sat on the other with Rene-Antonio's mother and grandmother.

Rene-Antonio's grandmother leaned forward and put her hand on my knee, drilling into my eyes with her gaze. Her head was tilted slightly and her eyes were creased, like she was listening carefully for a faraway sound. I could tell she was sizing me up, but she was doing so kindly.

"Do you believe in Jesus?" she asked, taking me off guard.

"Uh, *sí*," I answered. *"Yo lo creo."*

But there was so much more I wanted to say. Yes, I believed. I believed, kicking and screaming, that I liked my life just fine, thank you. Yes, I believed. And that belief led me to marry Christopher, despite all the facts saying it didn't make sense. Yes, I believed. And that belief had been carving out my being like a melon baller and filling me with the kind of love that would prompt me to seek out her grandson just hours after having something stolen from me. Oh yes, I believed in Jesus. And I believed in miracles too.

But my simple response sufficed for Grandma. She gave my knee a tight squeeze and told me how relieved she was, that there were many believers in the highlands where she lived, but that here in Antigua that wasn't the case.

*"Gracias a dios,"* she said, eyes closed and hands held high, "for bringing believers to be my grandson's godparents."

I felt a surge of love for that woman. I loved her bold question, her dignity, how secure she seemed in her priorities. Even though she and her family teetered on the brink of survival in a way that I could not imagine, I sensed this wasn't just about money for her. The most important thing for her was that her grandson should be surrounded by a cloud of believers.

She saw us for who we were, not for what we were worth in dollars.

While all this was going on between Grandma and me, Christopher was showing Rene-Antonio pictures, of San Francisco, of Tally, of our family and goddaughter. Rene-Antonio studied them intensely, then got out his school notebook and showed us his homework.

After a short while—too short—Gina said it was time to go. We exchanged tearful hugs and Grandma laid her hand on my cheek. Gazing at me intensely with her azure eyes, she said, *"Gracias a dios para ustedes. Vayan con dios."*

As we drove away, I watched in the rearview mirror to see the last glimpse of Rene-Antonio on his tiptoes, arms extended as far as he could reach.

*We stayed* in Guatemala three more weeks and would have stayed longer if I hadn't had a meeting to get to in Cabo San Lucas. The way north through Mexico was rougher than the way down. We both got food poisoning in Oaxaca, of all places, which put a serious damper on our culinary adventures for the rest of the trip, and Christopher spiked a dangerously high fever in Mazatlán before making the ferry crossing over to Baja. Our plan had been to camp for a week on the Bahia de la Conception, but the first night, despite the sugary sand beach, turquoise waves, and cush *palapas*, the temperature hadn't dipped below ninety.

"I'm ready to go home," Christopher said, lying spread-eagle in the sand trying to get cool. "You?"

I let that question sink in. The first thing that hit me was that I didn't know where home was. But I couldn't deny it; it felt like the adventure was behind us, like we were forestalling the inevitable.

"Yes," I said. "I'm ready too."

The next morning we packed up Rex and drove the remaining seven hundred miles through the Baja desert in two days, arriving in Tecate during early afternoon on the first day of July.

As we approached the Parque Hidalgo, just three blocks from the U.S. border, we rolled down the windows to get a better view. Heat rushed in and occupied the space, along with the scent that had become so familiar over the past eight thousand miles: a brew of dusty cement and earth and garbage and sweat and humanity. God, I loved that aroma. I leaned my head out the window and grinned in a contented-dog sort of way.

Christopher slowed Rex to a crawl. Park benches were crammed with men and women arguing and laughing and nodding, all fanning themselves under the broad shade trees and palms. Children darted about on the sidewalks playing made-up games or tugging on their parents' sleeves and, with pleading faces, pointing to the *paleta* cart.

I tugged Christopher's sleeve. "Let's go around one more time," I said. He nodded and I could swear I felt Rex wanting to linger too. The heat rose off the cement in a shimmer, giving a ghostly quality to the figures in the park. It was a timeless scene, and one we'd seen in nearly every town we'd driven through. What felt strange was moving away from it rather than toward it.

"I really want to do a paseo wherever we end up," I said vehemently, referring to the ritual where an entire town turned out for an evening stroll through the central zocalo, to see and be seen, to greet neighbors, to fan romance.

"We will," Christopher said, squeezing my hand and easing Rex past the square into the three-block stretch toward the border. So much emotion surged upward that it got stuck in my throat. *Where* will we do our paseo? And will anyone else in our town know to do it too? I had a box full of those types of questions buried in my heart, and it felt too heavy to carry. There was so much that I wanted to bring into our new life in America—and some I wanted to leave behind—but was it possible to surgically extract a tradition here, a memory there, while leaving an entire culture behind?

We rolled to a stop at the border booth and Christopher handed the woman our passports. Her eyebrows darted up as she thumbed through them and saw how many stamps we'd amassed during the past six months. Then she returned them with a genuine smile.

"Welcome home," she said.

As we rolled north over the border, tears filled my eyes. Christopher looked at me with a glimmer and said words that would reverberate in me for the next decade. "I have a feeling the real adventure is just beginning."

# BEIJING PEANUT NOODLES

*These cilantro-spiked peanut noodles are made from my memories of those we enjoyed in Antigua at Beijing Restaurant. Nowadays, this is one of my favorite "leftover lunch" dishes . . . the flavors are even better the next day.*

16 ounces dried linguine noodles

$^1/_2$ cup chicken broth

$^1/_2$ cup smooth peanut butter

3 tablespoons soy sauce

1 tablespoon fresh lime juice

1 to 2 teaspoons red curry paste (depending on how hot you like it)

2 garlic cloves, grated

2 teaspoons grated fresh ginger

Sea salt and freshly ground black pepper

2 tablespoons canola oil

2 bunches scallions (white and green parts),
    cut into $^1/_2$-inch pieces on the bias
1 red bell pepper, cored, seeded, and very thinly sliced lengthwise
$^1/_4$ cup packed cilantro leaves
$^1/_4$ cup coarsely chopped peanuts

Bring a pot of salted water to a boil and cook the linguine according to the package directions for al dente. Reserve 1 cup of the pasta water.

While the noodles are cooking, in a medium saucepan, heat the broth, peanut butter, soy sauce, lime juice, curry paste, garlic, ginger, and a pinch each of salt and pepper over medium heat for 5 to 8 minutes, whisking occasionally until smooth and heated through. Whisk in $^1/_2$ to 1 cup of the reserved pasta water to thin the sauce to the consistency of heavy cream.

While the sauce is cooking, in a medium skillet, heat the oil over medium-high heat. Add the scallions and sauté for 6 to 8 minutes, until blistered and charred in places.

Transfer the noodles to a bowl and toss with the bell pepper, the warm peanut sauce, half of the cilantro, and the scallions with their oil.

Divide among individual bowls, and top with the remaining cilantro and chopped peanuts.

SERVES 8

# CHAPTER 13

# ITALIAN LESSONS

APRIL 2001

I opened the oven door and hot air blew back tendrils of my hair. The turkey inside was perfectly bronzed, and our little kitchen, with its linoleum floors, Formica countertops, and laminate wood cabinets, emanated the homey scents of a Thanksgiving dinner. Only one thing about the scene felt odd: it was April.

Since coming back to the States nine months earlier, I'd gotten several more assignments from *Cooking Light*—among other publications—and discovered that the six-month lead time meant that I'd be grilling at Christmas and cooking turkey at Easter. But I didn't mind, aside from the fact that Thanksgiving was my least favorite holiday, which I now had to experience *twice* a year.

When we'd crossed the border nine months earlier, we had gone through reverse culture shock. The pristine highways and shiny cars, the abundance of choice at the supermarket, the posh little boutiques lining neighborhood streets: everything felt out of place and excessive. I kept thinking of the scene in *Cast Away* when Tom Hanks is rescued from the island and doesn't know what to make of the buffet at the banquet. So we settled in Ukiah—a gritty, pioneer-feeling town amid bucolic mountains and vineyard vistas two and a half hours due north of San Francisco—in an attempt to hold on to a simple life.

And then we tried to figure out what came next.

With the dream of opening a restaurant in Costa Rica gone, Christopher and I regrouped. We still wanted to pursue a food business but instead shifted our focus from a restaurant to a concept we named Flour—handmade pastas from the East and West with other prepared food for takeout. We'd designed the logo, written the menu, and done some initial market research for the business plan. The problem was, the research was making it clear that Flour wasn't going to work in Ukiah. So the question we were left with was where was Flour—and where were *we*—meant to bloom?

Between my consulting and writing work, and Christopher's occasional service training gigs, we'd saved up a bit of money to invest in Flour. We'd booked a trip to the April IACP conference in Minnesota to glean wisdom, and another to northern Italy in June to learn from the masters—chefs, *nonnas*, and pasta shop owners—how to prepare handmade pasta.


*We arrived* late into Minneapolis, but were happy to find an Italian restaurant open near our hotel. We wolfed down some sort of focaccia bread to start—we were famished—then finished off a dish of ravioli in meat sauce with a bottle of Dolcetto.

"Baby," I said, poking Christopher as we finished off the wine. "That's Bruce," I said, pointing to a table across the room with my elbow. "That's Bruce Aidells." Christopher turned his head, and I tugged at his sleeve. "Don't *look*."

"Fine," he said. "Let's say hi on our way out."

As we snaked through the tables I saw that Bruce was sitting with several bigwigs in the food writing world. One was even an expert on Italy.

"What did you think of the *schiacciata*?" she asked.

"It was good." I shrugged. "It hit the spot."

"It's good to see you," Bruce said with a smile showing through his thick beard. "I'm sure we'll see more of each other at the conference."

*The next* day, Christopher and I took front-row seats for a panel on food writing from other countries. There were four people speaking on different countries, including the woman we'd met the night before and Rick Bayless, the author of one of the cookbooks I'd lived by in Costa Rica.

Rick began by speaking about the sizzle of meat on open fires in Mexico, and I was back in Oaxaca seeing Clara's smile. He spoke of complex moles, and I pined for the ones we'd missed in Puebla. He spoke of the bustle and color of the markets, and I couldn't take it anymore. I squeezed Christopher's hand hard trying to stifle my sobs. That colorful, rich tapestry of life had been *our* life. Now we were back in limbo.

Then the woman from the night before took the floor. She opened with a story set at an Italian restaurant, in Minneapolis. She spoke about a couple who were so naïve and stupid (yes, she used that word) as to think that the fake *schiacciata* they'd been served had been the real thing.

"And this is what's wrong with the food world today," she was saying. "Traditional dishes are being bastardized and demeaned, and are happily accepted by unwitting idiots like that couple last night."

"Oh my God," I said, elbowing Christopher. "She's talking about us. But that's not what really happened! I didn't even *look* at the name of that dish!"

*I returned* to Ukiah rattled by the experience. On one hand, I'd find myself thinking, "I *am* an idiot. I've never been formally trained as a chef, I've never worked in a restaurant, what do I think I'm *doing*?" The next I came fuming to my own defense—*it was just focaccia, for God's sake*. In the end, I ended up completely disagreeing with the conference speaker's premise. To my mind, *she* was what was wrong with the food world. When people who are curious and eager and open to learn are stomped on and belittled by judgmental bee-yotches, it makes eating well something precious— not in a good way—and elite, which I didn't believe it should be.

*Two months* later on a blindingly sunny June day we arrived in Milan. We drove past field upon field of sunflowers that seemed, in our drowsy, jet-lagged state, to be nodding their frocked heads in welcome.

Our first stop, and destination for the next few days, was Villa Gaidello, a working farm and respected restaurant in the little town of Castelfranco, between Modena and Bologna.

We pulled up the long, stone driveway and were greeted by the owner, Paola, with a warm handshake. "I so sorry, I so sorry," she said, retracting her hands from ours. "I making *nocino* and the walnuts make my hands black." Indeed, Paola's fingertips looked as if they'd been dipped in black ink. "But no matter," she said, waving us out of the reception area with our bags and leading us to a stone guest room that looked as though it had probably once been a stable. "You get pasta lesson with Francesca, then you rest and come to dinner. Leave your bags here and I take you to Francesca in the kitchen." I was grateful Paola had a commanding presence, because every cell in my jet-lagged body wanted me to flop onto the feather bed and close my aching eyes.

Paola ushered us into another small stone building that seemed dim inside after the bright sunlight. "Ciao," she said, and then was gone, leaving us alone with Francesca.

Francesca was nearly as round as the ball of pasta dough sitting in front of her, with a flat paper cap—like a hollowed-out layer of cake—that we soon discovered was the head garb of *sfogline,* the women who roll out sheets of pasta, which are called *sfoglie* in Italian.

"*Perchè tropo* yellow?" I asked in broken Italian. It took a few back-and-forths, but eventually Francesca understood I was asking about the color of the dough, which was almost orange compared to the buff-colored pasta dough I was used to making with my parents.

"Aaah," she answered. "*È perchè delle uova.*" I understood, but I still didn't understand. I made pasta with eggs too, and mine didn't look like Francesca's.

As we talked, Francesca kneaded. Beneath her strong palms, the dough became a living beast, rising and falling almost like she were squishing a basketball with each push. After a good ten minutes, Francesca stroked the ball—which had become taut and almost shiny—with her thumb. "*Ecco.*" She nodded, motioning for us to feel the dough as well. "*È fatto.*"

"It's smooth," Christopher said. "It's not sticky at all."

"*Ecco. Ora facciamo le sfoglie,*" Francesca said, time to make the pasta sheets. She cut the giant ball into several smaller pieces and covered them with a dish towel. She dusted the worktable with flour as if she were feeding pigeons, and picked up a giant rolling pin longer than a baseball bat. "*Matarello,*" Francesca said.

At first, it was like she was taming the ball, willing it to just lie flat and not pop back into a sphere. Eventually the dough submitted into a flat disk. When it was about the size and thickness of a pizza crust, Francesca rolled the sheet back onto itself on the *matarello* and combined forces. She leaned against the edge of the sheet, which she'd dropped slightly over the lip of the table, and then pulled the dough gently with the *matarello* while rolling it back and forth, moving her hands from the center outward, pushing and stretching it so by the time the sheet was unfurled from the *matarello* it was twice as long and thin as it had been when she'd first rolled it upon itself. Then she flipped the sheet forty-five degrees to her left and began again. By this point, Francesca had broken a sweat and was letting out deep, raspy breaths. But just a few minutes later, she had completed a sheet of pasta about four feet round and so thin I could see my fingers through it when I picked it up.

Only nine more to go for the night.

As much as I wanted to see Francesca shape the tortellini for Il Gaidello's famed *tortellini in brodo,* I was raving tired. So after a good, solid nap within the cool walls of our "stable," we strolled back up to the restaurant and ordered two bowls of *tortellini in brodo.* Now let me just pause here and say that growing up, I was never much of a soup person. A meaty chili or even a split pea with big chunks of ham I could get behind, but I never got too excited about broth soups. So I was going into *tortellini in brodo* with low expectations.

And they were blown to smithereens.

My first mouthful of soup was a mix of pasta and broth and, I still can't believe I'm saying this, it was a toss-up as to which was more flavorful.

I studied the tortellini. It looked like Francesca had wrapped a thimbleful of stuffing in a cylinder made from a small square of pasta, and then tied it together in a knot—filling and all—and tucked under the edges. It looked like a disembodied belly button. It tasted like a meatball to end all meatballs sleeved in silk.

But the broth was ethereal too, richer in flavor than any liquid I had ever tasted, with just enough fat in it to give it real heft. It was like she'd poured the drippings and juices from a roast chicken *and* a roast beef together in a bowl and waved a magic wand to make it broth.

Paola ended our meal with little cut-glass tumblers of last year's *nocino*—the concoction that was making her fingers black. "It from black walnuts, peeled when they still young and cut in half, then soaking in alcohol and sugar for two months." She slid the glasses toward us. "Try it." I had to admit, I was curious. I couldn't imagine what a jet-black walnut liquor might taste like. I took a sip and it was viscous, nutty, and sweet, with perfumey, almost herbal notes I hadn't expected from so few ingredients. "Ah, that's the alchemy," Paola said.

After a good night's rest, we drove a half hour through hilly countryside to the town of Savigno. Whereas much of the region of Emilia-Romagna was as flat as the American prairie, southeast of Modena the land rose into soft, undulating hills called the Colli Bolognese. A man by the name of Alberto Bettini was to be our tutor for the day.

Like Paola, Alberto was short on pleasantries and got straight to business when we arrived. Dressed in a buttoned shirt, slacks, and knee-high rubber boots, he led us through the dark-paneled room that was both bar and shop—with aged balsamic vinegars and bottles of *nocino* on the shelves—through the dining room, and into the kitchen.

"You see this?" he said, pointing to a yellow plastic bucket full of wet gray clay. We nodded, clueless as to why he was pointing to a bucket of mud. "Come, come." Alberto motioned for us to follow him out the back door, so we did. He pointed to a gray streak on the side of the mountain. "I just get that clay from the mountain, and now two guinea fowl live inside." Christopher and I stared into the bucket, still drawing a blank, like when someone is pointing to a constellation in the night sky and you can't see the shape.

"Come, look, they in the oven now." He motioned us back inside and opened the oven door and everything made sense. Inside, nestled in a large roasting pan, were two lumps of gray.

I'd had fish roasted in a salt crust in the south of France once—on the same trip, I learned about how flavorful shrimp were with their heads on, and the beauty of a dry rosé—but I'd never encountered something encased in clay. "What does the clay do to it?" I asked Alberto.

His eyes sparkled. "It keep the juice in, and it give the flavors of the land, the salt, the minerals, the earth." Alberto's voice was soft, but he gestured broadly, as if taking in everything around us. "All those flavors going into the guinea fowl."

Alberto drew on the concept of what the French call *terroir*—the essence of a place and the effect it has on the flavor of grapes and a finished wine—to create his food. My strongest experience with *terroir* had been when my parents came to visit us in Costa Rica and brought a bottle of Simi Cabernet Sauvignon. We knew well the place where those grapes were grown; in fact, we'd spent our first anniversary in Healdsburg, not far from the winery, and used to escape from the city for long bike rides around the valley. When my dad pulled the cork on that bottle, the presence of the *terroir* was so strong I cried. I smelled the dusty, scrub-covered hills, and the eucalyptus trees swaying in the distance. I smelled the sun-baked earth and the ripe grapes crushed underfoot during harvest that I used to inhale on our rides. It was all there in that bottle. When I smelled it, when I drank it, I felt a connection between the earth of that place and my physical and spiritual being.

Alberto took us to another building where his mother and the *sfoglina* were rolling out pasta. Like Francesca's, the dough was nearly persimmon-colored. "What makes it so orange?" I asked Alberto. Like Francesca, he shrugged and answered, "The eggs," exchanging glances with his mother that reminded me of the way Alexi and his mother had exchanged "duh" looks when I asked about the fried eggs that first morning in Corfu. Why was it always the eggs, and how could *I* get me some eggs that color? "We make this into ricotta ravioli with balsamic butter sauce."

At that point, we were getting hungry. My mouth was watering so aggressively I made a little slurping sound to keep from drooling. Alberto sat us in the dining room, opened a bottle of Colli Bolognesi wine, which was light, plummy, and almost effervescent, and set down two parfait bowls in front of us with what looked exactly like a scoop of French vanilla ice cream drizzled with chocolate sauce.

My eyebrows shot up. "Dessert first?" I asked.

Alberto grinned. In the short time we'd spent with him we'd discovered he was a reserved, humble man of few words, and what words he did employ focused on doing justice to the food he was talking about. "It's a parfait of Parmigiano and cream, drizzled with fifty-year-old *aceto balsamico*." Christopher was off at the word *Parmigiano*, but I had to marvel at the work of art. I dragged my spoon across the top, and it was indeed like shaving soft ice cream. I brought it to my lips and it was creamy and unctuous in my mouth, but with the crunch and shatter from the crystallization of the cheese. Funny enough, the balsamic vinegar was so intense and complex as it cut gracefully through the richness of the cheese that in many ways it resembled a good dark chocolate.

None of Alberto's dishes were complicated or fussy. They just used the right amount of the best ingredients he could get his hands on. The lush slices of guinea fowl were no exception. There was a wild, gamey flavor surrounded by the essence of the hills themselves, a sharp, almost tangy minerality that tasted of earth and sea combined. I'd never tasted meat—let alone poultry—so complex.

We spent several more days learning from talented, gifted people throughout Emilia-Romagna, then shifted our home base to an inn in the hills across from the city of Orvieto, in the region of Umbria. Orvieto was a medieval city that sat upon a tall tuft of tufa rock. From the pool at Locanda Rosati, we could see the glowing rose marble façade of Orvieto's cathedral across the valley.

Giampiero Rosati, who owned the Locanda along with his sister and brother-in-law, Paolo, was yet another larger-than-life personality. The best way to describe Giampiero is to say that he took up a lot of space. He was a large man—yet fit—whose personality and constant gestures further amplified his physical presence. He wore a pair of big, square glasses that were never actually on his eyes, or above his head, but perched on his forehead, giving the impression that he could see things that others couldn't.

Paolo was the cook at Locanda Rosati, where he presided over a wood-fired oven throughout the afternoon. Giampiero, of course, presided over the communal table at dinner.

We took our places among the other guests, who came not just from Italy but from around the world, and enjoyed meal after meal of family specialties. These meals weren't fancy by any means—Paolo referred to them as "seasonal, rustic family recipes"—they were dishes like a zucchini frittata, and braised chicken and tomatoes, and chicken liver crostini. But they were simple and delicious and satisfying in a way that made my soul hum. It was similar, in many ways, to what I'd experienced in Greece.

It made me think about what that woman at the IACP conference had said about food traditions. And while I agreed that they're important, I felt more strongly than ever that they were meant to be a point of connection rather than contention.

Giampiero wasn't interested in preserving Italian tradition at the exclusion of others in some hushed, erudite manner (just the word *hushed* in the vicinity of Giampiero makes me laugh). On the contrary, he invited me to become a part of those traditions that stitched together generations, family, community, and history. And that experience became a part of me; it changed me.

When I returned home to write about the trip for a magazine assignment, I wanted to share it in a way that wouldn't make others feel smaller for not having had the experience themselves, but in a way that would invite them to the table with me.

# ZUCCHINI FRITTATA

*I vividly remember scribbling this recipe in my notepad as Giampiero and Paolo argued about the ingredients. Be sure to cook it over very low heat to get the creamy texture that makes it so special, even at room temperature. I've simplified the traditional flipping process (I can't tell you how many casualties I've had myself) by finishing the frittata under the broiler on a low oven rack, which maintains its custardlike consistency.*

1 pound zucchini
1 pound sweet onions
3 tablespoons extra virgin olive oil
$1/4$ cup minced parsley
Sea salt and freshly ground black pepper
8 large eggs, beaten

Slice the zucchini and onions crosswise very thinly, preferably on a mandoline. In a large skillet, heat 2 tablespoons of the oil over medium heat and sauté the vegetables for 10 minutes, until tender and just softening but not yet brown. Stir in the parsley, season with salt and pepper, and set aside to cool for 5 minutes. When slightly cooled, pour the vegetables into a large bowl with the eggs and mix thoroughly. Season again with salt and pepper.

Preheat the broiler to high and place an oven rack on the lowest position.

Heat a 10-inch nonstick sauté pan (if using the same one you used to sauté the veggies, wipe it out thoroughly) over medium heat with the remaining 1 tablespoon oil. Swirl the oil around the pan, then pour in the egg mixture, tilting the pan to spread it evenly. Reduce the heat to low and cook for 15 minutes, running a spatula around the edges and shaking occasionally, until the center of the frittata is set around the edges.

Transfer the pan to the oven and cook for an additional 5 minutes, until set in the middle.

Use an oven mitt to take the pan out of the oven and slide the frittata onto a plate. Scatter additional minced parsley over the top and serve warm or at room temperature.

SERVES 6

# CHAPTER 14

# IN THE FALLOW TIME

AUGUST 2001

Puffs of dust floated toward me as Tally trotted ahead down our gravel drive. We turned left on the one-lane road where a gently sloping vineyard butted up to a hill beyond, with views past the sycamore trees that lined the pond below all the way to Mount Saint Helena. Fragrant, sun-baked pulp from plums and apples carpeted the ground. Across the street from a tall brown house, a fig tree drooped with inky purple fruit.

We had moved, in July, to a tiny house on a back road in Healds-burg's Dry Creek Valley, not far from our favorite biking route. Christopher had gotten a job managing a restaurant at an inn in Healdsburg, and we both agreed the town was a better fit for Flour.

Just past the brown house we came to what I thought was a barn on the left, with two men standing outside beside several large square white plastic bins.

"Hi," one of them said with a smile. "You must be the new neighbor, up in Graham's place?"

"Yes," I said. "I'm Lia." The man extended a dusty hand and the sun sparkled on the specks of silver in his hair.

"I'm Gerry, your neighbor." He pointed to the house above the figs. "You should go introduce yourself to my wife, Jann," he said. "You'll love her—everyone loves her. She's been wanting to meet you."

"I'd love to," I said. "We haven't really met anyone here yet."

"You can go through that gate there," Gerry said. "Hang on, though, let me get you a bottle to take with you." He motioned for me to follow him into the barn—which turned out to be a small winery, smelling of yeast and fruit and toast—where he grabbed a dark green bottle. He slapped its side and handed it to me. "It doesn't have a label yet, but this is our Syrah. Enjoy." I took the wine and went through the gate, and not only did I walk home a few hours later with a bottle of wine and an armful of figs, I also walked home with new friends.

Christopher got home early that night, around 11:30, and I was waiting with a plateful of figs—which I'd stuffed with blue cheese, wrapped in prosciutto, and then drizzled with a bit of Alberto's aged balsamic vinegar—and a glass of Gerry's wine.

"Guess what happened today?" I said, aware that syllables seemed to be coming out faster than I was willing them. Before Christopher could answer I blurted, "I met our new neighbors."

"Hmmm," he said, biting into a fig.

"I met Gerry down at their winery—that's what we thought was a barn, down at the turn—and he gave me a bottle of their Syrah." I took a sip. "It's good, isn't it?" It was earthy and dusty, more French than Californian. "And Jann, his wife, is *awesome*. She's got this long copper hair and just feels like someone you've known forever. I was there most of the afternoon, just talking."

I'd learned that Jann and Gerry had three grown children and one grandson, that Gerry had been an executive in the healthcare world, and that they'd made the choice to step out of the fast lane and start over again as winemakers.

Within weeks, we became fast friends.

*Not long* after we met Jann and Gerry, Chris and Honore, who lived down at the end of our little road, came into the fold. Chris was a deep thinker with rural roots who worked for the *Wall Street Journal*. He reminded me of a cowboy poet. Honore was tall and willowy, with jet-black hair and intense blue eyes. She worked in marketing for a local winery and could describe the bejeezus out of anything she sipped. Honore's friend JoJo was living with them and was an apt completion of the trio; JoJo had a quick wit and a sass the size of her home state of Texas.

I can't remember a time when the seven of us left Dry Creek over the next six months. It was like, in the wake of the horrors of September 11, we all just wanted to cocoon ourselves in our soft, embryonic friendship and the welcome of each other's homes. And within that warm, safe place, deeply rooted friendships emerged.

We had Chris and Honore over for dinner one night in late October. It was chilly, the weather was flirting with the idea of fall, and we were all tucked into chairs and couches in front of the fire after dinner.

"So where did you guys move from?" Chris asked.

Christopher and I glanced at each other with a chuckle. "That's sort of a long story," Christopher said. "We lived in Ukiah for a year before moving here, and in San Francisco before that. But we took a seven-month road trip to Costa Rica and back between the two."

"That is so wild," Chris said. "That reminds me of an article I read on a flight recently—I even tore it out and brought it home

to Honore. It was of a crazy couple that left San Francisco and—"
Chris paused and his wise blue eyes went wide. "Wait a second, is
that a black Explorer outside?"

I started laughing. "It is."

"Is its name Rex?"

"It is."

"That was an article about *you two*?"

"It was," I said. "That article was one of my assignments on the
trip."

"How did you guys do it? *Why* did you do it?" Chris asked, which
was a question I'd been revisiting myself in the days after 9/11.

"We did it to live deliberately," Christopher said. "As Thoreau
says, 'to live deep and suck out all the marrow of life.'"

"It's true," I added. "We wanted to simplify in the sense of figur-
ing out what really mattered to us, and living by that, and letting
other, nonessential things go."

"Did you?" Chris asked.

"I think we did, then," I said. "But life seems busier, more complicated now. I feel like things aren't so simple anymore, especially now."

*One area* we were floundering in was church. We'd been nurtured
by wonderful communities in both San Francisco and Ukiah but
couldn't seem to find a home in Healdsburg. Part of the issue was
that we weren't newlyweds anymore, we didn't have kids, and our
day-to-day lives looked nothing like most of the congregation's.
People didn't know what to make of us. I could see the unease in
people's eyes the more they got to know of us. So we just stopped
searching.

Where we did find communion—the kind M. F. K. Fisher had described—was around the table. Nearly every night, I'd get a call from Honore, Chris, and JoJo beckoning me down the hill for dinner.

"But I'm working," I'd say. I'd been trying to pattern my days so that I could spend the hours Christopher was home with him, and then work while he was at work.

"You've still got to eat dinner," Chris would yell from the background. "Might as well be with us."

"But Christopher has Rex," I'd counter.

"Then we'll come up and get you," Hon or JoJo would say, and I'd hear wheels on the gravel minutes later, whether I'd consented or not. We'd all roll down the hill to their cozy home, and I could smell dinner cooking before even getting to the door.

Honore had no fear of complicated recipes on a weeknight. One night, Honore had her *Mastering the Art of French Cooking* open to blanquette de veau—a veal stew I remember my mother making, driving home the fact that it was a "fancy meal" from a French cooking course she'd taken—which we ate from bowls sitting on the couch while watching *Notting Hill*. Another time, Honore had Marcella Hazan's book open as she draped pasta into a pan, napping it with creamy homemade béchamel and chunky Bolognese sauce for a lasagna that was rivaled only by La Capanna's.

I returned the favor by inviting everyone over to our place when I was recipe testing. For an article on Latin American salsas and sauces for *Cooking Light* I served a Salva Vida–inspired feast of thin pork chops marinated in a vinegary *adobado* sauce that tinted the pork orange; a roasted *molcajete* sauce reminiscent of the ones we'd made with our classmates in Cuernavaca; and our own salsamole.

. . .

*I was* finding connection in nature too. My sanctuary had shifted from the four walls of a church to the woods and hills and vineyards of Dry Creek Valley. The larks and breeze became my choir, and the petals of each wild flower and pattern of each beetle my sermon. Prayers, rather than being sandwiched into a particular time slot, became an intimate, running conversation.

On long winter walks, Talisker and I would wade through swishy green grass that smelled like fresh-cut lettuce. We'd skip from stone to stone across babbling creeks, and stroll through rows of vineyards carpeted in sweet, earthy chamomile. We would trek up back roads to the tippy-top of wooded knolls with peek-a-boo views of the valley below. All seemed a feast before me.

In my youth, it was the chives around my parents' garden. Now I nibbled the young seedpods of wild fennel, which burst between my teeth with a fragrant, licorice sweetness. I pulled handfuls of bay leaves, moist with rain, from giant trees, and rolled them like miniature scrolls exuding the resinous scent of Christmas trees. I plucked stalks with leaves that looked like overgrown parsley and couldn't help but take a nibble.

We are, quite literally, one with the earth. The word *human* comes from the Latin word *humus,* which means "earth." The same six elements that make up 99 percent of the human body also make up the bulk of the planet.

Lord knows, I'm not the first to encounter the holy in nature. The twelfth-century German mystic Hildegard von Bingen spoke frequently of *viriditas*, greening from within through the yoking together of spiritual and physical health. "The Word is living, being, spirit, all verdant greening, all creativity. This Word manifests itself in every creature," she wrote. She believed that, whether from the seed of a dandelion or the seed of a human soul, we were all being called forth to "Become who you are; become all that you are."

The question I continued to ponder was, what was it that I was meant to become?

*One day* in mid-February, I was sitting with Jann in an Adirondack chair on her front porch, bundled in a blanket and sipping tea. My body was too sore to even think of going for a walk.

"How are you doing?" Jann asked.

"Not great," I said. "We just found out that Flour fell through."

"You're kidding! I thought that was a done deal."

"So did we," I said. Christopher and I had spent nearly two years working on a business plan for Flour and had expanded the concept to be a co-op with a local organic grocer, a fishmonger, and a bakery. We'd even drawn up plans for the space with an architect. And then, after months and months, we found out that the landlord rejected our deal. "It just seems like everything has come to a grinding halt yet again and there's a big, gaping void in front of us now." I shifted on my chair, unable to get comfortable. "And I'm just so tired of hurting."

Back in Ukiah, a yoga teacher had told me about fibromyalgia, and the way she'd described it had been a perfect fit to what I'd been feeling. I learned that fibromyalgia affects the connective tissue of the whole body, which was why I often felt like I was wearing a suit that was too tight. Other times, during what are called "fibro flares," the pain concentrates in certain areas like the ankles, elbows, knees, and hips.

The good news was, I had challenged the lupus diagnosis and

gotten it reversed; the doctor agreed with me on the thought that I had fibromyalgia and not lupus. The bad news was, the suffering was almost constant.

Fibromyalgia is a bit of a chicken and egg. There's pain that comes with fibromyalgia, but there's also exhaustion, hopelessness, and depression. Personally, I think it's a cascading effect. The pain sets in and it becomes exhausting to do normal, everyday things. Literally to sit up in a chair takes effort. Standing up from said chair when your hips feel like someone has popped out the joint, rubbed it all down with sandpaper, smacked it a few times with a sledgehammer, and popped it back in again becomes a sort of torture. Dealing with that kind of pain—in whatever form it happens to be manifesting itself at a given moment—is bound to exhaust anybody. And when everybody around you seems to be gliding through life, you start to despair.

Jann reached over and squeezed my hand. "Look at those vines out there, Lia," she said. "What do you see?"

"A bunch of bare vines."

"Exactly," Jann said. "That's what it looks like to us, because we don't see any shoots or leaves or fruit right now. Yet this is the most important time of the year for them. This is when their roots soak in all the nutrients from the soil. This is what makes it possible for them to send out their leaves and bear their fruit."

I sat in silence and let her words sink in.

"Maybe, my friend," Jann said, squeezing my hand again, "you're in a time of fallow too. Maybe you're supposed to be deepening and nourishing your roots right now even more than *doing* any particular thing, so you can bear fruit when the time is right."

Jann's words resonated deeply with me. When we moved to Healdsburg, we dug up our garden in Ukiah and transported the tomatoes and eggplant and peppers in gallon containers to our yard in Dry Creek. One by one, they died. I wanted them to take off in full bloom, but their roots, I discovered, had been starving in poor soil.

I began to wonder if I'd been imposing the same unrealistic expectations on myself. I wanted to shoot forth into new ventures, but maybe the soil of my soul wasn't ready. Maybe I was supposed to wait for something else, and work on growing deeper roots in the meantime.

*I noticed* something else that year too. While I loved that our tribe treated our times together as a celebration (Jann had a saying that life was celebration enough for a glass of bubbly each day), I discovered I felt groggy and spent and sore for days afterward, and I wondered if the lavish food and copious amounts of wine could be exacerbating the fibro. I hadn't made the connection before because the food we ate was all *good* food—things like roasts, potatoes from the garden, good cheeses and charcuterie, and homemade sauces.

So I began pitching articles to my editors like "Food Myths," debunking common, but wrong, beliefs about nutrition, and "Worldly Advice," on how the healthiest people in the world live, as a thinly veiled guise of getting access to the experts and answers to the questions that plagued me.

It turned out that no matter whether I was interviewing someone from Harvard or Penn or Athens or Paris, the advice was all the same: eat a *lot* of different veggies, with a good amount of healthy oils and whole grains, and treat protein like a condiment for flavor and texture rather than as the main attraction. They also said to embrace celebrations as part of the natural cycle of scarcity and abundance—echoing what the grapevines in winter had taught me.

My problem wasn't that I was eating the wrong things. It was that the right things were in the wrong proportion on my plate. For most meals, two thirds of my plate would be covered with meat, with grains and vegetables filling the rest, and I wasn't balancing out the celebratory feasts with moderate meals during the week.

By the end of the year, I had the answers I needed. The only problem was, I wasn't sure what to do with the advice. I'd gotten much more comfortable with vegetables than I ever thought possible, but I still wondered how in God's name I was going to fill plate after plate with them, day after day, without going batty from boredom.

So I gave myself a gift that New Year's Day. I gave myself a year to figure out *how* to eat the way those experts had told me to. Not being a slave to the scale, not being plagued by a sense of deprivation or beating myself up for slipping a pizza in the oven every once in a while. I was in it for the long haul, and ready to know, ready to *feel* what it would be like to eat in a way that would bring joy, give me energy, and take away my pain.

## GRILLED PROSCIUTTO-WRAPPED STUFFED FIGS

*If you can find fresh figs, this is the recipe to make with them. If you can't, this will also work with pitted Medjool dates. You can make these indoors too by popping them under the broiler for 2 minutes instead of on the grill. If you happen to have aged* aceto balsamico, *like we had from Alberto's, use it in place of the vinegar-honey reduction.*

$\frac{1}{4}$ cup balsamic vinegar
1 tablespoon honey
6 figs, halved lengthwise
1 ounce blue cheese
6 pieces of thinly sliced prosciutto, cut in half lengthwise
Freshly ground black pepper

In a small saucepan, combine the balsamic vinegar and honey and heat over medium heat. Bring to a gentle boil for 3 to 5 minutes, until it reaches a syrupy consistency.

Gently press against the cut side of a fig with your thumb to make an indentation. Break off a bit of blue cheese about the size of the tip of your pinky finger and press it into the indentation. Wrap the fig half with a slice of prosciutto and place on a serving platter. Repeat with the remaining figs.

Heat a grill to medium heat. Place each fig half flesh side up on the grill grates and cook for 2 to 3 minutes, until the prosciutto has crisped and the cheese is bubbly.

Transfer back to the serving platter, drizzle with the vinegar-honey mixture, and top with a generous grind of pepper.

SERVES 6

# CHAPTER 15

# ALWAYS THE ALTERNATE PATH

## JULY 2004

I'd cobbled together a makeshift raft out of two pool noodles, one beneath my head and one beneath my knees, and lay floating above the warm, mineral-laden water. I could see the treetops swaying in the breeze and could hear nothing except the slow, rhythmic sound of my own breath amplified underwater.

It was perfect. I was at a Zen retreat center in a remote crevice on top of a mountain in the Ventana Wilderness.

I'd been gripped by a strong desire for a spiritual getaway to digest all the ways God had helped me grow in the past eight months—in the past eight years—and this retreat center was just an hour from Earthbound Farm in Carmel Valley, where I had conveniently just been for another *Cooking Light* assignment.

I'd fasted all day, wishing to physically empty myself in order to be filled spiritually. Christopher and I had discovered, in the years since we'd returned from Costa Rica, that simplification wasn't an external thing as much as it was a manifestation of what was on the inside. When we were centered and focused spiritually, the important things stood out clearly, decisions came more easily, life felt doable. When we lost that focus, life felt out of control.

Over the past few months, I'd also found a correlation between how centered I felt and what I consumed. When I ate things I knew I didn't want to—heading to the drive-through or plowing through a bag of potato chips—I'd eventually realize I was running away . . . from myself, from life, from God. And vice versa; when I consistently ate the way I was striving to—finding joy in a plate filled with peak-of-the-season vegetables—I found myself filled with an inner stillness that helped me remain centered moment after moment, day after day.

But getting to and maintaining that focus took tending. Which is what brought me to the mountaintop.

*The next* day, I sat in the garden at the base of a sunflower that must have been twenty feet tall and went through a half dozen old journals, looking for patterns, and praying over which ones to cultivate and which ones to let go of.

As I read, I noticed how often I berated myself for changing course. I saw echoes of what I'd been told when I was younger, that I was flighty, noncommittal. But now I saw that I wasn't so much *changing* course as *correcting* course, based on new understandings, or, increasingly, how I was feeling led by the Spirit.

So I wrote myself a note of compassion. *You are constantly evolving, and new things are revealed every day. Life isn't linear, so stop trying to live it like it is.*

I'd started to let go of things a few months earlier, during an orientation for a hybrid online/onsite MBA program I was accepted to

at the University of Florida. By the time I'd gotten down to Gaines-
ville and met my classmates, I was in a full-blown fibromyalgia flare.
When we drove out to a challenge course the first day, I struggled
just to stay clearheaded enough to keep up with conversation.

And then they led us to a ropes course.

My body was throbbing with exhaustion as I climbed the first
two rungs of the rope ladder, which led to a platform high above
where we were supposed to walk across two wobbly ropes to another platform. I looked up. I reached for the next rung and my arm
screeched with pain. But I couldn't stop. Everyone was cheering me
on. What would they think? How could I let my classmates think
I was a quitter or, worse, weak? But then I felt that irrational calm,
and an ancient promise was whispered into my mind.

*"My power is made perfect in your weakness."*

I hung there, three rungs up on that rope ladder, people's cheers
echoing in my ears, and I thought of Jann's wise question: what
if this time in my life wasn't about proving how strong I was, but
about growing roots into a deeper strength not of my own?

And then, for the first time in my life, I let go. I admitted that I
couldn't do it all.

I climbed down from the ladder, and even more of a miracle, I
didn't berate myself for doing so. Instead, I was grateful for all I
*could* do, recognizing what a big push it had been just to get there at
all. And I walked away from that challenge course feeling like I had
conquered what I was meant to conquer.


*The afternoon* on the mountaintop had become swelteringly hot and
the cicadas were in full chorus. I tucked away all of my journals but
one and walked down to the bathhouse on the creek. I was tempted

to keep my swimsuit on, as some women had done, but decided against it, slipping into the warm, mineral-fed stream as naked as the day I was born. In eight months, I had lost nearly twenty pounds just by reshaping what was on my plate, and felt more at home in my body than I could ever remember. I felt lithe and strong and somehow just the right size as I sat on a boulder, the soft water caressing my legs, and captured a few remaining thoughts.

It wasn't just my body and being that was changing, our geography had changed too. We'd bought a little 1922 bungalow in town, with slanted wood floors, built-in cabinets with glass doors, and two cozy window seats. As much as we hated to leave the country (although we were only ten minutes away from our friends in Dry Creek), it felt good to have a place of our own to call home.

And the MBA program wasn't the only new beginning on the horizon; I'd begun to work on a novel, called *I Land Home*. I never expected to write a novel. But then a strange, "what if" scenario had floated through my head one day—what if I'd stayed in Greece and married Alexi?—and morphed into a story all its own. Within a day I had a sixty-page outline, and I was now a third of the way through the manuscript.

I looked down at my journal and wrote one last line that felt like a whisper on the paper before plunging back into the creek. *Lord, am I supposed to be a mother?*


*Four months* later, in late November, I was in Julie's kitchen in Denver with her two boys, Cole and Cooper, standing on chairs beside me. I had them pulling the needles off rosemary stems for a paste I was making to rub on a pork loin, which I was going to roast with a bunch of root vegetables.

up at me with a smile that lit up his whole face. "I *love* being a kitchen helper, Auntie Lia! I want to be a kitchen maker just like you when I grow up."

Julie sidled up beside me with a chuckle. She hummed into my wineglass, taking a long sniff as I smashed a clove of garlic for the paste. "I'm with you, Cole," she said. "If you can make the house smell like it does when Auntie Lia's here, I'll support you being a kitchen maker all the way."

I smiled. Not everyone was comfortable with someone coming in and taking over their kitchen, but Julie had given me carte blanche long ago. This visit, though, was special. Julie was nine months pregnant, and she and Steve had invited me there for the birth of their daughter, Kennedy Lia.

The following day, the day before Kennedy Lia was born, I had an agenda of my own. I'd made an appointment with Lois, a spiritual director whom Julie had once met, to discuss the matter of parenthood, or, rather, lack thereof. I felt it was time once and for all to close the door on adoption, and, for whatever reason, I felt Lois could help me.

The next morning, the snow crunched beneath my feet, and it was so cold and crisp it felt like the air would shatter as I opened the door to Steve's Caddy. I sat behind the wheel for a beat before starting the car, thinking, *What am I doing?* I mean, did I really think I was going to get anything out of an hour with a woman I didn't know with a question as large and looming as "Are Christopher and I meant to adopt?"

I backed onto the road and pulled onto the highway, the blue sky almost blinding it was so bright. The jagged white peaks of the Rockies marched over the horizon, bringing back a memory of the first time I'd seen them. I had been six years old and Mom and Dad had brought Russ and me to Colorado to visit Mom's best friend in Steamboat. When we'd landed in Denver the mountains had seemed close. But then we began driving and it was like the mountains receded farther and farther while at the same time growing larger and larger. The peaks were magnificent, yet always just out of reach. I had a similar feeling as I pulled into the parking lot, like I could sense an intimate presence that was very near, yet cloaked in something majestic beyond me.

I walked into the office and took a clipboard to fill out the orientation form. Looking back, I think part of the reason I was going to see Lois was to somehow validate my path; to make my choice of being childless as worthy as Julie's choice of motherhood.

I pressed the pen to the paper on the clipboard and the tip exploded. Annoyed, I pulled another one out of my purse and began to fill out the form. The pen dried up three lines in. I was in tears, frustrated, as I fished out a third pen, in a third color, and saw that my form looked like something between a tie-dye and a finger painting. Couldn't I at least *seem* normal, just this once?

Just this once, as I sat there with the burning question people never seemed to stop asking, I just wanted it to be easy. I wanted someone to pat me on the back and say, "The answer is in room 102," and send me on my merry way, rather than point me toward yet another emotional, spiritual, soul-searching trek through the mountains.

So I walked into Lois's office with my tie-dyed/finger-painted form and explained my frustration with how God always had me on an "alternate path," expecting her to commiserate. Instead, she surprised me by saying it was all, quite frankly, "poppycock."

She went on to tell me that my life was rich and colorful and patterned by the movements of God's hand, not stuffed into a box of worldly expectations.

We spoke about children and she didn't say much new, emphasizing that many people live very fulfilling lives without kids, and that if we did decide to adopt, it would need to be a decision we both made together.

Next she prayed over me, for God to give me clarity, to speak to my heart, and to align Christopher and me. Then we sat in silence. And in that silence came the kind of revelation where eons of information are conferred to every synapsis of your being in a millisecond. In that silence I felt, I knew, that I would be a mom as surely as I knew there were mountains on the horizon. But I also knew that I had a long journey ahead, not only to becoming a mom, but to finding the desire to be one.

I was sobbing so hard it choked out the tears.

"I feel like there's something you're supposed to tell me," Lois said calmly.

I looked up and tried to steady my voice, speaking something so piercingly precious and powerful—for what it was, for the fear that I'd misinterpreted—that I wouldn't tell a soul or even voice it in my journal for more than a year. And when I did speak, it was barely a whisper. "I think I know the answer," I said. "I'm going to be a mother."

# ROASTED PORK LOIN WITH ROOT VEGETABLES

*This roasted pork loin is always a showstopper and is perfect with roasted root vegetables. I love to make this when I visit Julie and her family in the winter, because the scent itself brings her so much joy. She always says, "The house smells like Lia!"*

3 garlic cloves, smashed

Sea salt and freshly ground black pepper

1 teaspoon fresh thyme leaves

1 teaspoon fennel seeds

$1/_8$ teaspoon ground allspice

1 teaspoon ground coriander

$1/_4$ cup extra virgin olive oil

$2^1/_2$-pound boneless pork loin roast

10 cups (1-inch cubes) mixed root vegetables (such as turnips, parsnips, sweet potatoes, carrots, celery root, and rutabaga)

2 cups thickly sliced yellow onions

3 thyme sprigs

2 tablespoons cider vinegar

Pound the garlic to a paste in a mortar and pestle with a pinch of salt and a grind of pepper. Add the thyme leaves and fennel seeds and continue to pound to a paste. Mix in the allspice, coriander, and 1 tablespoon of the oil and rub the mixture all over the pork. Cover and refrigerate for at least 3 hours or overnight.

Preheat the oven to 425°F.

In a large bowl, toss the root vegetables and onions with 2 tablespoons of the oil and a generous pinch each of salt and pepper. Spread the vegetables in a large roasting pan and lay the thyme sprigs on top. Transfer pan to the oven.

When the vegetables have roasted for 15 minutes, turn them with a sturdy spatula. Sprinkle the pork with an additional pinch of salt, heat a large skillet over medium-high heat, and swirl in the remaining 1 tablespoon olive oil. Sear the pork on all sides, 3 to 5 minutes total, and transfer the pork to the oven (push aside the veggies to make room in the pan).

Roast everything together for another 25 to 35 minutes, until a thermometer poked into the thickest part of the pork reads 140°F.

Remove the pan from the oven, transfer the pork to a cutting board and tent with foil for 15 minutes. Toss the vegetables again and return the pan to the oven.

When the vegetables are caramelized on the outside and tender on the inside (some will be slightly charred and collapsed), remove the pan from the oven and pour in the vinegar. Toss to coat the vegetables, scraping up any bits stuck to the bottom of the pan. Season with additional salt and pepper if desired.

To serve, slice the pork into $\frac{1}{4}$-inch slices and serve on a platter with the vegetables.

SERVES 6

# CHAPTER 16

# RETURN TO CORFU

## MAY 2005

I stood at the front door with my heart pounding in my throat. The village was just as I remembered, and this house with its whitewashed walls and heavy wooden door was just as it had been fifteen years earlier. What was I doing coming back? What was I doing bringing Christopher here? Would Mama even remember me? Surely I had exaggerated how much the Kourtesis had meant to me and how much I had meant to them.

But there we were. I squeezed Christopher's hand and knocked on the door. Seconds later, Mama swung it open and there were the same wide, beautiful dimpled smile and sparkling eyes I remembered so clearly. I had expected Mama to have aged into a withered Greek widow; Matina had told me that Spiros had passed on a few years after I left Corfu. But I swear, the woman looked younger than when I'd lived with her.

She took my face in both of her hands and her eyes got teary. "*Lia, agapi mou*," she said. (Lia, my love.)

I had brought Christopher back to Corfu for two reasons. The first being that I had wanted to share the place—and the people—

that had meant so much to me, that had defined my ideals around food and life and love all those years ago. The second being that I was nearing the completion of my novel, *I Land Home,* and thought it a good excuse to submerge myself in the setting.

I'd reached out to Alexi's sister, Matina, to let her know we were coming. We'd kept in touch via infrequent letters over the years. Quite frankly, I wasn't sure how welcome we would be. After all, I was the one who didn't come back.

Mama opened the door to welcome us in and Matina pushed her way to the front, enveloping me in her strong arms, as beautiful and commanding as ever.

"This is my husband, Christopher," I said to them. Mama made a clucking noise and turned away. Matina held out her hand.

"Welcome," she said. "I am Matina."

We walked in and all stood in the kitchen around the table. *The* table. The table where Alexi first brought me home to Spiros's *pastisada.* The table where we sat for innumerable meals together. The table where Alexi proposed. And there I stood with my husband and Mama and Matina and her husband, Yannis, and their kids.

It was surreal.

"You must be Yannis," Christopher said, holding out his hand. "I'm Christopher."

"Good to meet you, Christopher," Yannis said, then folded me into a bear hug. "Lia, Lia, Lia," he rumbled in a voice that reminded me of Spiros. "It so good to see you."

I introduced myself to the kids, who spoke English just as well as their mother. Evagalia, who was named after her grandmother and was called, ironically, Lia, was around nine and Pantelis was two years older, and both had warm eyes like Yannis and beautiful smiles like Matina.

We sat down at the table and Mama brought out a heaping platter of salt cod fritters and a big bowl of golden *skordalia*, which made
my eyes water as much from nostalgia as from the pungency of the
garlic. "You're a writer now," Matina declared, as she always did so
authoritatively.

"I am," I said. "I write about food. I'm writing about Corfu," I
said.

"Pfff," Matina said, waving a hand at her body. "We're all gain-
ing weight here in Greece," she said. "We have fast food now, we
have McDonald's, like in America. And we have fat bodies like in
America too." She waved at me. "But not you, when did you get so
skinny?"

I laughed, "When I started eating like you Greeks."

Mama chuckled and poked me, saying something in Greek. Matina translated with a chuckle herself. "She said we'll get you fat-
tened up by the time you leave."

The fritters were puffy and crunchy, and the *skordalia* was thick,
pungent, and creamy, a meal in and of itself. Mama brought out a
bowl of boiled beets and greens tossed in olive oil—from the ouzo
bottle, of course—with a little salt and pepper and a squeeze of
lemon, and then mussels in an oniony tomato sauce whisked with
a bit of feta and milk, all tossed with thick spaghetti. By the end of
the meal I was stuffed, and so happy. These were the foods I remembered and the foods I pined for, and the people I loved.

"There is much going on during Holy Week," Matina said. "You'll
join us." We hadn't anticipated being in Corfu during the weeks before Easter, and welcomed the opportunity to experience Orthodox
Holy Week. No meat, though, until Easter Monday's lamb.

"We'd love to," I said, and Christopher nodded in agreement.
"Just tell us where you want us and when."

I'm sure you're wondering, so I should fill it in here. Christopher and I had stopped by Moda Car, the gas station and café that Alexi and Yannis owned, the day before seeing Matina and Mama, on our way home from a provisioning trip to Corfu Town. I'd expected Alexi to be gray, and maybe semibald like his father had been. But he was as handsome as ever, and as brazen. Matina had told me that Alexi had failed to tell his wife that we were there, which had sent her into a tailspin. I couldn't blame her.

It was the oddest sensation being there with Christopher and Alexi. With Christopher, I felt grounded and sure and ... adult. With Alexi, there was a frisson of teenage-esque excitement that surprised me. Thank God my husband had not one ounce of jealousy in his bones.

We had sat down to beers and Alexi said, "So, what happen?" which I took to mean, "What's happening in your life?" I brought him up to date on the main points of the past fifteen years, and he did the same. But when Christopher went to the bathroom, Alexi leaned across the table and said, "I mean, what happen? Why you not come back?" It became clear from the get-go that there was a good deal of unfinished business, for both of us.

*I'd wanted* Christopher to experience village life as I had. So I found a small apartment in the village on the northern side of the crescent beach of which the Kourtesis lived at the southern end.

We spent the next couple of days in our little village. Our house was dark, damp, and a little depressing, so our landlady showed us a hidden perch up the mountain, an abandoned outdoor café tucked amid some olive groves, with a carpet of perfumey pine needles and gorgeous views of the beach and the Kourtesis' village crowning the southern promontory. It had three iron benches in a semicircle on a cement block, half shaded, and was the perfect place to while away the day writing, reading, and drawing.

One day, I made *tzatziki* and beef *keftedes*—like little torpedoes of ground beef seasoned with onion, garlic, and spices—which we packed up and took as a picnic to our perch. Another day, we went to Corfu Town to explore. We found Hrisomallis Mezedopolis, a simple restaurant with prim white paint, plate-glass windows, and heavenly scents coming from a spit in a little appended room in front. We took a seat among a cluster of old, iron-footed tables on the sidewalk outside. Christopher ordered pastitsio, a classic Venetian dish—similar to lasagna—with a rich Bolognese-esque sauce and light, fluffy béchamel baked with noodles that were somewhere between macaroni and penne. I ordered *sofrito*, pounded veal dusted with flour and pan-fried, then layered with garlic and parsley and slow-cooked in a vinegar broth until it was falling-apart tender and saturated with flavor. I groaned with pleasure on my first bite and our waiter pointed to his grandmother in the kitchen. "She make it," he said. "She the best cook."


*Wednesday afternoon* we climbed the steep steps at the top of the hill in Kato Garouna to the church, where we were supposed to meet Matina and Mama at 5:00 for a special service. But the door was locked and only two old women sat outside. Moments later, we saw Lia bounding up the stairs. "Would you like to go see my grandfather?"

We followed her down the stairs and drove to the cemetery, where we found Mama surrounded by all of her young grandchildren: Lia and Pantelis; Alexi's children, Spiros and Eleni; and

Alexi's other sister Effie's youngest daughter, also named Lia. The white marble of the headstones glowed in the late-afternoon sun and the poplars made a shushing sound. Mama was perched on the edge of Spiros's raised grave, with a marble headstone that bore his photo behind a pane of glass.

Mama was telling the children that Spiros had been a great man; I agreed. Mama and I squeezed each other's hands and it occurred to me that she and I were the only ones there who had actually *known* Spiros, in the flesh.

The kids played around, walking on the edges of graves while Christopher chased and goaded them. Mama leaned over to me, pointing at the empty rectangle next to Spiros's. "That's mine," she said in Greek. "That's where I'm going."

I patted her on the back. "Not for a long time, though," I said, and she nodded in agreement.

After coffee and halva at Mama's house, our whole troupe tromped up to the village square and then up the stairs to the church. I had a Lia on both sides of me and we all joked that we were the "*Thia* Lias," the three Lias.

Mama nodded toward the back, where we stood for an hour while the priest and three other men swiveled a giant Bible back and forth and read in a monotone chant. Candlelight cast shadows on the carved statues, and I became drowsy from the incense. In my semiconscious state, the saints seemed to move in the flickering light. In fact, all of it was coming to life for me in a new way. The chants and hymns and icons and formalities had all seemed staid and dead to me before. Now a circuit was connecting, these rhythms and ceremonies—as timeless as the seasons—boring a deeper well into my faith.

After church, well past dusk, we all made our way to Matina

and Yannis's house, a lovely three-story home up the street from the Kourtesis', on the corner of the two main streets of the village. Matina was finishing the *taramasalata* and, unable to help myself, I dragged my finger through it, just as I'd done to her father's *skordalia* the first time. "It's smoky," I said to Matina. "Why is that?"

Matina busted out one of her Sphinx-like smiles and said, "Because here on Corfu, we use smoked herring roe, which makes our *taramasalata* better than anywhere else in Greece."

The adults corralled the children and set down big platters of fried calamari, shrimp in a gorgeous tomato sauce, the *taramasalata,* and a Greek salad. Mama set down a big bowl of *horta*—wild greens she'd collected that day—that was swimming in a pool of inky red olive oil.

"The *horta*," I said to Matina. "Why is it red?"

"We call it *tsigarelli*. Here on Corfu we add hot paprika to our *horta*, which makes it—"

I cut her off. "—better than the *horta* in the rest of Greece."

"You're learning," she said, patting me on the cheek.

It was one of those nights where it was easy to forget there was a language barrier. Conversation and laughter—lots of laughter—flowed as freely as the wine, and I was struck by how the kids gobbled up things with tentacles and squishy fish eggs and spicy greens just as enthusiastically as the adults did. There was no "kids' table" here, no mac and cheese. It was 10:30 at night, and the table was full of three generations feasting side by side.

*Friday evening* in Sinarades, the torches we'd seen propped on walls all over town were lit, crackling and whooshing in the breeze and making the dusk seem darker. The eerie shadows, the smell of kerosene, all gave it a feel of being set back several centuries in time. We followed the crowds down our alley toward the main street and saw a boy coming toward us carrying an oversized cross. Behind him were a dozen others carrying huge torches, followed by the church choir singing laments and, finally, the marching band. We fell into place behind the procession with the rest of the town, all of us carrying candles, and wound down the main street to the turnabout and then back up our alley. The procession felt holy and macabre all at the same time. Which, I guess, is exactly what Easter is meant to convey, especially on Good Friday, when Jesus was crucified.

After becoming a Christian I found Easter celebrations to be watered down. The fact of Jesus's horrid death and the miracle of his resurrection gets diluted when it has to compete with someone in a fuzzy white suit with big ears and colored plastic eggs.

Here, though, these visceral enactments brought a mystical dimension that breathed life into that deep, earthy way I'd experienced God when I was a child. In the same way that food on Corfu was simple and more real and grounded in the earth, so were my experiences with Christ.

We got up early the next morning to see the "throwing of the pots" in Corfu Town, a spectacle people came from all over Greece to see. We found a place away from the crowds and plopped down on the grass. At 11:00 precisely the people on the balconies with red drapes hanging over the banisters throughout town began to drop clay pots and amphorae out of their windows. Some were huge and filled with water. They made a big plopping noise when they hit the ground, and the crowd went wild with applause. Supposedly, this tradition came between Good Friday and Easter Sunday to emphasize the passing nature of worldly life compared to the eternal nature of the Spirit. It was also to symbolize a sort of "out with the old" philosophy: getting rid of what is no longer needed in order to make room for new life, a metaphor that spoke to me on my ongoing quest to weed out the unessential, even if I didn't have any pots to throw.

By Easter Sunday, every butcher's window showcased whole, flayed lambs ready for Monday's feast. Matina had invited us to yet another procession with the family on Monday morning and told us to meet them at the village pub. We found Matina and Mama with Effie—Matina's older sister—and her husband, Demetrius. They were with their daughter Lia and her older sister, Fae, who had been four when I'd lived there, who was now all grown up and beautiful, visiting from college.

The procession began. Men in frocks held up large banners of icons, like those in Sinarades on Good Friday. They chanted something in Greek, then started on a narrow path up the mountain with the rest of the villagers—and us—falling in behind. We climbed the eastern slope, past big bushes of wild sage, broom, goldenrod, and wild oregano. Then we wound up through a forested area dense with squat purple lupines, ferns, and little daisies, and out again onto the dusty path with views down south to Lefkimmi shimmering in the heat.

We turned the last corner and walked through a stone archway into a sort of garden in front of a church. Everyone was sitting on a low stone wall that we learned was the ruins of a twelfth-century monastery. Beyond there was a vineyard and, of course, olive groves, and then stunning views of the sea and Agios Gordios and north all along the western coast, as far as the Ropa Valley.

We were winded, and I took a seat on the stone wall next to Alexi and his children. "I'm eager to meet your wife," I said. "Why didn't she come?"

Alexi shrugged. "She couldn't make today."

"I remember when you first brought me to the top of the mountain," I said, looking around and taking it in, breathing in the scent of minty, sagey scrub and salty tang from the sea. "It's just as beautiful now as it was then." I could see Mama joining the villagers in the old church beyond the trellis, but I wasn't in any hurry to leave the view.

"Come." Matina motioned to me and Christopher and led us down another path to an even older chapel—a little one carved into the rock among the olive groves, apparently built for a lesser saint. We ducked inside. Its far side was hewn from bare rock, and both sides of the church were lined with the golden iconic paintings of saints.

It felt ancient and holy, yet somehow lived in. I could picture David hiding from Saul, or Samuel hiding from God there. Churches felt to me like rigid, straight-backed chairs. That cave-chapel felt like a well-worn leather armchair. It was a place you could sink in and just *be* with God, rather than having to watch your manners.

*Later that* day we went our own way, finding seats in the town square, where the butcher was spit-roasting several lambs, unleashing a heavenly scent of charred fat with every sizzle and pop. I was drooling. Christopher sought out a bottle of wine, coming back with a water bottle filled with pale yellow liquid. I walked up to the butcher with the rest of the crowd, took a piece of butcher paper, and held it up in front of my face to protect it from splattering juice.

But something remained for me to do before leaving. As wonderful as it had been to reconnect with Matina and Mama and meet all of the children, things had been strained between Alexi and me, and I wanted to make them right. We agreed to meet at Moda Car on Wednesday afternoon.

I walked in and Alexi was behind the bar. Even after all these years, there was something so familiar about him, the way he moved, his expressions. He made us both coffees and sat down next to me.

"First, I want to say, I have a delete key in my head," he said.

I sat with that for a moment. "I'm sorry, I'm not following."

"If I don't care for someone, I just delete them from my mind. I just forget them." He made a whooshing motion with his arm, and I wondered if he had deleted me, if that was why he seemed so uncomfortable with me around. But then he looked me in the eyes. "In all these years, I never deleted you."

He apologized for things that didn't need apology, and I was able to set him straight. And I explained in better detail than was ever possible on the phone or paper why I didn't come back. Some of it had been external forces, but some of it had been about us too. I'd felt then and felt even more strongly now that the very things Alexi loved about me were also the things he struggled most with—my independence, my fire, my passion.

I hadn't realized how much I needed to tell Alexi how much he had meant to me and what a big impact he had had on my life, and to hear the same from him. We gave each other a long hug, and I walked out feeling a closure I hadn't even known I needed.

Later that afternoon, I took one last walk down the mountain to capture lingering notes for *I Land Home,* while Christopher waited for me at the bottom. It was drizzly and gray and the ground smelled of moist humus and wet leaves. On the way down I picked a bouquet of wildflowers and walked into the cemetery. I sat down on the edge of Spiros's grave and set the bouquet beneath his photo, laying my hand on the cool marble.

"Thank you, Spiros," I said. "For sharing your family with me, your town with me, your culture." I swallowed the lump in my throat and whispered, "Thank you for sharing your love with me."

Then I walked down the mountain to where my husband was waiting.

## MAMA'S SALT COD FRITTERS

*Salt cod is a traditional ingredient in many Mediterranean dishes. Ask for it at your fish counter—they'll often have a box in the freezer—or order it online. When I'm missing Greece, this is the recipe I turn to most often. I remember hovering over Mama at the kitchen counter, trying to lock on to what she was putting in the bowl and what the consistency of the batter should be. Serve these with the Skordalia from Chapter 1.*

1 pound dried and salted cod
1 cup all-purpose flour
2 tablespoons baking powder
$^1/_2$ cup extra virgin olive oil

Soak the salt cod in cold water for 24 hours, changing the water at least five times over the course of the soak.

Drain the fish and pull it apart into shreds into a mixing bowl. Add the flour and baking powder and stir to coat the strands. Then drizzle in 1 cup water and mix well.

In a large sauté pan, heat the oil over medium-high heat until a crumb of bread sizzles immediately. Working in batches, spoon $^1/_4$-cup mounds of batter into the pan (the batter will be roughly the consistency of pancake batter, with stringy strands of fish), leaving a bit of room between each to allow browning. Cook for 3 to 5 minutes per side, flipping carefully with a spatula, until each side is well browned. As each fritter is finished, remove to a plate lined with paper towels and repeat with the rest of the batter.

SERVES 8

# PART III
## STARTS

*Visible to everyone, the first true leaves of a tomato plant pop out, followed by a stem and branches. Yet an equally important action occurs below ground, where no one can see, as the roots continue to grow and deepen in preparation for the plant to bear fruit.*

THE NEW SEED-STARTERS HANDBOOK

*I want to beg you, as much as I can, to be patient toward all that is unsolved in your heart, and try to love the questions themselves like locked rooms.*

LETTERS TO A YOUNG POET, #4, RAINER MARIA RILKE

# CHAPTER 17

# CALL OF THE WILD

AUGUST 2005

Thunder rumbled off the granite peaks. I stood on a pile of boulders that straddled Piute Pass—at 11,800 feet and high above the tree line—in California's John Muir Wilderness. Nasty, dark clouds swirled just overhead and my heart beat so hard in my chest I was nauseous. Below me a cluster of women in brightly colored rain gear urged me on to where they were standing across a wide, moorlike basin dotted with lakes and wildflowers.

I was the tallest thing around . . . and I am *terrified* of lightning.

Alison, my editor at *Cooking Light,* had given me an assignment to write about Carole Latimer, the queen of wilderness cuisine and the owner of a backcountry adventure company for women called Call of the Wild. At the time it sounded like fun, but I was having second (and third and fourth) thoughts.

"Come on, Lia," I said under my breath. "You can do this. You *have* to do this." I took a deep breath and took off down the glade with a battle cry like Mel Gibson in *Braveheart.*

But I made it. We made it. The clouds broke on the other side of the pass, and the giant mound of Mount Humphreys glowed like a Chinese lantern in the lingering mist. When I could see past the pinpricks of terror, the scene was actually quite bucolic. Purple lupine, delicate tiger lilies, columbine bonnets, and lipstick-red shooting stars dotted the meadows, which were crisscrossed by babbling creeks and hemmed in by snow-streaked cliffs.

Ten miles in we made camp in a beautiful close of evergreens at the foot of the Glacier Divide with a branch of the Piute Creek just steps to the south. To the west was a broad plate of granite looking out toward the Pinnacles—jagged mountains that looked like a row of shark's teeth.

I loosened up considerably over dinner, which was much better than I'd expected: ginger soup with fresh zucchini, beef curry, and creamy cucumber salad. Over the next three days, I learned all about Carole's dehydration techniques and organizational strategies for a camp kitchen (I was totally going to adopt her method of folding a piece of mesh over a clothesline to use as a drying rack).

Come day four, it was my time to leave. The rest of the ladies were staying on for the full week, but I had other deadlines at home I needed to tend to, so I waited behind for the team of pack mules while everyone went off to hike for the day.

I had a lovely late morning and early afternoon, reading in camp and doing a sort of improvised yoga on the big granite expanse overlooking the Pinnacles. But around 2:00, I noticed big, dark thunderheads tumbling in from both sides of the canyon, followed by rumbles that sounded like cannon shot. I ran back to camp and got there just as the torrent began. There was a vicious slash of lightning. I took off my watch and threw it several feet from me, wanting to get away from any sort of metal. Then I semisquatted between two big pine trees, unable to remember whether I was supposed to be close to a tree or far away from a tree to avoid getting hit.

My fear of lightning may have been acute, but it wasn't entirely unfounded. When I was a sophomore in high school, I went on a ski trip to Colorado. Halfway up the mountain on the chair lift, a storm blew in that was howling so hard I couldn't hear my boyfriend next to me. On our descent, I was making wide snowplow traverses down the empty mountain just trying to remain upright in the powerful gusts.

And then, *zing.* A bright flash and I felt like my body had been plugged into a socket and all my hair burned off. In fact, the first thing I screamed to my boyfriend when I realized I was still alive was, "Is my hair still there?" (It was.) As far as anyone could ascertain later, lightning had struck one of the chair lift poles and I had been caught in a current between that pole and another across the slope. I was lucky to be alive. My head was hot to the touch for hours. But it left me with a lingering (irrational) fear that, maybe, the lightning accidentally missed that time and wouldn't be so careless the next.

So my fear of lightning in the Sierras had solid cred, which only got stronger once the pack mule team arrived (finding me in my pee-like squat). "Get your rain gear on!" the man yelled over the tumult. "It's gonna be a long, wet ride!"

"What?" I asked, mortified. "We're not really riding down in *this,* are we?" I asked, gesturing at the ruckus going on around us.

The man chuckled, and I worried for a moment that I was facing not only a giant thunderstorm at ten thousand feet but a madman as well. "Oh yes we are, we gotta get this stuff down the mountain."

I glanced behind him, and there were five other mules laden with gear and another pulling up the rear with another rider. "I'm Mike," the man yelled. "And that there's my daughter, Gracie." I nodded at both of them, drawing solace from the fact that Mike had his daughter with him. I mean, you wouldn't bring your daughter into a situation that spelled death, would you? "Now get your rain gear on!" Mike bellowed, and I did.

We climbed out of the enclosure and up toward the pass, above the tree line with no cover whatsoever. It was raining in sheets, and thunder and lightning seemed to come from all directions. "We got a perfect storm here," Mike yelled. "One's coming from that way and another's coming from that way and they're crossing right over the top of us."

"So it isn't dangerous for us to be out in this?" I bellowed back, fixated—through the veil of rain that ran off the brim of my hat—on the shod hooves of the mule ahead of me.

Mike looked back over his shoulder. "Oh, sure it is. Heck, just a few months ago we was doing something just like this with one of Carole's people and lightning struck a pack mule. It fell over dead, and the woman on the mule behind it had to be flown out by helicopter."

I really couldn't speak after that. But I spent a good long time—it was a four-hour ride out of the wilderness with no break in the thunderstorms and even a deafening landslide for good measure—trying to let go of my fear of death.

I'd been pondering the pots the Corfiots had thrown out of their windows, asking myself what I was still holding on to that needed to be tossed. All the usual answers came up: the desire for worldly possessions and comforts, the desire for recognition and acceptance.

But there on that ride, when I was convinced beyond a doubt that the chances of making it off that mountain alive was in the single digits, I realized that there were some other bedrock assumptions that God might want me to bash open too. These were the ones that

I held like cards close to my chest, not showing them to anyone, *especially* not God.

So I closed my eyes, held the reins in my numb hands, and one by one, handed over the whole well-worn deck.

None of those cards belonged to me anyway. If God saw fit to strip me of comforts, so be it. If He saw fit to withhold success in my career, so be it. If He chose to take those I loved, so be it. And if He chose to take me in a doozy of a thunderstorm on a mule on a mountain, so be it.

I would not cling, I would trust. And I would not be afraid any longer.

*Not long* after turning in the Call of the Wild assignment, I got another e-mail from *Cooking Light*. Only this one was from the editor in chief asking if I would consider hosting a television show for the magazine.

I'd made a couple of stops in Birmingham—where *Cooking Light* is headquartered—on my way down to my classes in Florida to get to know the people I worked with, and Mary Kay told me in the e-mail that she'd recognized my ability to think on my feet.

I was flabbergasted. I'd never done any television before. We hadn't even *owned* a television since we'd left San Francisco. I was flattered by the offer but highly unsure. Just a year or so earlier, Christopher and I had been talking about me pursuing a cookbook. By then, I had built a solid reputation as a food writer and recipe developer, and writing a cookbook would have been a natural next step. But I said no for two reasons: first, I wasn't yet clear on what I was being called to write, and I didn't just want to write a book for the sake of having a book. Second, I knew that writing a cookbook meant seeking out media opportunities to promote it, and that prospect sent me into a cold sweat.

But just before that call from Mary Kay, I'd been out on a walk. It had been raining for weeks and the eucalyptus smelled so strong it was like someone had opened a jar of Vicks. Around a bend where Jann and I used to gorge on summer blackberries, there was a small pond with a waterfall feeding into it that I could feel reverberating beneath my feet.

*Deep calls to deep in the roar of your waterfalls.* The psalm floated through my mind like a whisper, and I stood there letting deep call to that deep, sacred space beneath my sternum. I sensed I was supposed to take note of something important.

I looked down at the pond and saw four little humps on a log. When I moved, three of them plopped into the water. But one turned toward me and stuck its head out into the sun. It was a turtle coming out of its shell and reaching its head toward the light.

That was it. I was being called to move out of my shell—out of my comfort zone—toward the light, even if I wanted to stay hidden safely below water.

So when that call came from Mary Kay, I thought, *Is this how I'm supposed to get out of my shell?* And I stuck my neck out and said yes.

*The next* couple of months were a whirlwind. I made a demo reel to send to *Cooking Light,* and it made its rounds though Time, Inc. I began working with an agent on *I Land Home.* And just before I graduated from my MBA program in April, my team won an entrepreneurship competition for a business that I'd brought to the table, and I was invited—and enthusiastically encouraged by my professor—to present at a national competition for venture capital money.

There were many—too many—possibilities on the horizon, and I was grateful for the three-week hiatus Christopher and I had planned in Spain and Italy just after graduation.

We spent the first week in Seville eating every sort of tapas known to man (toss-up for favorite between the *boquerones* and the *jamón Serrano*). The second week we split between the Costa Brava with friends from San Francisco and Venice with Jann and Gerry, where we'd rented a little apartment close to the Rialto Market and literally bought so much food we couldn't eat it all (much to Gerry's chagrin). We made balsamic braised *cipollini* onions, stuffed squash blossoms, braised baby artichokes, salt-and-pepper shrimp . . . but we threw in the towel before we got to the sole meunière. So now we joke that we left our soles in Venice.

The last week, we met up with Chris, Honore, and JoJo at a villa we were renting in southern Tuscany. We had an epic time (there were Moroccan daybeds on the terrace by the pool overlooking a gentle valley with grazing sheep and grapevines . . . need I say more?). We made epic meals. One night, we marinated fat pork chops in a paste of garlic and rosemary and grilled them over an open fire, then served them beside zucchini and garlic cooked over low heat with several glugs of local olive oil so that it melted into a sort of confit. I even shorted out the entire electrical system of the villa when I soaked salt cod (for Mama's Salt Cod Fritters) in a leaky vessel.

But as incredible as it all was, my mind was elsewhere. I was constantly distracted by a little voice whispering, "It's time." To which

I kept whispering back, more and more insistently, "For *what*?" I lay there on those posh Moroccan daybeds silently praying, holding each option up and saying, this one? TV? *I Land Home*? Business? Or was it option D, born of a desire that had suddenly and unexpectedly burbled to the surface just a few weeks earlier ... to become a mom? I gazed out at the sheep grazing on the hills (we called it Sheep TV). These things were too tender to pull out to the general crowd over an afternoon aperitif, so I pondered them alone, with God, watching Sheep TV. I couldn't say yes to all, but what if I said yes to the wrong one?

I eventually admitted to myself that I already knew the answer. There were times I doubted that God had told me I'd become a mother, feeling so far from that promise in Lois's office that I wondered if I'd heard right. But now I knew. It was time to say yes to adoption. The question now was how to tell Christopher.

*When we* returned home that summer, I found the strength that allowed me to boldly declare my news to Christopher. The irrational calm. I knew my job was to trust, to speak, and to let go, and let God take care of the rest.

Christopher wasn't ready. He retreated into his cave and sealed the door shut. Over the next few weeks I had several conversations with God that went something like this: "You told me to do this and I did it, and I'm absolutely not going to meddle, so you better get on it," and "OK, God, I did my part, so now it's time to do your part." Pause. "But if you don't—I mean, if Christopher never comes around—that's OK too, because I did my part by being faithful, and that's all you've asked me to do ... right?"

Then one night in bed at home, I got a surprise. I was just about asleep when Christopher rolled over and pushed my hair back from my face.

"Honey," he said. "You awake?"

"Hmmm," I said, not really wanting to wake back up.

"I've been thinking—a *lot*—over the last two weeks about what you said about adoption."

My eyes flew open. "You have?"

"I'm not there yet, but—" I could see Christopher's eyes glistening. "But I even started envisioning a baby cuddled up with us over the last few days."

"I'm speechless," I said, taking his hand. "And I'm scared."

"I am too. I think we'd be silly not to be."

"It feels huge and overwhelming, but I think it's what we're supposed to do. It's not about being comfortable, it's about growing in the way we're meant to be grown."


*Two weeks* later, Christopher returned from a leadership retreat. I had made a simple dinner of pasta with broccoli sauce—one of our favorites to come home to—and lit candles all over the house. I poured wine and turned on Abbey Lincoln, waiting for Christopher to come through the door. We had a tradition of creating soft landings for each other when we came back from retreats—or any place where there would be stories to tell—to create the space to let the stories unspool without being rushed.

I saw his headlights and heard the car pull to a stop and greeted him at the door with a kiss. "Welcome home," I said, handing Christopher his wine.

"Hmmmm," he hummed in contentment. Then he sat down on the couch, leaned back, and started weeping.

"What's wrong?" I asked. "What happened?"

"Honey," he said, standing back up and dragging his foot across the ground. He took a step over the invisible line he had drawn and said, "I'm past fifty percent." He looked like a deer in headlights. "I'm ready to be a dad."

⸎

## ORECCHIETTE WITH BROCCOLI SAUCE

*This dish—which has turned into our go-to "welcome home" meal in one form or another—was originally made for us in Costa Rica by our friend Vittoria, the night she told us about Finca Ipe. It's one of those ridiculously easy, one-pot meals that's both nourishing and satisfying.*

Sea salt

16 ounces dried orecchiette pasta

1 pound broccoli crowns, cut into bite-sized pieces

5 garlic cloves

3 anchovy fillets

$1/4$ teaspoon crushed red pepper flakes (optional)

$1/2$ cup extra virgin olive oil

$1/2$ cup freshly grated Romano cheese

Bring a large pot of salted water to a boil.

Add the pasta and cook according to package directions to al dente. Six minutes *before* the pasta is done cooking, add the broccoli to the pot and push down to submerge.

While the pasta and broccoli are cooking, pound the garlic and anchovies to a paste in a mortar and pestle with a sprinkle of salt (alternatively, mince them finely, sprinkle salt over the top, and drag the side of your knife over the top to mash them into a paste).

Transfer the anchovy paste to a bowl, add the red pepper flakes (if using), and whisk in the oil and 2 to 3 tablespoons of the pasta water.

Drain the pasta and broccoli in a colander and return it to the pot. Toss with the sauce for 30 to 60 seconds to coat well; the broccoli will break apart and become part of the sauce. Add the cheese and toss again.

SERVES 6 TO 8

## CHAPTER 18

# HER NAME IS NOEMI

SEPTEMBER 2006

I pulled the pan out of the oven and slipped the skins easily off the beets, revealing shiny orbs of garnet and the palest shade of pink. Then I sliced each into thin wedges and scattered them atop the thick asparagus spears I'd roasted and laid out like an extended tic-tac-toe. A douse of garlic-lemon vinaigrette, a light crumble of blue cheese, and dinner was ready.

I took it to the table outside, where I'd already lit candles that flickered off our fruit trees. Christopher and I had spent nearly six months the previous summer re-landscaping our yard from the ground up. Where there had once been grass and concrete, there were now potted lemon and lime trees, a fig tree espaliered against the house, a pineapple guava tree, lime-green striped yucca, and spiky purple salvia. Likewise in the back, where there had once been a series of dilapidated railroad ties and wood chips, there were now four lush garden beds surrounding a circular fountain that we almost had working.

I set my plate down next to my journal on the table and walked back to the garden in the waning light to see what herbs I could find.

I grabbed a handful of basil and chives, which I tore into pieces and sprinkled over the vegetables. I sliced into the asparagus, speared a wedge of beet, and hummed out loud at the sweet, earthy flavors kicked up by the zing of the vinaigrette. Then I leaned back and laughed. Just eight years ago I wouldn't have touched anything on my plate but the cheese.

Oh, how things had changed.

I scribbled in my journal while I ate, and the enormity of how much had shifted in our lives became even more evident.

*Saramaya,* I wrote. Over and over. It was the name I was secretly harboring for our daughter, guarding it, testing it, praying over it.

Once Christopher had gotten to 51 percent, things began to move quickly. In my Bible study that week we looked closely at Moses crossing the Red Sea. He parted the sea, sure. But then he ushered everyone across as quickly as possible. It wasn't like he had everyone stop and have a picnic on the dry riverbed. The point was, there are times in life—many times—where we are invited to wait. But there are also times when we must move swiftly.

I sensed God saying *go.*

Of course, I argued with Him all the way home. "You're sure you're not saying *no*?" "How can I go to Christopher and tell him we need to move on this now without seeming like I'm manipulating things? I mean, he just said *yes.*" "What do I even do to go? I have no idea what to do next!"

But the answer was the same. A steady, calm, unchanging, unfaltering *go.*

I walked in the front door somewhat shell-shocked and told Christopher I had something to tell him.

"Um . . . you know how Moses parted the Red Sea?" I began. Always a good place to begin a big discussion. And then I told him that I felt God was giving us our marching orders. Now. God bless him, here's what my husband said.

"You're the jib, baby. I trust you, and I trust God."

When we were in Costa Rica, Christopher and I had made a map. Looking back on it, I think it was our way of trying to literally find solid ground during a very ambiguous time. We had "islands" that were different aspects of our lives—writing was an island, some sort of joint business was an island—we had "gauges" for indicating where we were emotionally, physically, spiritually. And we had a sailboat. I was the jib and Christopher was the mainsail.

According to Bernoulli's law—the law that governs both hydrodynamics and aerodynamics—what gives a sailboat movement isn't direct force from the wind. Rather, when wind funnels past a sail (or a wing), the force of resistance decreases and the boat moves in that direction. The faster the air funneling past the sail, the lower the resistance and the speedier the forward movement. Adding a jib funnels the air faster past the mainsail and makes the boat move quickly.

We had both decided that Bernoulli's law was an apt metaphor for the roles we had. I tend to feel the stirrings of the Spirit first—that is, I catch the wind—and funnel it to Christopher, the mainsail, who adds the forward locomotion.

So in terms of adoption and Moses and the Red Sea and *go*, Christopher had just caught my wind, and he was ready to run with it.

We didn't have the slightest idea what to do next, but we trusted that God did. I had Googled a few international adoption agencies over the years but had been put off by the "these kids are waiting for a family" photos. It felt more like adopting a pet than entering into a sacred pact where souls are brought together as a family—because we wholeheartedly believed that that was what was happening. We wanted to find an adoption agency that both knew their stuff and believed there was something mystical, something holy, about the whole thing.

So we talked to someone who pointed us to someone else who knew of a couple in Healdsburg who had adopted a child from Guatemala. We called them up and went for a visit, and then we called their adoption agency—Heartsent.

*The morning* we drove down to the East Bay for our orientation, both of us were so nervous we couldn't eat. "Do you think she's born yet?" I asked Christopher. "Where do you think she's from?" Christopher just kept driving.

I was excited, too, to meet others who loved Guatemala as much as we did, and to hear their stories. In fact, Heartsent handled adoptions from several different countries, and I was eager to meet such a diverse crowd.

We pulled up to a nondescript 1970s office building and were ushered into a room that felt like a children's classroom. We put on tags with our names and the country we were hoping to adopt from, and then we mingled. Right away I realized I'd been naïve about a few things. As we talked to people and heard their stories, I discovered there were some potential parents who were there not from a place of joy, but with a broken heart. They saw adoption as the last card they'd hoped and hoped and hoped they wouldn't have to play. And for them, my heart broke. I wasn't even a mom yet, but I wanted to go give those weeping women with sad, sad eyes hugs and say, *Go home. This isn't right for you, at least not right now. Please don't bring a child into your pain.*

We took our seats in plastic chairs and listened to a presentation about each of the countries Heartsent works in. They even handed out a little matrix, outlining how long it took to adopt from each country, how much each cost, what age of a child you could reasonably expect. And then, after I'd heard several people speak, it clicked. Most people there weren't sure yet where they wanted to adopt from. They were looking for a right fit for their families among that matrix in the same way my dad looked to *U.S. News & World Report's* "Best Places to Live," evaluating such things as tax rates and employment rates. These were the tangible, logical points upon which many people made decisions, and I respected that.

It also made perfect sense that Christopher and I were there working backward from Guatemala. That's the way *we* worked.

In fact, since our Salva Vida trip we'd been back to Guatemala twice to see Rene-Antonio and had already grown our Guatemalan "family." We had supported a scholarship fund for children of the women in a highland organization called AMIDI through our local Slow Food chapter. And in one newsletter update, I read that the first of the scholarship recipients had just graduated from high school—a major accomplishment in Guatemala. I was thrilled . . . but then I thought, *What now?* They had worked so hard to get there; what if they wanted to go on to college?

So I'd called up Marilee, the woman who had founded the scholarship fund and was close friends with the women in AMIDI, and I'd asked her that question. It sparked a thoughtful conversation among the AMIDI members, and resulted in Christopher and me partnering with Mayra, the daughter of the AMIDI leader, Ana Maria, to help pay for Mayra's college education.

And a partnership it truly was. Marilee kept us updated on Mayra's progress and hardships, and I felt like we were on a path together. When she needed money for Internet access, we tightened our belts and gave it to her. When I had trouble getting up in the morning or getting motivated to work, I thought of Mayra walking a mile down a steep, rugged mountain in the dark just to catch the bus.

I was discovering something about radical giving. When we're cajoled to give from a shallow place of "should," it can bring about the bitter fruit of an I'm-better-than-them pity, or a false piety (*Aren't I a good person for doing that?*). But when we start by nourishing the soul in order to establish deep roots in who we are and what we're made for, we're able to act nimbly when the Spirit calls, less encumbered by our own ego.

Everything about Heartsent—including the leader of the Guatemalan program, Kelly Jo—made us feel that they were the right fit for us. So we made an appointment with Kelly Jo to start the process, and she gave us a big, fat, empty binder.

"Why is it empty?" I asked, turning it over in my hands.

Kelly Jo chuckled. "Trust me, it won't be empty for long."

"But can't you just give us the paperwork we'll need to fill out, so we can get a head start?"

"We'll just take it one step at a time," she said calmly. "Together."

The first step was to meet with a social worker for what, in adoption parlance, are called "home studies." I gathered later that many people looked upon home studies defensively, as if the social worker were an inspection agent looking for something wrong ("Tsk tsk tsk, there's no child lock on that cabinet—two points off for you").

Christopher and I, on the other hand, felt like we were being thrown into the world of parenting with virtually no preparation at all. I mean, how were you supposed to learn this stuff? What a baby's cries mean, how to feed them, where to put the changing table, what kind of gear do you need. We *pummeled* our social worker with questions, oblivious to any notion that she might think, *Hmmm, these folks don't seem to have a clue.*

We got a call in late October from Kelly Jo during which she gave us a status update in her usual let's-get-down-to-business tone. "OK, we've got everything in to Guatemala and now need to wait for the I-171 form. I'm anticipating four or five weeks, but you never know."

"Then what?" I asked.

"Then you'll be cleared for a match."

Kelly Jo had made it clear to us from the get-go that it would likely be a longer wait for an infant girl, as we'd requested. So she suggested checking in after a couple of months' wait to see if we felt differently. Then, if we were chomping at the bit, we could change our request to a boy. But first, we had to get the I-171.

Just when we thought that everything had been turned in, Kelly Jo called again. "You need to redo your police clearance forms. The notary crossed her seven and it looks too much like a one."

"You're kidding."

"Sorry, nope."

Three more tries—the chief of police used the wrong date, there was another crossed seven, and Kelly Jo made a last-minute decision to have Christopher and me do separate forms instead of filing a joint one—and two weeks later, we *finally* had all the paperwork together.

"OK," Kelly Jo said. "I'm turning everything in. Like I said, it could be up to four or five weeks before we get the I-171, and then the real wait for a match."

. . .

*Four days* later, on November 17 to be exact, the phone rang from Heartsent.

"Hello," I answered.

"Liiiaaaa," Kelly Jo said, in a tender drawl that I'd never heard come out of her before. My heart started beating so wildly that my fingers went numb and I almost dropped the phone.

"Oh my God, oh my God, oh my God," I said, running into Christopher's office. "I know what you're going to say. Hang on, putting you on speaker."

I sat cross-legged on the floor beside the phone while Christopher came to sit beside me, looking thoroughly bewildered.

"OK," I said. "Go ahead."

"We've got your daughter, you two," she said. I collapsed over my knees, sobbing, too overwhelmed in that moment to even ponder the fact that what was supposed to have taken months and months had taken days. "Her name is Noemi de Leon, and she was born eleven days ago." In that heartbeat, Saramaya evaporated and Noemi de Leon became our daughter. "She's beautiful, you guys. And from the sound of it, she's so your daughter—feisty and strong and sweet."

I didn't think I could cry any harder, but I did. How could I feel such a fierce, tangible love for a being I hadn't even met yet?

Noemi was living in Guatemala City with a foster family. "They're awesome," Kelly Jo assured us—she did onsite visits in Guatemala three times a year, so she knew all the foster families, children, and lawyers personally.

When we got photos of Noemi a few days later we saw the sweetest waif of a girl with long, skinny legs and arms, café au lait skin, and a head full of black hair. She had a gaze that already seemed to say, *Trust me, I know what I'm doing.*

I took her photo with me wherever I went. When we went to Ikea for a nursery run, we propped the photo of Noemi up on the handle of the cart. When I went to buy clothes for her with Julie, I held her photo up to the outfits to see if they were the right colors. And every evening, I'd sing to her and kiss her photo good night before setting it on my nightstand—or sometimes under my pillow, where I could hold it—never wanting to be more than a few inches away.

Christopher and I took photos of ourselves to send to her foster mother, Virginia, so she could show Noemi. We bought a little tape recorder and recorded ourselves reading poems and children's stories and singing songs so she could get to know our voices. We sent essentials like clothes and diapers every other week.

Thanksgiving came quickly and we turned down offers to visit friends. We wanted this Thanksgiving to be about our little family.

I asked Marilee to suggest a Guatemalan dish to make for our Thanksgiving celebration and she suggested *pollo en jocon*, a chicken stew made with tomatillos. So I bought two pounds of tomatillos from the Mexican market and carefully peeled and chopped each one. Then I sautéed them with onions and set them to simmer with the chicken. I'd picked two avocados earlier in the week so they'd be perfect for Thursday and mashed them with onion, chile, and lime juice, then stirred in diced jicama. Christopher and I lit candles and sat on the floor with our feast laid out before us and our little girl, Noemi de Leon, in a picture frame in the middle.

It was, hands down, the best Thanksgiving ever.

༄

# POLLO EN JOCON

*Pollo en jocon is a chicken stew from the Cobán region of Guatemala, traditionally served over rice with warm corn tortillas. This recipe is adapted from one my friend, cookbook author Sandra Gutierrez, gifted us with shortly after we brought Noe home. The stew can be prepared ahead of time, chilled, and reheated before serving. It also freezes beautifully for up to 2 months, as does the leftover chicken broth.*

1 (3- to 4-pound) chicken
2 scallions (white and green parts)
6 garlic cloves
Salt and freshly ground black pepper
20 large tomatillos, cleaned of husks, rinsed, and dried
$\frac{1}{2}$ large yellow onion, cut into thick slices
1 green bell pepper, quartered and seeded
1 plum tomato
2 serrano chiles, stemmed, halved lengthwise, and seeded
1 bunch cilantro (about 3 cups, packed)
1 tablespoon vegetable oil

Place the chicken in a large pot with the scallions and 2 of the garlic cloves and cover with cold water. Add a generous pinch each of salt and pepper, bring to a boil over medium-high heat, and skim off any foam that has risen to the surface. Then reduce the heat to medium-low (it should still be bubbling, but not very vigorously) and simmer for 50 to 60 minutes; the legs and wings should come off easily when grabbed with tongs. Remove the chicken and reserve the liquid. Let the chicken cool enough so you can handle it, then remove and discard the skin and bones and shred the meat (you should have about 7 cups).

Heat a *comal* or large cast-iron skillet over medium-high heat. Working in batches, add the tomatillos, onion, bell pepper, tomato, serrano chiles, and the remaining 4 garlic cloves, roasting them until they are charred all over. Transfer them to a large bowl as they're done.

Working in batches in a blender, purée the roasted vegetables and cilantro with enough chicken broth (about $1/4$ cup) to blend smoothly; it should be about the consistency of salsa.

Heat the oil in a Dutch oven or large pot over medium-high heat. Add the tomatillo sauce (careful, it will splatter) and stir well. Reduce the heat and simmer the sauce for 5 minutes; it will darken slightly. Add the cooked chicken and 1 cup chicken broth, stir well, and simmer the stew for 15 minutes. Serve over steamed brown rice.

SERVES 6 TO 8

CHAPTER 19

# REDEFINING CONTENTMENT

MARCH 2007

W e sat in white plastic chairs in a dirt yard in Antigua, Guatemala, watching two men hammer the tin roof onto what was becoming a house right before our eyes. The men, and the women cleaning up around the site, were part of a Common Hope team, there to build the house that Rene-Antonio's mother and grandmother had worked so hard for.

Rene-Antonio sat beside me. We clasped all four hands, practically vibrating we were so excited to be together again. He had grown into a handsome young man, almost as tall as I was. Maria Elena and her mother came out of the wooden shack that was serving as their current home carrying a plate of fat, ruby-hued watermelon slices and wearing smiles that mimicked the shape of the rinds.

"What an amazing coincidence we're here the day your house is being built," I said.

Rene-Antonio's grandmother gave a solemn nod and pointed up at the sky. *"Benediction de Dios,"* she said. (It's a blessing from God.)

I didn't disagree. We didn't even know that Maria Elena and her mom had been working toward a house. What were the odds that the one day we were there in Antigua was the same day they'd be building it? A blessing indeed. And a celebration. No champagne served, no fancy pâté or canapés. Just sitting in that little circle of plastic chairs spitting watermelon seeds and wiping the juice off our chins made us feel like we were all a part of what was happening there that day. And we were. We were family, feasting together.

And yet, all that was icing on the cake. Because the real reason we were in Guatemala was to meet Noemi for the first time. We still wouldn't be able to bring her home for another several months— Kelly Jo wasn't kidding when she said we'd fill that folder full of paperwork—but we'd passed the stage where we were given clearance to meet Noemi. Starting the next morning, we'd have four whole days together cloistered within our hotel.

They had recommended the Marriott, which was close to the airport and town. But we'd said no, remembering how awkward we'd felt there amid so many adoptive families all those years ago, and instead booked a room at a hotel that was part of the Latin American Quinta Real chain that we'd splurged on a couple of times when traveling through Mexico.

When we returned from Antigua that evening, votives flickered everywhere, illuminating the rich, sunset hues of the plaster walls and the sacred art peeking from every niche. Big wrought-iron chandeliers and rough-hewn wooden tables complemented frilly plasterwork, like decorative icing on a cake.

I had brought collapsible fabric cubes that now sat in a neat row beneath the picture window, each holding different necessities. One with clothes, one with bottle accoutrements, one with diaper necessities, one with toys and stuffed animals. Around midnight, we realized in a panic that we had no way to sterilize Noe's bottles, so Christopher took a cab to the Guatemalan version of Walmart to buy a bottle sterilizer.

And then the sun rose on the day we would meet our baby.

My knees shook as we walked across the covered portico toward the lobby. The chilly breeze carried the scent of honeysuckle, and I untied my linen shirt from around my waist and pulled it on over my sundress. We turned the corner and walked down the stairs to the lobby, and there they were. A beautiful Mayan woman holding a little bundle of blankets with pastel stripes, and peeking out, a head of black hair. Noemi. She was *here*.

I had a hard time catching my breath.

"Virginia," Christopher said, walking toward them. *"Soy Cristobal, y Lia."*

Virginia nodded at two butter-colored leather chairs, inviting us to sit down. *"Y esta es su hija. Su Noemi."* (This is your daughter. Your Noemi.) Virginia smiled in a wise, matronly way as she laid Noemi—just under four months old—in my arms and positioned the bottle in my hand.

She. Was. Beautiful. Her eyes were closed and she was sucking away at the bottle, oblivious to the immensity of the transfer that had just taken place, that all of our lives in that moment had turned on a pinpoint. I brushed Noe's cheek with my pinky and her eyes opened slightly. She gazed right into my eyes, grasped my pinky with her tiny little finger, and slipped back into bottle bliss.

For anyone who doubts the love of a mother toward her adopted child, let me just tell you that I would have taken flaming arrows while being dragged by a galloping horse through glass shards scattered over burning coals for that little girl lying in my arms. She was

238 · LIA HUBER

my daughter and I would love her with all of my might until the end of time, pure and simple.

Christopher had to lead me back to the room by my elbow because I couldn't take my eyes off Noe. Her perfect little cheeks, her soft bushy eyebrows, her plump pink lips, the little pigtail poking off the top of her head.

We got to the room and I passed her to Christopher, and, I swear, the man glowed. He walked around bouncing Noe, talking some silly baby talk while she giggled and pulled on his nose. We put her on the bed, on a piece of fabric we'd bought in Antigua to make into a bumper for her crib, and just watched her gurgle and coo and grab at the air.

I sat cross-legged in front of her and let her grab my fingers, pulling them back and forth. Then I *brzzzzzzed* with my lips and she did the same.

"Honey!" I said, surprised. "She just copied me. She just *brzzzzzzed*."

"What?" Christopher came rushing over as if I'd said she'd quoted Shakespeare.

"Watch." I leaned toward Noe. *"Brzzzzzz."*

Sure enough, Noe got a determined look on her face, pressed her lips together and made a little *brzzz* of her own, sending droplets of spittle all over her chin.

Now, if you had told me a year earlier that my definition of contentment would be watching a petite three-and-a-half-month-old baby spit raspberries for twenty minutes straight, I would not have believed you. But as I sat there on the bed with Noe, there was no place on earth I'd rather be.

That night, Christopher ran some water in the bath and tenderly held Noe's squirmy little body as he cupped water over her to rinse, speaking all the while in a soothing, fatherly tone that I hadn't even known existed in him until now. I stood in the doorway, my heart ballooning to the size of the room and beyond.

On our agenda the next day was to master the sling. We'd watched the video that had come with it a few times back home and practiced putting it on and taking it off. But this was for real. With a baby. With *our* baby.

I put the sling over my right shoulder and left it with lots of slack. "OK," I said to Christopher. "Put her in."

He was holding Noe like a hot potato with his arms outstretched.

"No, no, no," I said. "Put her head up *here*, by my elbow, and lay her bum *there*." Christopher turned Noe around and laid her in the sling as I directed. I cinched it up so that she lay just at the top of my belly. The fabric was taut around Noe's diaper-clad behind, and she was curled up against me in a fetal position. I patted her back softly and felt the rise and fall of her breath.

After a few practice tries aided by Christopher, I became quite adept at maneuvering the sling on my own. I could fold down the outer edge so Noe could see out, or fold it up to make a little co-coon. But, always, Noe had one hand poking out to grip my pinky, even when she slept.

Because we didn't have much experience with babies, and be-cause I was terrified that I would "do it wrong," and because we'd already read a half dozen how-to-parent books, I made a chart of what needed to happen and when. Feeding, here. Nap, here. Chang-ing, here. Bathing, here. As much as I would have loved to hold Noe all day long, the schedule dictated otherwise. It was astounding to me how much time was filled up on that grid just from the basics of care and feeding. The reality of parenthood—of motherhood—began to set in . . . how was I supposed to slot *my* life into that jam-packed little chart?

Naps were a little tricky. Noe much preferred sleeping in the sling, or gazing out at the world from Mama's tummy, to lying immobile in the crib. And, boy oh boy, did she let us know. Our petite little girl had a not-so-petite set of lungs.

There were times we'd give up and I would put her in the sling, or Christopher would take her onto his chest where she would fall sound asleep, leaving big drool marks on his shirt. And, in true new-parent form, Christopher and I got less and less sleep as the days wore on. You can literally track what day it is in our photos by how dark the circles are under our eyes.

One night, when Noe wouldn't stop crying and I was completely exhausted, I lay in bed and quietly wept.

Christopher rolled over and hugged me. "What's going on, honey?" he asked, in a sleep-slurred voice.

"I'm sorry," I said, taking in sharp breaths to try to stop crying. "I didn't want to wake you up."

"It's OK," he said. "I'm awake."

"I just don't know if I can do this," I said. "What made me think I could do this? What if I have a fibro flare and can't get up for Noe in the morning? What if my body hurts too much to pick her up?" I was sobbing again.

"God made a promise, remember? He'll never give you more than you can handle." He kissed my forehead. "And we're in this together. We're partners in this—we're *parents* in this. You won't be doing this alone." I nodded into Christopher's chest, sniffing. "I love you," he said.

"I love you too."

Noe was still wailing and the timbre had turned from *I'm just try-ing to put myself to sleep, Mommy* to *OK, now I'm really working myself up into a tizzy.*

"I'm going to take Noe for a walk," I said. I gave Christopher a kiss and stood up to put on the sling. "Come here, sweet pea," I said as I eased Noe up and into its folds, surprised at how easy the move-ment had become. "Let's go for a walk."

I ambled through the empty hallways and open courtyards, bouncing Noe with each step to the tune of "Hush, Little Baby." I sang not only of mockingbirds and diamond rings, but of alley cats and porcupines and kitchen sinks. Twenty minutes later, she was fast asleep, tucked tightly against me in the sling, holding my pinky.

*The days* with Noe went way too fast, and the evening when Vir-ginia's daughter, Susi, came to pick her up came way too soon. I began to panic on the way to the lobby for our rendezvous. How in God's name was I going to walk away from my daughter? Susi and her sister were there, sweet, competent, beautiful young women who hugged me compassionately when I took Noe out of the sling. I would rather have given my heart up than hand over my baby that day. In fact, that was exactly what it felt like I was doing. We kissed Noe's face, her sweet little nose. I kissed each of her fingers and *brzzzzzzed* one last time. Then I handed her over to Susi.

"Take good care of her," I said. "I know you will."

Susi took Noemi into her arms. Then she took my hand. "We'll see you soon."

We waved good-bye and turned back toward our room, and the sling hung against me, lifeless and inert. My knees buckled as we turned the corner; I could barely breathe, I was sobbing so hard. Christopher picked me up and held his arm around me as we walked back to the room. I wept all through the night and all through the next morning and all the way to the airport.

Until we were rear-ended in the taxi.

Christopher and I flew forward and hit the back of the front seat; we were fine, it was just a fender bender. But even while it was happening I thought, *Thank God Noemi isn't in the car with us.*

The first thing I said as we got out of the taxi, while the driver was hailing us another, was, "We're staying at the Marriott when we pick Noe up." Christopher agreed.

The shock of the accident had temporarily stanched my tears, but my crying resumed as we were standing in line to check our bags.

"Seven bags," Christopher said with panic in his voice. "Our video camera! We must have left it in the cab!"

The video camera with footage of our precious girl. The video camera with the cooing and gurgling and *brzzzzzzing* that I was counting on to sustain me until we could bring Noe home for good. "You have to find it," I said desperately.

"I know," Christopher said. "I—"

"Excuse me." An elegant Latina behind us in line held out her cell phone. "Do you need to call someone?" She dialed the Quinta Real for Christopher and they told him they'd send someone to the crash site to look for the camera. I stayed in line while Christopher waited at the entrance.

"Excuse me," the woman said again a few moments later. "My friend and I are faith healers," she said, looking at me with a tender gaze. "May we pray over you?" Now, this may sound like a strange thing to occur in line at an airport. And, in retrospect, it was. But to me, right there, right then, it seemed blatantly obvious that these women were angels coming to me just when I needed them.

I nodded, trying to hold back the tsunami of tears working its way up my chest.

Each laid one hand on me and raised the other into the air. Loudly, publicly, they called down blessings from God and asked that He would comfort me and answer my prayers. At a point in my life not too many years earlier, the scene would have mortified me. But I stood there, feeling my shoulders soften and my breath ease. When I opened my eyes, Christopher was running toward me, holding the video camera high.

## WATERMELON AGUA FRESCA

*Agua frescas are one of the delights of Latin America. Cold water is blended with fruit to make a super refreshing drink—somewhere between a juice and a smoothie. This one, made from watermelon and lime, always reminds me of that watermelon feast we shared with Rene-Antonio and his family.*

4 cups seedless watermelon cubes or balls
2 cups cold water
2 tablespoons lime juice

In a blender, blend all ingredients until smooth.

SERVES 4

# CHAPTER 20

# REAL FOOD IN REAL LIFE (WITH BABY)

MARCH 2007

I swished the glob around my mouth, trying hard not to gag. Then I shook my head. We were playing Name the Baby Food. "Come on," JoJo goaded. "Lord's sake, you're a food writer! You should be able to name a simple baby food."

She was right. As one of *Bon Appétit*'s Restaurant Reporters five years earlier, I had reviewed the restaurants of star chefs. I had described silken sautéed foie gras and diminutive quail legs wrapped with cords of fried potatoes. Yet for the life of me, I couldn't put words to what was in my mouth. I couldn't even figure out what it was.

Jann, Honore, JoJo, and our friend and host, Christine, had all pitched in to throw me a baby shower—a high point that I desperately needed after returning from Guatemala—and JoJo had set out a lineup of high-end organic baby foods to blind-taste as a game. I was 0 for 5. Bananas supreme, chicken lasagna, mac and cheese, they all tasted like moldy mashed potatoes to me.

Ten years earlier, when Julie had thrown a wedding shower for me in Manhattan, I didn't have many friends. Or at least, not many who were within spitting distance of New York City. About a half dozen of us gathered then, and of those six, two were family friends and one was a guy friend who dressed in drag to crash the party.

For this shower, thirty women from all areas of my life— including Mom, Julie, and Janis, who flew in for the occasion— had gathered to celebrate the expansion of our family. They were excited about the path I was pursuing. But most important, they loved me for who I was.

I took a seat in a nook by the window and nibbled on the *pâté de campagne* and grilled pork loin that Honore had made, soaking in the staggering blessing of the women around me. How, I marveled, had life—how had *I*—changed so much in ten years?

*The game* got me thinking in the days and weeks after the shower. Making the shift from processed food to real food had had such a profound impact on my health and my life. The more I thought about it, the less sense it made to start our daughter's life with processed food from a jar.

So I looked into what it would take to make my own baby food. Not all that much, it turned out. It was just a matter of steaming or roasting some vegetables, puréeing them, and freezing them in ice cube trays. Defrost a cube or two as needed and there you had it.

As I began to tell acquaintances that I'd be making Noe's food instead of buying it, some got excited. But some dismissed me as a fanatic, somehow inferring that my decision was a judgment on theirs to buy baby food in a jar.

"No, no, no," I wanted to retort. "It's no big deal. It's actually really, really easy to make, and it's cheaper too." But they wouldn't have any of it. For them, my cooking real food instead of buying something in a jar got me consigned to a pigeonhole I didn't want to be in. Foodie.

*A month* after my shower, Christopher and I flew to Isla Holbox, a tiny island off of Mexico's Yucatán coast, to celebrate our tenth anniversary. Our last evening, after three blissful days napping in hammocks on the beach and hunting for shells for Noe, we walked hand in hand to the end of the beach. Palm fronds crackled in the hot breeze while waves lapped softly on the shore. We turned off at a restaurant and took a table set up against a low stone wall, facing out toward the sunset.

"You're burned," I said to Christopher with a chuckle, pressing my thumb into his forehead and leaving a white mark.

"You're not much better," he said, moving the strap of my sundress off my shoulder to reveal a white strip.

The waiter brought our Dos Equis and I clinked Christopher's bottle with mine. "Here's to becoming parents," I said, leaning over to meet his kiss. This trip was our last hurrah. Kelly Jo had told us it was only a matter of weeks before we'd get clearance to bring Noe home.

"Here's to a pretty spectacular year in general," he said, clinking my bottle again.

"I know." I paused on that thought, watching the water shimmer like a golden landing strip leading up to the sun. "I feel like this is going to be a big year. For obvious reasons—Noe—but I'm also feeling like God is preparing me for something. I just don't know what yet."

"Well, what do you think it is?" Christopher said. He smirked. "You are the jib, after all."

"Ha." I paused, taking a sip of beer.

"I guess I'm feeling like I want to write about more than just fancy restaurants or the latest superfood or diet hype."

"OK," Christopher said, making room for a plate of grilled shrimp. "Go on."

"I just feel like it's time to find my own voice. I've spent my career writing about places, and then about food and wine, and then about health, all in other people's voices—magazines, companies. But I've been through *a lot*, and I've learned a lot, and I feel like I have a lot to share. I just don't know what it looks like yet. A book? A blog?" I squeezed lime over the shrimp and took a bite; it was garlicky, smoky, and juicy.

I poked at Christopher with the shrimp tail. "Remember when Aunt Judy and Uncle Norm came for dinner with their friends, and I roasted a chicken and some vegetables and they couldn't believe how good it was? Remember how they kept insisting that I shouldn't have gone through all the trouble of spending all day in the kitchen? And I was like, but I didn't spend all day. I rubbed a chicken with some salt and pepper and tossed veggies with some olive oil and threw it all in the oven for an hour. But they wouldn't believe me. Well, I want to write about how a roast chicken can nourish you down to the marrow in your bones, and how rainbow chard makes your body smile from the inside out, and how it's something all of us have the capacity to do and enjoy, not just rich people or foodies."

Christopher chuckled.

"What?" I asked, reaching for another shrimp.

"Do you realize you just verbalized exactly what Clos du Bois has hired you to do?"

A smile crept up my face. He was right. A few weeks earlier, Clos du Bois, a winery based in Healdsburg and a client of our friend Chris, had said they were looking for someone who "sucked the marrow out of life," traveled with a sense of curiosity, and was inquisitive about everything to start a first-person blog for the brand.

"You have to call Lia," Chris had said. Two weeks later, the Swirling Notions blog was born. I'd picked the name as a subtle nod to the thoughts we ponder as we're swirling wine in our glass. But it had a double entendre. As we came closer and closer to bringing Noemi home—more papers, more notarizations, more lawyers— the thoughts and snippets of where the Spirit was leading me were swirling around in there too.

As the sun dipped below the horizon, Christopher leaned toward me and took my hands. "The great news is you've got the canvas now to work all those thoughts out."

In early June, not long after returning from Holbox, we got the call from Kelly Jo. Finally, we could bring Noemi home.

*We had* vowed not to go pink with our daughter so she wouldn't have any preconceived gender roles thrust upon her (fast-forward four years and that was thrown back in our faces, along with handfuls of sparkles and glitter). We'd had a bumper and skirt made out of colorful Guatemalan fabrics that we'd bought in Antigua, and painted an old bookshelf bright, lipstick red. I sat cross-legged in the middle of her room and it felt still and womblike. I tried to imagine what it would be like to have her there, with her smells and coos and burbles.

But one more thing needed to be done before we brought Noemi home. It was time to say good-bye to Rex. He was of an age that he needed more and more maintenance, and he was guzzling gas. So, on the last day of May, we bought a white Toyota Highlander Hybrid with tan seats and named her Mae.

She couldn't have been more the opposite of Rex. Where Rex epitomized adventure, Mae felt upscale soccer mom. Truth be told, I still felt more Rex than Mae. What did that say about me? I wondered. Was I really ready to be a mom?

*We left* for Guatemala on Father's Day. Christopher and I had silly permagrins the entire flight down. We had put together a photo album of our time together in February and showed it to anyone within a five-foot radius. And, yes, we did book a room at the Marriott—both of us wanted to be close to town to minimize taxi time. But there was a silver lining. Our old friend Ben Villegas— the same Ben who'd taken us under his wing in Mexico City—was now general manager of the Guatemala City Marriott. He and his wife, Cecilia, were tickled pink to hear we were becoming parents.

Our meeting with Virginia and Susi was different this time. When I saw their faces I recognized the grief—it was the grief I felt when I'd handed Noe back to them four months earlier. As joyful as the day would be for Christopher and me, it would be filled with loss and emptiness for the two of them, and I wanted to honor that.

"Thank you, Virginia," I said, cradling Noe in the nook of my arm. "Thank you for being a part of our family."

In a similar way, I'd felt an invisible tether to Noe's birth mother throughout the entire adoption process, my joy at each step tempered by what I imagined the pain must be on the other side of the equation.

I poked Noe's cute little nose, and she blinked and smiled. Once we were together again, it was like we had never been apart, except for how much she'd grown in those four months. I slipped Noe back into the sling and she cocooned herself against me. She slept like that all through our meeting at the consulate the following day. The man who gave us our final sign-off glanced over the edge of the counter and looked at her little tuft of hair. "She's a happy little one." His eyebrows shot up when he looked down at the paper. "And a lucky little one to be growing up in Healdsburg."

The rest of the day we lounged by the pool while Noe smeared mango all over her face. She and Daddy took a nap beside each other on the bed, and her entire length, from head to toe, took up about as much space as Christopher's forearm. By the time we were ready to go to dinner with Ben and Cecilia, Noe had gotten fussy. At seven and a half months, her first tooth was coming in, and even though we were equipped with frozen teething rings and homeopathic gum gel, she just was not a happy camper, which meant Christopher and I were stressed and on edge too.

"I'm sorry," I said to Ben and Cecilia, trying to shush Noe from crying. Christopher glanced self-consciously at the tables around us.

"Nonsense!" Cecilia said. "Let's get her shoes off, she'll feel more comfortable." She slid Noe's shoes off and massaged her little feet, and Noe's cries turned instantly to coos.

"So you leave tomorrow?" Ben asked.

"We do," Christopher said. "Home to a whole new chapter in life."

"You are going to love parenthood," Cecilia said. "Although I'll tell you, being a grandparent is even better." She was making little *choo choo choo* noises at Noe and tapping her nose, and Noe was giggling wildly. A large part of me was grateful for Cecilia's ease with Noe. But there was a slight part of me that was berating myself for not instinctively knowing the right thing to do. Would that come in time? I wondered.

Noe started to fuss again. Cecilia eased Noe's fist out of her mouth and dipped a breadstick in her wine. "Here you go," she said.

Ben chuckled. "I used to do that with Ben Jr. all the time."

A couple of dips and a couple of bites later, Noe had calmed and was starting to nod off.

"Works like a charm," Ben said.

Whether it was the wine, or Noe's quieting, or Ben and Cecilia's wise command of the situation, Christopher and I began to calm down too. By the time we got on the airplane the next day, we felt more natural and relaxed with Noe. So what if she cried? She was a baby. Now we knew to take her shoes off.

We were exhausted when we landed at SFO, and grateful for the comfort of Mae, who held Noe's car seat snugly and carried us home safely. I sat in the back and played with Noe and sang her lullabies when she cried. When we pulled up to our house, there was a big poster on the front porch from Auntie Jann. "Look what this says, baby," Christopher said, bouncing Noe in his arms.

WELCOME HOME, NOE! WE LOVE YOU!

Then we set Noe's feet on the ground for the very first time on U.S. soil, in Healdsburg, at our home.

Noe settled into home from the get-go. She slept through the first night in her crib (Christopher and I had set a mattress in her room just in case) and cooed her way throughout the days. I, on the other hand, was knocked completely out of whack. Between the million changes large and small that had come with being a new parent, I felt like my life had been replaced with someone else's.

I would start the day in a panic, flipping through my mind how I was going to get everything done as I lifted Noe out of the crib and changed her diaper. During her naps, I'd frantically scribble schedules, trying to shoehorn my work—Swirling Notions, several magazine articles, and the last edits for *I Land Home*—in between feedings and changings and play times, I found with a baby that most of the day went toward the connective tissue of actual tasks, to conquering the in-between, and I found it draining beyond measure.

And it wasn't just Noe's schedule, it was Christopher's too. Christopher started a new job with a winery in Napa and, because of the hour commute each way, was gone from 6:00 a.m. to 6:00 p.m. Our entire marriage I'd been used to time alone—on my own schedule and my own terms—when Christopher was gone, followed by an intensity when we were together. Now there were scattered, amorphous blocks to my day and a hard stop at 6:00 p.m. when Christopher walked through the door. Every night. Expecting things to be tidy and dinner to be cooking.

It may sound ungrateful on the heels of bringing home our wonderful little girl. It may sound selfish, but sometimes I felt as though I was disappearing. Between the frantic pace of work, the constant focus on Noe, and Christopher being gone all day and home every evening, there was no time, no space to listen to that still, small voice of God. Heck, I couldn't even hear my own voice.

Of course, millions of working moms before me had found themselves in just this predicament. Looking back, it probably would have made sense to hit pause on my career, even for a moment. But at the time, it didn't feel that neat and tidy—if I gave up the opportunities on my plate, would they ever come back again? So I did the only thing I knew how to do, which was to push on through it all, consumed with insecurity, feeling like I was doing everything wrong.

. . .

*One morning,* six weeks after we'd brought Noe home, I got a call from the winemaker at Clos du Bois saying that they'd just brought the first grapes in. "Do you want to come join us for the traditional harvest kickoff toast?"

My answer, of course, was yes. And I did. These were exactly the moments I relished writing about. But I looked at Noe, covered in scrambled eggs and frijoles, and felt a million years old. She'd been teething and I'd been up for most of the night soothing her and rocking her. Christopher slept. He had a job to go to.

"Come on, sweet pea," I said to Noe as I wiped her down with a wet cloth. I pulled her out of her high chair and tugged on her jean jacket. "You're coming to work with Mommy."

It had been foggy when Erik called, but by the time we finally got up the road to Clos du Bois, there was just a chalk line left floating below the bumps of Mount Saint Helena and Geyser Peak. The vineyards themselves had a sort of green-gold, Sauvignon Blanc–esque sheen to them in the morning sunlight.

"Just in time!" Erik called, as I pulled Noe out of her car seat and swung her into the sling. He handed me a glass of orange juice and I suddenly felt horribly self-conscious of my worn sweater and hasty ponytail, let alone the fact that I had my baby strapped to me in a sling. They'd reassured me several times that they wanted me just the way I was—new mom and all—and yet I couldn't help but cower at the perception that bringing a child into the mix was just plain unprofessional.

"So this is little Noe?" he asked, tucking down the edge of the sling to play with her fingers.

"The one and only," I answered. Trucks were pulling onto the crush pad one after another, overflowing with sunny green grape clusters that were upturned into the press. Pale yellow juice dripped through the holes into the bin below. There was an excitement, an effervescence, palpable there on the crush pad. I looked around at the clusters of people—vineyard workers with bloodshot eyes and caps askew; the marketing and sales crew in office garb; and me, the new voice of the brand, in jeans and a baby in a sling.

I rubbed Noe's knuckles and tried hard to soak in the beauty of the moment. Maybe I wasn't being unprofessional. Maybe this really was part of the whole.

"Cheers to the 2007 harvest!" Erik called, lifting his glass.

I raised my glass to the others, leaned down to kiss Noe's fuzzy little head, and whispered, "Cheers to a new season indeed."

## GARLIC-LIME GRILLED SHRIMP

*Whenever I make this dish I think of our time on Holbox. While these shrimp definitely make a delicious dinner, they're also terrific as finger food for a party. Keeping the shells on retains the moisture and adds flavor.*

$1^1/_2$ pounds large shrimp, with shells

3 garlic cloves, grated

$1^1/_2$ tablespoons extra virgin olive oil

Sea salt

$1/_8$ teaspoon crushed red pepper flakes

Zest and juice of 1 lime

To butterfly the shrimp, cut each down the back with a pair of sharp scissors and rinse out the vein. In a small bowl, whisk together the garlic, oil, salt, red pepper flakes, and lime zest. Toss the shrimp with the garlic-lime mixture, massaging it under the shells. Cover and let marinate for 30 minutes.

While shrimp is marinating, heat a grill to medium-high heat (you could also use a grill pan and cover with a large lid to approximate a closed grill).

Press each shrimp onto the grill flesh side down to fan it out. Grill for 5 to 7 minutes, or until just opaque. Transfer the shrimp to a serving platter as they are finished. Squirt lime juice over the top just before serving and season with additional salt if needed.

SERVES 4

# CHAPTER 21

# IT'S ALL CONNECTED

FEBRUARY 2008

L et's get everything you're going to need together," Julia, the publicist, said.

"I don't know if they told you, but I've never done this before," I replied, not having the slightest clue what I would need to do a live cooking demo. Although the *Cooking Light* show had fallen through, I'd stayed on Mary Kay's radar. A month earlier, she'd called to ask if I would be a television spokesperson for the magazine, doing segments on news shows and the like. We decided I would fly to *Cooking Light* headquarters in Birmingham for media training and then go from there. Only I'd just found out that "media training" meant doing a live cooking demo on Fox News at 10:00 that morning.

Julia looked up. "You've never done TV before or you've never done a cooking demo before?"

"Neither." I didn't have the heart to tell her I didn't have a television either, and hadn't even *seen* a live cooking segment on TV in nearly a decade.

"Oh." Her eyebrows shot up to her hairline. "Well, you're going to be making Hungarian goulash."

"Hungarian goulash? So this isn't one of my recipes."

"Ah, no. It's a segment on braising. I thought this Dutch oven would look nice on camera, and this bowl would be good for the hero shot."

"Hero shot?" I asked.

"The *cooked* dish," she said. "That we need to make now so we'll have it to show on the segment." She stepped back and took a breath, then leaned against the counter. "OK," she said. "Here's how it goes. The host is going to introduce you and the dish. She'll probably ask a question, you answer it. And at the same time, you'll start cooking, and say what you're doing as you're doing it."

So my "media training" consisted of making Hungarian goulash, for the "hero shot," in the *Cooking Light* kitchen as Julia coached me. I browned onions and beef in olive oil, trying to explain each step. "Nope, you've got to look at me . . . hold your body sideways, but look forward . . . remember, you can't turn your back to the camera." I added the spices and tomatoes to the pan and went to turn the heat down, expounding on the principles of braising. "Don't say 'um' so much. . . . You can't clank the tongs on the pot or it'll be deafening in the microphone. . . . And for God's sake, don't say 'connective tissue' on camera."

Two hours later, I did it all again on live television.

I was still highly skeptical of pursuing TV, so I made myself a deal; I'd try it to see if (1) I was any good at TV and (2) I enjoyed it or hated it.

After several more test shoots at the *Cooking Light* headquarters, when the producer approached me and remarked I was the best she'd ever seen ("How long have you been doing this?" she asked, to which I answered, with a big, full belly laugh, "Since about three hours ago"), I felt like I could answer yes to question number 1.

What surprised me was the answer to number 2. I actually had *fun*.

*A week* later, I was bundled under a blanket on our couch on a blustery winter morning when Noe, now a year and a half old, was playing at the little wooden stove we'd gotten her for Christmas.

"What do you have there, sweetie?" I asked her. She was slicing a wooden carrot held together by Velcro into a pot.

"I magging zoop," she said.

"Soup?" I rubbed my tummy. "Mmmmm."

I watched her putter around, taking swigs of "moo juice" from her sippy cup, and felt like my smile would fall off my cheeks it was so wide.

Noe started to dip her ladle into the pot, but then stopped, navigating around a chair to claim the missing ingredient. Salt. My heart swelled. Not only was my daughter adding veggies to her soup, she was seasoning it too, just like Mama. She tottered back to the stove and gave a few generous shakes over the pot, then ladled the soup into a teacup and brought it to me. Her eyes twinkled as she held it out and I went to sip it like tea. "Way!" she said, realizing something else was missing. "Spoo." Noe rummaged around in the wooden oven (which also functioned as her china cabinet and pantry) until she found a spoon and brought it over to me proudly. "Eat," she declared. And I did.

· · ·

*But for* all the happy moments Noe had brought to our lives, I continued to struggle. I told Jann and Honore that I felt like I was spinning like a top, but I found an even better fit in Elizabeth Gilbert's metaphor of a gyroscope, one of those gizmos where rings spin in different directions, yet the whole remains remarkably stable around a central force.

It was like life kept adding whirling rings on top of all that had come with adjusting to our new family dynamic: Tally died of cancer in March; with Christopher in an office and Noe in daycare, I was *constantly* sick; and then there was the call from my doctor about another abnormal test. They put me on a "light" dose of chemotherapy, just in case.

For the first time in my life, I struggled with bona fide depression. Once a month my mood would plummet so fast and viciously within the course of twenty-four hours that it would feel like I'd fallen down a well. One day, I stood on the sidewalk in front of our house watching a moving truck lumber up the street and had to exert quite a bit of will not to step in front of it. And that flat-out scared me. So I went to my doctor and he strongly suggested going on a once-a-month antidepressant for three months.

I hemmed and hawed at first. Shouldn't I be able to get past these waves by fixing my gaze on the steady horizon? Weren't antidepressants just the easy way out? Truth be told, nothing felt easy about where I was emotionally, and I eventually decided that, perhaps, God wanted me to wear a life vest through the rapids.

Three months of antidepressants and marriage counseling later, I had some semblance of solid ground beneath me once again. I learned something about a gyroscope too. As wonky and out of control as it may look, there's always a place of stillness.

At the center.

I was beginning to realize that we're not promised things will be easy, or that life won't be a struggle. What we *are* promised is a deep, abiding joy in *any* circumstance when we are deeply rooted in that center, no matter how many rings are spinning. So I cultivated the practices that would keep me grounded—yoga, prayer, meditation, and eating well.

*The swirl* of obligations kept coming. I signed with an agent for a cookbook. I was invited to a string of symposiums and conferences on nutrition, sustainability, public health, and food policy. I was even asked to moderate a panel at one of them, at the University of California, Davis. When I was there, a reporter asked to interview me and I got into a conversation with her assistant. The woman was sputtering with indignation at all she'd been learning at the conference. She was appalled, she was angry, she was unintelligible . . . exactly as I had been. As I listened calmly, and asked questions, and even shared some opinions, I realized that not only was I finding my voice, I was entering into a bigger conversation.

*At the* end of July, Christopher, Noe, and I flew out to Maine to meet my parents and brother for a week at a lovely house they'd rented on the St. George River for my dad's seventieth birthday (I was also celebrating an all-clear from my doctor after the three months of chemo). The house was a white Cape-style home with a sloping yard down to the dock. Colorful lobster pots bobbed in the glimmering water beyond the trees, and the flat, stark-yet-lush landscape reminded me of an Andrew Wyeth painting.

Which, it turns out, wasn't that surprising, given that Wyeth frequented the area. In fact, when Christopher, Russ, Dad, and I went on a quest for lobster that afternoon—Mom stayed home to play with Noe—we were led down a country road, past the Olsen House that was the backdrop for Wyeth's famous painting *Christina's World*. And when we found our lobsterman—white-haired and mustached—on the dock at the end of the road, his name was Sam Olsen; his father was the last person to be born in the Olsen House.

"You want hard shell or shedders?" Sam asked.

Now you may think that question might have stumped me. But in doing due diligence on how to cook lobsters, I'd run across some strong opinions on the merits of hard-shell versus soft-shell lobsters, which are lobsters that have just molted.

"I've heard that hard shell are better," I said. "That the claw meat is tough in soft-shell lobsters." The guys wandered along the dock, shaking their heads in a "here she goes again" gesture.

Not three words into my sentence, Sam had begun to shake his head too. "I beg to differ. To me, them shedders have meat that's more tender and sweet."

I shrugged my shoulders. "Then I guess we'd better try both. I'll take five of each."

We decided on the way home to go Mexican with the lobsters, splitting and grilling them, and basting them with cilantro-lime butter. We picked up tortillas, avocados, and onions, and Mom and I set to making guacamole while Noe and Russ watched *Pete's Dragon*.

"So what have you been learning at all these conferences, honey?" Mom asked.

"I don't even know where to start," I said, peeling the onion. "I guess the first thing is just how strong the science is behind all that I've been discovering on my own about real food."

"Oh?" Mom asked.

"I mean, look at my life since I started eating real food and stopped eating junk food. I lost the weight that I could never get off before, almost without trying; the lupus diagnosis was reversed; and the pain from fibromyalgia is basically gone. Plus I've got energy—like, constant energy—like I've never had before."

"I know," Mom said, smiling across the island at me. "It really is a miracle."

"Yes, it is," I said. "But I'm finding out there's solid science behind it all too. Did you know that, beyond the big nutrients of fats and proteins and carbs that we tend to focus on, plants have these things called phytonutrients?"

"I've never heard of those."

"They're what give foods their flavor and taste and smell." I wiped my eyes and chuckled. "They're what's making me cry right now mincing this onion. And they've got really powerful anti-oxidant, antibiotic, and anti-inflammatory properties—which is probably why they've helped my fibromyalgia so much." I was on a roll. "As far as scientists can figure, phytonutrients outnumber macronutrients by ten thousand to one. Every food scientist and researcher I talked to at these conferences—and for the articles I'm writing—all said that they don't really know much about or understand phytonutrients yet, but they do know how powerful they are."

Mom mashed the avocado into the onion I'd minced. "So what do they do, these phytonutrients?"

"Crazy powerful things. Preventable illness—in healthcare they call cancer, diabetes, heart disease, and Alzheimer's the Big

Four—makes up eighty percent of the illnesses treated in America and *ninety* percent of healthcare costs. Just eating more vegetables and healthy fats can drastically lower the risk factors for *all* of them. One statistic I remember is that for every additional half cup of vegetables you add to your plate, you'll reduce your risk of heart disease by up to four percent. I mean, that's a big deal."

Mom had paused her mashing. "I had no idea vegetables could do all that." She smirked. "I thought they were just for torturing children."

"Ha ha," I said. I sliced a lime and squeezed it into the guacamole. "One of the scientists talked about a 'pipeline of obesity' that he says will take thirty to sixty years to see the full impact. He was saying that as the kids who are battling obesity age, mortality rates and chronic disease are going to soar. It really puts things in perspective. This isn't just a theoretical debate for foodies. He actually said we're talking about life and death."

"You're inspiring me to lay off the potato chips," Mom said.

"Hey," I said. "We've all got to start somewhere."

*That evening* we fired up the grill while molten sunlight gilded the river and ignited the lobster pots strewn along its surface. Noe and I sat on the porch making up a new version of patty-cake called Lobster Man. Then she tromped around the yard with Gampa while Christopher, Russ, and I split and grilled the lobsters. True to Sam's word, the shedders were succulent and sweet—although *everything* was so good, there was nothing left over for the birthday meal I was planning for the following night.

The next morning I brought Noe with me to Sam's to pick up

more lobsters—hard shell this time, so I could use the shells for stock. I was planning a spin on the shrimp fettuccine with caramelized onions and corn that I'd made for Swirling Notions the previous year, making fresh gnocchi instead of using fettuccine, subbing lobster reduction as the liquid, and, of course, using lobster meat in lieu of shrimp.

I pulled up to Sam's dock and he gave a wave. "Which were the winners?" he asked.

"You were right. The shedders were awesome." I spotted three huge bins next to the lobster crates and peeked over the side with Noe. "What are these?" I asked.

"Herring," Sam answered. "They're good fish." Sam shook his head. "It's a shame we dump billions of pounds of perfectly good herring into lobster traps to catch lobster rather than selling the herring themselves. Or sardines for that matter. Both are good fish. Just think how many more people we could feed." I couldn't have agreed more. I'd learned that eating lower on the food chain—smaller fish instead of larger fish, plants instead of animals—was a big deal in terms of both our own health and the health of the planet.

*Driving back* to the house past small farms with cornstalks and tomato vines and the broad leaves of zucchini plants, pointing out chickens and goats and an occasional cow to Noe, made me think of what I'd learned about organic and sustainable agriculture too. Farms like these were the picture of what many scientists believe is the best way to feed the world.

I used to think of soil as just dirt. But it's infinitely more complex than that. Soil is an entire ecosystem in and of itself—a teaspoon of compost can contain up to five *billion* microbial life forms—and many of the farmers and scientists I met at these conferences considered it the most vital resource on the planet.

Farms like the ones we were passing respect the importance of healthy soil. They use compost from the plants and animals, and techniques like companion planting, cover cropping, and crop rotation to keep the soil healthy and pests and disease at bay, all without chemicals.

On the flip side, "conventional" farms are more like factories. The people who run the companies who run those factories value yield and efficiency. They grow one crop on vast tracts of land (called monocropping), which depletes the soil, so they add synthetic fertilizers made with petroleum that inject the soil with large doses of nitrogen, phosphate and potassium (known as N-P-K), which increase short-term yields. The plants that grow in these increasingly depleted soils tend to have weak immune systems, so the growers spray them with chemicals to ward off pests and disease, or plant genetically modified varieties that have an insecticide built into the seed itself. And the waste from this concentrated monoculture— whether corn or wheat or cattle—results in vast amounts of pollution and runoff, polluting waterways, creating "dead zones" in rivers and oceans, and contributing nearly 25 to 30 percent of global warming. By contrast, crops and animals raised organically *sequester* up to 40 percent of carbon dioxide.

"But what about feeding the world?" I'd asked the panelists at one symposium. "We keep hearing that it's going to take genetic engineering to do that."

It turns out that's not true. Especially when facing catastrophes like drought or severe weather. Studies were showing that organic farming—farming that cared about the soil as much as the plants itself—had 13 to 28 percent *greater* yields than seeds genetically engineered to withstand drought. In other words, the beautifully complex pattern that nature had already set in place performed better under stress than the one we have devised.

I was seeing a pattern here. Five billion microbial life forms in soil versus the grand three N-P-K we humans have mastered. Tens of thousands of phytonutrients that we don't yet understand, versus the grand trio of proteins, fats, and carbs. It seemed to come down to trusting that nature was designed to work a certain way (even if we don't fully understand how), versus trying to engineer the bits and pieces we think we've mastered to perform the way we want them to.

Interestingly, not only is the word *humus*—soil—the root word for *human*, it's also the root of *humility*. From all I'd learned and observed, it seemed that humility was required to nurture a healthy, connected ecosystem (just as it was to nurture a vigorous faith). Engineered ecosystems, on the other hand, severed connections and were based on *hubris*.

In fields like math, science, and engineering, elegant solutions are ones that achieve "the maximum desired effect with the smallest, or simplest, effort." I was seeing an elegant solution in all that I'd learned, one that would slash rates of obesity and disease, radically lower healthcare costs, go a long way toward feeding the world, and turn the tide on global warming. It was so simple it was almost ridiculous, and I certainly wasn't the first to spot it. Eat more plants—vegetables and whole grains and healthy fats—and less meat, and choose food that's grown and raised sustainably.

And do it humbly, in a way that brings joy and love to the table.

·   ·   ·

*I got* back to the house and boiled the lobsters while watching Noe play Frisbee (it was really more like chase the Frisbee) with Russ in the yard. We didn't have a mixer, like Chef Mark had used all those years ago, so I pulled out the lobster meat and set the empty shells on plastic bags. Then I let Christopher have at them with a hammer before transferring them to a big stockpot. I added water, onions, and a bunch of herbs from the garden and brought everything up to a long, slow simmer. A couple of hours later, it smelled like the sea had been captured in that pot.

I pushed the shells down, skimmed the foam, and turned up the heat to reduce the stock. I loved making reductions. I loved how you could concentrate flavor to its very essence, and use it to bring a deep, rich, vibrant element to other things.

I felt like that was what was happening to me too. I'd spent months—years, really—struggling to refine what I felt I was supposed to say, filling up notebook after notebook of thoughts and ideas and expressions and words, and little by little I reduced them down into a proposal for a cookbook that I'd handed off to my agent just before coming to Maine. Now I was hoping that what I had to say would go out to season other people's way of thinking, way of looking at food, way of looking at the world.

I took the potatoes out of the oven to peel and thought of Spiros's all those years ago as they scalded my fingertips. Then I grated the potatoes into a dough, which Christopher and Russ rolled into long strands and cut into gnocchi the size and shape of a fingertip. Mom made a salad while I cut the kernels off several ears of corn. Then I doused a large skillet with olive oil and sautéed the corn with mushrooms and diced onion until all was sticky and caramelized, stirring in a pat of butter and deglazing it all with Chardonnay at the end before ladling in a cup of that elixir-like lobster reduction.

When the gnocchi started bobbing in the pot I hit the corn with some cream—just enough to give the intense flavors of the dish something to cling to and add a bit of body—and folded in the lobster meat. Then I drained the gnocchi and tossed it with everything, finishing it with chopped tarragon that seemed to lasso all the scents together.

I set the dish of pasta on the table while Christopher poured wine, smiling back at Dad's beaming face. "Happy birthday, Dad," I said, leaning over to kiss his cheek. There was a deep hum of contentment as we talked about lobsters and Sam, and our adventures with the eighth generation of grocers at Fales Market up the road, where we'd gotten the corn and potatoes.

Looking around the table, at everyone's faces in the flickering candlelight, I breathed in the scent of briny lobster and sweet corn and minty tarragon and felt like I was breathing in the whole of everything—this little corner of Maine, the beauty of being with my family, and the gift of being whole again.

## GNOCCHI WITH MUSHROOMS, LOBSTER, AND CARAMELIZED CORN

*This dish was an all-out feast for my dad's seventieth-birthday celebration in Maine. If you can't get your hands on lobster, just substitute clam juice for the lobster stock, and shrimp for the lobster meat.*

## LOBSTER STOCK

Shells from 3 pounds cooked lobster (reserve the
  meat in a separate bowl for the sauce)
1 medium yellow onion, quartered
1 carrot, roughly chopped
1 celery stalk, roughly chopped
4 garlic cloves, smashed
5 thyme sprigs
2 tablespoons extra virgin olive oil
Sea salt and freshly ground black pepper
1 cup dry white wine
2 tablespoons tomato paste

Preheat the oven to 425°F.

In a large roasting pan, toss the lobster shells, onion, carrot, celery, garlic, and thyme with the oil and salt and pepper and spread out evenly. Roast for 20 minutes, until the lobster shells become fragrant.

Remove the roasting pan from the oven, pour in the wine, and add the tomato paste, scraping up anything stuck to the bottom of the pan. Transfer everything into a large stockpot and bring to a lively simmer for 5 minutes, then add enough cold water to cover the shells by 2 inches.

Bring the stock to a simmer over medium heat (it will take a while), then reduce the heat to medium-low to maintain a simmer for 45 minutes. Strain through a fine-meshed strainer, return the stock to a clean pot, and bring back to a simmer for another 30 minutes to concentrate the flavors. Season with salt and pepper.

## GNOCCHI

2 pounds russet potatoes

Sea salt

2 large eggs, beaten

$1^1/_2$ cups all-purpose flour, plus more for dusting

Place the potatoes in a saucepan and cover with 2 inches of cold, salted water. Bring the water to a boil and reduce the heat to medium-low. Cover the pot and simmer for 30 to 40 minutes, until you can easily pierce the potatoes with the tip of a sharp knife.

Transfer the potatoes to a plate and let them cool enough to handle. Peel the potatoes and pass them through a ricer (or grate on the finer setting of a box grater) into a large bowl. Let the potatoes cool and mix in the eggs and a generous pinch of salt.

Sprinkle the flour into the potato mixture and use your hands to mix it together (don't overmix), so that all the flour is incorporated and the dough comes together into a rough ball. Knead the dough in the bowl for another 30 seconds, until it becomes a smooth ball.

Dust the counter with flour and pull off a piece of dough about the size of a baseball (cover the bowl with a kitchen towel so the remaining dough doesn't dry out). Place the ball of dough on the counter and roll it out between your fingertips and palms into a rope about $3/_4$ inch thick. Use a knife or pastry cutter to cut the rope into 1-inch pieces and transfer them to a cookie sheet lined with a flour-dusted kitchen towel.

Repeat with the remaining dough, using additional cookie sheets and floured kitchen towels as necessary to hold the gnocchi in a single layer.

SAUCE

2 tablespoons olive oil

1 ounce pancetta, minced

4 cups sliced wild mushrooms

2 thyme sprigs

Sea salt and freshly ground white pepper

Meat from 3 pounds cooked lobster*

2 tablespoons butter

$^1/_4$ cup finely chopped shallots

2 ears shucked corn, kernels removed from the cob and reserved

$^1/_2$ cup dry white wine

1 cup lobster stock or clam juice

3 tablespoons heavy cream

Tiny dash of nutmeg

2 tablespoons minced tarragon

*Or use 1 pound large shrimp, shelled and deveined. Heat 1 tablespoon butter over medium heat and sauté the shrimp until just opaque. Lightly dust with salt and pepper and add to the pan when the lobster meat is called for.

Bring a large pot of salted water to a boil.

In a large sauté pan, heat the oil over medium-high heat and add the pancetta, mushrooms, and thyme. Sprinkle with salt and pepper and sauté for 10 to 12 minutes, until the pancetta is crisp and the mushrooms are well browned. While the mushrooms are cooking, tear the lobster meat into $^3/_4$-inch pieces and place in a large bowl. Add the pancetta-mushroom mixture to the bowl with the lobster meat.

Melt the butter in the same pan and add the shallots and corn. Sauté for 10 to 12 minutes, until the shallots are well bronzed and the corn is tender and browned in places. Add the wine to the pan and deglaze, cooking for 3 to 4 minutes until the liquid is almost evaporated. Stir in the lobster stock and let simmer for 5 minutes.

Reduce the heat to low and add the cream and nutmeg to the pan. Add the lobster and mushrooms and toss to coat. Simmer for 2 to 3 minutes to thicken the sauce slightly.

While the sauce is simmering, carefully drop the gnocchi into the boiling water, pushing down with a slotted spoon. When they bob to the surface, after 3 to 4 minutes, skim them out and transfer them to a large bowl.

Pour the sauce over the top of the gnocchi, add the tarragon, and gently toss to coat. Season to taste with additional salt and pepper and serve in warmed pasta bowls.

SERVES 6

# PART IV
## *FRUIT*

*At last, we see the first little marbles of green fruit emerge from the tomato plant's blossoms.*

THE NEW SEED-STARTERS HANDBOOK

*The fruit of the Spirit is love, joy, peace, patience, kindness, goodness, faithfulness, gentleness, self-control.*

GALATIANS 5:22–23

# CHAPTER 22

# SURRENDER

SEPTEMBER 2011

I looked out the airplane window over downtown Manhattan and couldn't help remembering the scene from ten years ago. Then, on my way to meet up with my brother and dad to surprise Mom for her sixtieth birthday, I had been flying over the still-smoldering ruins of the Twin Towers. The whole world seemed to be crumbling.

Now, ten years later, it was just my own little world that was rubble.

Both the cookbook and *I Land Home* had met with rejection in the wake of the economy crashing (on the very day the cookbook proposal went out). So I'd decided to forge ahead and launch my own website—Nourish Evolution—a place where people could explore how we nourish ourselves, others, and the earth we share, through the food we eat. The only problem was, it had taken forever and cost a fortune to build, and my original revenue model hadn't panned out. We were deeply in debt and banks kept cutting back on our credit. Being broke—having no money and no cushion—was like getting a tooth pulled when the anesthesia hadn't kicked in.

The stress had brought out the worst in Christopher and me. He blamed me for not making money, so I threw myself into wrenching some sort of income out of Nourish Evolution and in the process ended up ignoring the deeper needs of my family.

And then Dad called with news that flipped my world on its head. Mom had had a stroke.

I cringe now to think that, in the days before Dad's call, I had been annoyed by Mom's barrage of e-mails with subject lines like "Christmas menu" and "What do you want to eat?" *Can't she just wait until I get there to talk about all that stuff?* I thought. *Doesn't she know I'm busy?*

But those e-mails came to a grinding halt the evening of December 7, when Mom was pulling holiday serving dishes out of the hutch and Dad was watching TV in the other room. Mom knew what was happening as soon as she hit the floor. Dad came running and called 911 when he saw her contorted face and contracted body, and my mom, ever the pragmatist, mumbled through half of her mouth, "I'll be fine, just give me an aspirin."

But she wasn't fine. In fact, an area of her brain the size of a plum would never be the same again, leaving her paralyzed on the left side of her body. Ten months had passed since that night, and now we were on our way to celebrate the miracle that Mom had made it to her seventieth birthday.

The plane began its descent into JFK and I reached over Noe, who was glued to *Finding Nemo* on the screen in front of her, and took Christopher's hand. We'd hit our lowest point about seven months after Mom's stroke, in July. I'd come back from a week-long conference and there were no candles lit. No welcome home. Christopher's eyes were bloodshot and when he looked at me it was with a scowl. I was somewhat surprised he was even there. Judging from our phone calls that week, I'd half expected to find him packed and gone. Quite honestly, I'd felt so pummeled from taking the brunt of the blame for our financial situation that I was tempted to pack and go myself.

But we didn't.

Thankfully, Christopher was humble enough to call on our friends for help, and slowly, carefully, we began to heal. Frankly, I was shocked by the irrational calm I felt moving through it all, and knew it was because I was held in place by the practices that kept me pointed toward the center axis among all the spinning rings of my life.

During that time Christopher tended to the wounds that were beyond me to salve, and I sought to gain perspective and rein in my all-consuming drive to succeed. (I met with a monk who had a culinary bent and he put it this way: "You know what a lovely spice cardamom is? But if you use too much of it, it destroys the flavor of everything. Beware of too much cardamom in your endeavors, Lia.")

After all we'd endured, Christopher and I were reaping the rewards of a richer relationship, which was unexpected and deeply satisfying. The connection and intimacy I'd wanted so badly back in Costa Rica was finally coming about, but only after a time of intense testing.

It reminded me of making a braise. When you initially sear the meat it looks good, it smells good, but it's still raw inside, like in the early days of a relationship. Then you add a bit of liquid and a slow, constant heat that builds pressure in a confined space and breaks down all the tough fibers and (sorry, Julia, I'm saying it) connective tissues. If you peek on it too early, the meat seems impossibly dry and tough and it's easy to think you've overdone it; it's tempting to want to toss it out as worthless, beyond saving. But that's just because all the juices have taken a temporary leave and the cells have contracted. If you leave it longer, then everything relaxes into where it's supposed to be, resulting in something tender, complex, and delicious.

*When we* got back home to California, we faced some hard decisions. Nourish Evolution didn't look like it was going to hit the targets I needed to keep it going. And while enticing opportunities were coming in from all over—offers to be a blogger for big-name publications, hints at a column, steady television appearances, interest in both books "with just a few changes"—we still had a problem. How in God's name, I asked, was I supposed to support my family?

The answer came, of all places, in the bathroom. I was brushing my teeth one morning when, I kid you not, the bridge from the Christmas song "O Holy Night" (where it says "fall on your knees") burst into my mind in full chorus. I stopped short and listened, and there it was again.

So I did. I fell on my knees, there on my worn white bathmat with toothpaste smeared all over my chin. I can't say I'd ever fallen on my knees before, and I didn't really know what to do, so I tucked into a sort of child's pose. *Here I am, Lord,* I whispered in my head. *I'm listening.*

*Stop spending and stop worrying,* He said.

Now, over the years I've noticed that there are certain telltale signs that help me discern when it's God speaking and when it's me. One of them is how my body feels when God speaks. When it's me giving myself some sort of existential pep talk, my breath becomes faster and my body becomes tense. But when God gives some directive or promise, this preternatural level of calm comes over me.

So I stopped spending and stopped worrying. Or I tried to anyway.

Funny enough, after so many years struggling to simplify, now, under the crush of our finances, following the directive to stop spending came more easily. I started filling our plates with a lot more beans and whole grains from the bulk bins, and cutting back on meat. I stopped buying the expensive condiments I collected like most women collect shoes, and instead started making pastes and rubs and pestos from scratch (Noe loved pounding garlic and herbs in our "Recuerdo de Oaxaca" *molcajete*). And I learned how to stretch everything. Vegetable scraps would turn into vegetable stock. Roast chicken would turn into three meals—the dark meat served with veggies and a whole grain the first night, the white meat in a salad the second night, and the stock made from the carcass as soup the third night.

The irony was, none of this economizing felt like a loss.

We tend to perceive loss as something negative. Lord knows, I've feared loss my whole life. But I was learning that God is in the loss too. He's not in the worry about it, but He will meet us there in the midst of the loss itself.

One day, a few weeks after we'd gotten back from Maine, I was on a walk with Noe when I got a call from my doctor's office; there had been a complication with the chemo and they were questioning the all-clear.

When we got home, I turned on a Noodlebug and put Noe in front of the TV. Then I closed the door, walked back to my office, and railed at God.

"How can you do this?" I yelled at him, grabbing the denim "dammit doll" that my friend had given me and whacking it against the walls as hard as I could. "Why are you doing this now?" As the dam of fear broke and words and tears came flooding out, I could hear God answer as clearly as if He were in the room with me, and it was not the gentle, calming voice that I'd heard in the past. It was a rebuke.

*Because I'm not there, Lia,* He said firmly. *I am not in your fear. I am not in your worry. I am here, waiting for you, in hope and light and life. And you need to come to me here if you want me to be with you.*

It brought me up so sharp that my gasp choked off my tears, dammit doll in midair. I sat down and took a deep breath. He was right. I had done a piss-poor job of guarding my heart and mind, and I had ended up in the land of fear.

Until then, I'd viewed simplifying as saying yes or no to external opportunities. But I was realizing that it's more than that. In order to keep the soil of my soul nourished, I needed to thin my thoughts too. Noble traits like perseverance and compassion were growing in me right alongside my shortcomings (like perfectionism and resentment and fear). Now it was up to me which thoughts, which traits, which patterns I would weed out and which I would nurture to fruition.

I'd also assumed that the fruit God wanted me to bear was directly tied to accomplishments. But what if the fruit He was bearing through me was the *who* He was making me into? Viewed from that angle, good and bad, success and failure in a traditional sense had no power. What did was how I chose to deal with those circumstances.

· · ·

*In the* months after Mom's birthday, and as the year wound down, I was content to hit pause on Nourish Evolution except for keeping up a weekly e-mail. Yet, ironically, just as I was taking my foot off the pedal, a project I'd been working on for years suddenly sprang to life. Jennifer and Jen, the producer and director from ABC, and I had become friends over the few years that I'd been doing television, and the three of us had talked about doing my own show, *Nourish*, a couple of years earlier.

We had gone to lunch and talked in earnest about what it would take to pitch a show to their boss, Maggie, the executive producer of ABC in San Francisco. "Everyone you've worked with wants this to happen, Lia," Jennifer had said. "I think it's time we put together a treatment, and Jen and I will present it to Maggie. It's a long shot, and I'm not going to lie, it's a long, long process. But I think it's definitely worth a try."

So I put together a treatment—essentially an explanation of how I saw the show flowing and what an episode would look like—and Jennifer and Jen presented it to Maggie. And then, months later in November 2011, Maggie called and said she liked the concept, and that she'd like to meet me about going into production on a pilot for a series.

"What if her vision for *Nourish* is totally different than mine?" I asked Christopher over dinner the night before. "I just don't want it to be all flash and no substance."

Christopher looked me square in the eyes and I was taken aback by how much life was in them again, how much love, where before there had been pain and anger. "This is bigger than that, honey. This is bigger than Maggie, this is bigger than you. Remember, it's not about a TV show. It's about changing people's lives."

The next day around noon, I checked in at the lobby of the ABC building, just steps away from the parking lot that had housed the farmers' market where I'd met Bruce Aidells over a decade earlier and had the conversation that launched my career in food writing.

I'd always been ushered into the green room by the studios on the main floor, but this time, Jennifer brought me upstairs, through a hallway decked with framed posters of television celebrities, toward the executive offices.

"You want to hear the funniest thing about all this?" I said to Jennifer, dropping my voice to a whisper. "Don't tell Maggie, but we don't even have TV."

"You're kidding," she said, her laugh bouncing off the walls. "See, I think that's why you come across as so genuine. Because you really are, you're not trying to act like someone else."

We walked into Maggie's office with its view of the bay, and she shook my hand and gestured toward the couch. "It's a real pleasure to finally meet you, Lia," Maggie said. "You've been doing excellent work, and more than once, these two"—she gestured at Jennifer and Jen—"have sat right there on that couch and told me how what you'd covered in a segment changed the way they looked at food."

"I didn't even know what kale was before Lia," Jennifer said. "Now I make it for my family, like, three times a week."

"I thought I was buying healthy bread just because it was tan," Jen said. "Now every time I buy a loaf of bread I flip it over and look for the word *whole* first."

"You see?" Maggie said. My heart was thumping and the whole scene felt surreal. "The angle I see this show taking, Lia—" This was it, I thought. This was where she was going to throw in something gratuitous like a dancing dog or cooking cat to capture viewers. *"The thing that I think is so unique to what you bring to the table, literally, is that it has the potential to change people's lives for the better."*

I was stunned. Had she really just said those words? The words I'd been waiting to hear from publishers going on half a decade? The words that I'd just heard from Christopher and that I'd heard over and over again when I would cry out to God, "What do you want me to do?"

And He would answer back, *I want you to nourish people.*

*I left* the office and pointed Mae south, down the peninsula, past the Santa Cruz Mountains toward Big Sur, where I was headed for a solo retreat. I was grateful for the big pause to take everything in. As I was cutting through Salinas Valley toward the welcoming crescent of Monterey Bay, a stormy, mercurial sky loomed behind the mountains. I rounded a curve and a burst of sunlight punched through near the coast and illuminated the dark canvas with the most glorious rainbow I'd ever seen. It was so strong it painted rainbow stripes on the black-and-white cows grazing among the emerald hills.

I pulled to the shoulder to bathe in its sight.

I felt like Noah—the man in Genesis who had persisted year after year in his epically crazy venture (a theme that hit a little too close to home in my own life)—had dipped his finger in the water of time and it had made a ripple all the way through to the present day, to the rainbow in front of me. Now it was my turn to remember all the times God had delivered on His promises to me, no matter how far-fetched they seemed. Over and over again He'd proven that the brightest, most intense rainbows shine amid the darkest skies.

✿

# ASIAN CHICKEN NOODLE SOUP

*I've grown to love brothy soups ever since that awakening with the* tortellini in brodo *in Italy. I find them invigorating and comforting all at once.
This one leans into the Asian flavor palette, which is a nice change of pace
from the traditional chicken noodle. Although I've written this recipe as a
stand-alone, I'd actually make it a couple of days after roasting a chicken.
Then I'd use any leftover chicken in lieu of the (expensive) boneless, skinless
chicken breast, and refrigerate or freeze the remaining broth to use later instead of boxed stock.*

6 whole cloves
2 unpeeled yellow onions, halved
5 large garlic cloves, unpeeled
1 cooked chicken carcass
2 carrots, chopped into 3 pieces each
8 whole star anise
1 cinnamon stick
2 1-inch pieces fresh ginger, bruised with the heel of your knife
1 or 2 dried Asian red chiles
Sea salt
$1/_4$ cup fish sauce
3 cups thinly sliced shiitake mushrooms
1 cup julienned carrot
2 cups thinly sliced napa cabbage
6 ounces rice vermicelli, cooked 3 minutes
    in boiling water and drained

2 raw boneless, skinless chicken breast halves, cut
   into paper-thin slices across the grain (freeze
   for 20 minutes to make slicing easier)
$\frac{1}{4}$ cup packed cilantro leaves
$\frac{1}{2}$ cup thinly sliced scallions (white and green parts)
1 lime, cut into 8 wedges

Poke 3 cloves into each onion half and char the onions and garlic in a large stockpot over medium-high heat for 2 to 3 minutes, until well colored but not burned. Add the chicken carcass and 6 quarts cold water and bring to a boil. Skim off the foam, gray crud, and fat as they rise to the surface. Lower the heat to maintain simmer and cook for 45 minutes to 1 hour, or until there isn't much foam being produced any longer.

Add the chopped carrots, star anise, cinnamon, ginger, chiles, and a generous pinch of salt. Reduce the heat so the broth gurgles a few times each second. Let the broth cook at this low heat overnight or for at least 8 hours (yes, you could totally do this in a slow cooker).

Skim the broth one more time and strain through a fine mesh strainer or a colander lined with cheesecloth. Rinse out the pot and add 8 cups of broth back, along with the fish sauce, mushrooms, julienned carrot, and cabbage. Bring the soup to a vigorous simmer and serve.

To serve, divide the vermicelli, chicken breast (the heat from the broth will cook the slices through), cilantro, and scallions among 8 large bowls. Ladle soup into each bowl and finish with a squeeze of lime juice.

SERVES 8

# CHAPTER 23

# COME TO THE TABLE

JULY 2012

We walked from stall to stall and I tried to tease a smile from each purveyor as I combed through their produce. Was their cauliflower snowy white with crisp green leaves? Was their chard perky or limp? I settled on a woman who had arranged her tomatoes in neat little rows and continually fluffed her cilantro and who obviously took pride in what she sold.

"*Tres kilos de cebollas, por favor,*" I said. "*Y cinco kilos de chayote.*" The woman, clad in a brightly colored *huipile*, packaged them up carefully and placed them in my oversized market bag.

Christopher and I were in Antigua, Guatemala, as part of an eight-person Vision Team for Common Hope. Kellen, our team's director, had brought us to the market to provision.

"That's a *lot* of vegetables," Kellen said.

Since food was my forte, Kellen had charged me with cooking lunch for sixty kids at the grade school in San Rafael—a chicken soup that I intended to heavily stud with vegetables—and teaching a cooking class for teens later in the week.

"We'll need them. I'm going to use the onions and the squash in both the soup and the class." I smiled. "I'm going to teach the kids how to make melted squash and onions, and garlicky sautéed chard. I was thinking we could serve them like a bruschetta, on pieces of toast."

Kellen, a blond-haired, blue-eyed young man from Minnesota, nodded, nonplussed. "Give me the bags then," he said. "I'll carry them."

Five weeks earlier, when Christopher had said he wanted to serve on a Vision Team, I'd bristled that he wanted to go on an adventure without me—without Noe. Then, when he'd asked me to join him, I insisted that I had to stay home to hold down the fort. But in time, and with prayer, something became clear.

*I wasn't supposed to hold down a fort, I was supposed to build my family.* And I knew that building my family meant sharing the experience in Guatemala with Christopher.

As things tend to do when we heed a call from the Spirit, things out of my control fell into place to make it possible. Dad called to say he'd be arriving the week before the trip to stay with us for a month (Mom had moved to an assisted-living facility in Healdsburg and Dad was driving out from Connecticut after selling the house). Honore insisted that they and the Forths would be happy to help take care of Noe.

And so it was that Christopher and I became part of the team.

We'd settled quickly into a routine in Guatemala. Christopher and I would get up early and take our yoga mats onto the rooftop deck to do a morning sun salutation. I was so used to doing yoga with my eyes closed that when I opened them to the sight of Volcán Fuego's silhouette in the distance, framed by scarlet bougainvillea along the side of the building in the soft morning light, it always took my breath away. Then the rest of our crew would meander up to the rooftop and grab a chair or a stump as we slowly assembled into our circle, everyone carrying cups of steaming coffee to keep warm in the chilly mist.

With little conversation, we would all put our mugs down and join hands, heads bowed, to lift up morning prayers. Melissa, the leader of our Vision Team, would follow with scripture and a poem or other creative tidbit along with a theme for the day, handing out threads for us to add to our wrists. Each day, we took another color thread as a reminder for the intention we'd set in the morning, and each day the cord became thicker, stronger, more full of dimension.

Tuesday afternoon, we all came back from San Rafael in a glow. It had been the poorest town any of us had ever seen, with open sewage pits behind homes made of cane, and the majority of kids barefoot, missing teeth, and obviously malnourished. But the connections we made there—through cooking and serving that chicken soup with the chayote, playing impromptu soccer matches with the kids, and decorating flip-flops—were as rich as the soup itself.

*At two* o'clock the following afternoon, I stood by the door of the kitchen on the Common Hope campus in my chef's jacket. Two assistants and I had set up chopping stations along the counters by the stove. Everything was ready.

Three minutes later, a line of teenage boys in jeans, T-shirts, and hairnets, and girls in their *huipiles* and *trajes* filed through the hallway, about a dozen or so total.

"Wow," I said to the translator, Barb. "There are a lot of boys."

"They're excited to learn," she said. "A lot of them hope to become professional cooks."

I shook the hand of each one as they entered. In typical teen form, they either met my gaze with nonchalance or avoided it altogether, like they had something more pressing and relevant to do.

Barb introduced me and I saw a few eyebrows go up when she got to the magazine and television part. Eyes darted toward me and away before I could catch and hold a line of sight.

And then I took the floor. *"Buenos tardes, amigos!"* I said. "Who here *loves* vegetables?"

Everyone was guarding their expressions in the way teens do, yet a few of them let their faces crumple into disgust. No one raised their hand.

"Excellent," I said. "Because I love challenges." I caught the flicker of a grin on a few lips. "I guarantee that you are going to walk out of this kitchen loving vegetables. Specifically, chard and chayote." At the mention of chayote, a couple of kids made gagging expressions. "Does anyone know *why* it's important to eat vegetables?" Shoulders shrugged, and I went into my spiel about phytonutrients.

"But first," I said, picking up a knife, "I want to show you some basic knife skills, because you've got a *lot* of vegetables to chop." I grinned sardonically and they giggled. I showed them how to mince garlic, and how to dice an onion. "Notice that my knife doesn't sound like *chop, chop, chop* on the cutting board," I said, banging my knife on the board. "It sounds like *swish, swish, swish* as I move in a smooth motion from tip to hilt." They were craning over one another to watch my movements with the knife, and I noticed that one particularly petite girl with a long ponytail was hiding behind a handsome boy with brown-blue eyes. I leaned around him and smiled at her. "Does that make sense?" She ducked back into the crowd like a frightened fawn.

And then we got to cooking. I had one group peel the chayote

290 · LIA HUBER

and dice the onions, and another zip the chard leaves from the stems and slice the garlic.

One boy raised his hand. "I don't like onions."

I smiled. "Don't worry, you will when we're done with them."

I set two large sauté pans on the burners and heated olive oil in them, explaining that the oil could be any they had in their own kitchens. I showed how they needed to get the oil hot before adding the vegetables, so the vegetables would sear and caramelize, and made sure they didn't hover over the pans pushing things around. "Now," I said, smelling the telltale savory scent of when the crust was forming and browning had begun. "Now you want to take the spatula and scrape underneath these chayote, to flip them over so the other parts will brown." A few stray pieces of squash and onion fell onto the counter as the boy flipped, and I caught sight of another boy picking them up and tucking them into his mouth. The boy who had declared he didn't like onions. I caught his eye and cocked my eyebrow.

"What can I say?" he said. "It's really good."

The girl who was cooking the chard looked like she'd just discovered a pot of gold at the end of the rainbow. "How are you doing?" I asked. "It looks great."

She looked up at me with bright eyes. "I didn't even know what chard was before today, even though I see it at the market all the time. And now I know how to cook it."

"Have you tasted it yet?" The leaves were a perfect wilt, with the slightest bit of syrupy gild binding them together with the sticky slices of garlic. She shook her head.

I reached for a fork and fished out a bite. She took the greens into her mouth and her eyes went wide for a beat, then closed as she let out a hum. "*Que rico,*" she said. (That is delicious.)

Another group of kids were slicing loaves of bread to toast. I could see them concentrating on the movement of the knife, gliding it forward and back instead of chopping down. I laid my left hand over the shy girl's and curled her fingers into a claw, while Barb helped translate. "Hold whatever you're cutting like this, so you don't accidentally cut your finger. That way you can guide the food toward the knife as you slice as well." She nodded up at me and went back to work, slowly, deliberately making even slices, trying to acclimate her hand to the strange position.

Our time was almost up. "OK," I said. "Half of the bread team, help the chayote team top half the toasts. The other half, help the chard team top the rest of the toasts."

As the kids scrounged for serving platters, I noticed how the vibe had changed since the beginning of the class. The kids ribbed one another and laughed openly, coming up to me to ask a question or share an opinion.

We brought trays of the veggie-topped toasts out to the dining room, and the kids snapped them up so fast they barely made it out the swinging doors. I went back to the kitchen for napkins and caught two boys picking at the remnants from the bottom of the pans. They stopped and looked like I'd just caught them with their hands in a candy jar. I burst out laughing. "Didn't I tell you you'd walk out of here loving vegetables?"

The toasts were gone from the platters by the time I got back out to the dining room, and the kids were licking their fingers.

"What do you say?" I asked. "How do you feel about vegetables now?"

"*Rico!*" they yelled, amid full-on belly laughs. "We love them!"

· · ·

*That night,* Common Hope's strategic director, Jeff, and I were thinking big. Jeff and I had struck up a friendship when he'd come to our barracks the first night, hearing of the impromptu cooking class I was holding for our crew. He told me how much he loved cooking and was boasting about his knife skills when, at that exact moment, he sliced a deep gash in his finger. It was deep enough to be painful, but the irony of the timing was so absurd that we both laughed until we couldn't catch our breaths.

"I'm telling you," I said. "I'm seeing the same stumbling blocks here as I do in the U.S. Obviously poverty plays a role, but when you pick away at that, it's really that moms don't think their kids will eat vegetables, so they don't learn to cook them. But the truth is, kids *love* vegetables when they're cooked a certain way."

"I couldn't agree more," Jeff said as he took a bite of the Thai chicken and eggplant dish I'd made that night for our crew. "Economically, it doesn't make sense. A family could buy several kilos of fresh vegetables from the market for what it would cost to eat the convenience food so many are turning to."

"What if we started a program to teach teenagers—and parents who were interested—some basics of sound nutrition and how to cook a variety of vegetables? We could even work in how to grow their own vegetables in a garden bed."

Christopher set a beer in front of me and took a seat. "Eat, honey," he said, and I realized that I'd had my fork poised above my plate for the past five minutes. He looked at Jeff. "Once the words *what if* come out of her mouth, you're done for." I leaned toward him and he planted a kiss on my lips.

.  .  .

*Our last* morning, we lingered over hugs up on the rooftop, while Volcán Fuego spat steam into a cloudless blue sky. We fingered our bracelets—seven strands strong now—and marveled at how we were ever supposed to go back to a "normal" life after that week.

Then we ambled down the concrete stairs to a crowd awaiting us in the courtyard for the week's closing ceremonies. One by one each of us were called forth individually and presented with a weaving by someone who had been particularly impacted by us over the course of the week, along with a tale of how and why.

When my name was called, the boy with brown-blue eyes stepped up and held out a yellow weaving. "Thank you, chef," he said. "For opening our eyes and teaching us that we *do* love vegetables." I smiled and squeezed his shoulder.

After the ceremony I was talking with Jeff about the plan we had begun hatching the night before when I felt a tiny arm encircle my waist. I looked down and saw the shy girl beaming up at me.

"I wanted to tell you, chef," she said. "This morning, as I was cutting potatoes, I made a *swish, swish, swish.*"

I swiveled around to enfold her in a hug, missing my own daughter as I did so, wondering if this is what it would feel like to hug Noe when she's a teenager. I nuzzled my nose into the top of the girl's head and smelled wood smoke in her hair, picturing the stifling fire she undoubtedly cooked those potatoes over this morning.

Nothing truly earth-shattering happened that week, but seeds were planted and lives—including mine—were altered however slightly from the course they had been on by new discoveries, new connections, new openings, and new beginnings. I'd learned, yet again, that when we move toward something we're meant to move toward, we grow in exactly the ways we're meant to grow.

The intertwining roots of real food and deep faith are what healed my body, helped me understand who I am, and, ultimately, gave my life purpose. Standing there in the courtyard of Common Hope that morning I felt more confident than ever of what that purpose was: to invite *everyone* to be nourished, no matter what nationality, race, economic status, faith, or even where they stood on food. Because the truth is, we all come with something to learn and something to share.

I looked up and caught Christopher's eye. As we prepared to leave I knew, as always . . . the journey had just begun.

## GARLICKY SWISS CHARD TARTINES

*These are the tartines that my class of teenagers in Guatemala couldn't get enough of. More proof that* anyone *can learn to love vegetables when they taste this good.*

2 tablespoons extra virgin olive oil
12 cups cleaned, destemmed, and chopped
   Swiss chard (about 3 bunches)
4 garlic cloves
Sea salt and freshly ground black pepper
4 slices rustic bread

In a large sauté pan, heat 1 tablespoon of the oil over medium heat and swirl to coat the bottom of the pan. Add the Swiss chard and toss to coat. Cook for 3 to 5 minutes, until the chard is well wilted.

Pour in the remaining 1 tablespoon oil. Grate 3 of the garlic cloves onto the chard, sprinkle with salt and pepper, and toss several times to distribute the garlic and coat the leaves evenly. Cook for 3 to 4 minutes more, until the chard is wilted and the garlic is fragrant.

Toast or grill the bread until slightly charred on the edges. Cut the remaining garlic clove in half and rub each of the toasted slices with the cut sides of the garlic halves. Top each evenly with the chard.

SERVES 4

# Afterword: Volunteers

Each spring, I pull out a pad of paper and carefully plan out my garden beds. I'll put the eggplant there, I decide, and the tomatoes there and the peppers there. Then I'll scatter arugula and basil in between the rows as a sort of living mulch.

But no matter how carefully I plan, tomato seedlings always pop up wherever they please, as if to color outside the lines of my perfect design.

Volunteers, a gardener calls them: plants that sprout from the seeds that were sown not by my hand directly but by fallen fruit from the previous season that had rotted and nourished the soil in their decay.

This past summer, while working on this manuscript, I couldn't help but see a parallel between the volunteers in my garden and the volunteers in my life. So much of *Nourished* is about how beauty I never could have fathomed on my own has grown up out of failed plans and dashed hopes.

Take Noe. The sweetest fruit imaginable sprouted from a seed I did not sow. When Rex was broken into all those years ago, the scattered seeds of compassion and giving eventually blossomed into the yes that became our family of three.

This is the kind of girl Noe has grown up to be. For several years after Gammy moved into an assisted-living place out here, Noe chose to forsake trick-or-treating on Halloween. Instead, entirely of her own volition, she would take candy to each of Gammy's neighbors, knocking door to door in a sort of Santa-meets-Robin-Hood Halloween tradition.

Nowadays, Noe is in the throes of tweenhood, and the sweet days of holding hands and hugs are behind us. For now, anyway. But in its place is sprouting an independent, *fuerte* young woman who wholeheartedly owns her Guatemalan heritage while working through how to straddle the two worlds that define her. I am in awe of my daughter, and live in a perpetual state of gratitude that I am her mother.

Take Christopher. For years, he looked at the challenges that plagued his formative years as something rotten. And then, against all odds and logic, Christopher walked right into the epicenter of that pain—and right into where he felt God was calling him—by volunteering at a local rescue mission, working with men in recovery. In doing so, he has healed wounds from his childhood and profoundly affected many others in their own healing. A year later, he made a leap to working full time at the mission, while at the same time going through a two-year spiritual direction training program. Since then, he founded Everyday Monk, with a focus on teaching men spiritual practices to deepen their faith.

For my part, the business setbacks of the early years provided fertile soil for a new start. I gained a much clearer vision of what Nourish Evolution was, and how it could best serve others (I was even named Entrepreneur of the Year by the International Association of

Culinary Professionals just as I had begun letting go of everything). Now, through our online programs, content, and Nourished Radio podcast, we're empowering tens of thousands of people each year to make a lasting shift from processed food to real food in real life. My dream is to roll out programs in low-income areas throughout the United States and countries like Guatemala.

Our enduring relationship with Guatemala through Common Hope and AMIDI continues to flourish from those early seeds too. Rene-Antonio graduated from high school and was awarded a scholarship to university, which he deferred, choosing instead to work at a pharmacy to help his mother support a young man that he and his family had taken in off the streets.

Mayra graduated from college three years ago and is now a social worker, teaching classes on social and human rights and empowering communities. And remember the kitchen at the school in San Rafael, Guatemala? Where we cooked the soup? We ended up sponsoring Victor—the son of the woman who ran the kitchen— who went on to trade school to become a baker (he's promised to bake me a cake the next time we visit).

Looking back over my life, over what could appear to be failure or barrenness, I never stop delighting in how—if the soil is right— volunteers always sprout. These insistent, unplanned-for gifts of grace fill me with the confidence to keep going and give me hope when times are tough for a flourishing yet to come. I hope, dear reader, that they will for you too.

# ACKNOWLEDGMENTS

I am indebted to so many people who appear in and who helped me with this book. Let me start by thanking the incredible members of Cook the Seasons and followers of Nourish Evolution. You are the ongoing expression—the "volunteers"—of all that is in this book.

Thank you to my amazing agent, Janet Kobobel-Grant, who nurtured the seed of this book, challenged me to take it so much further than my original vision ("You want me to write *what*?"), and expertly guided it to the home I was so craving with Convergent Books.

Big thanks to the phenomenal team at Convergent. David Kopp, I swear there were times I felt you had a periscope into my soul. Derek Reed, thank you for giving me the "thesis statement" mantra. Andrew Watson, thank you for letting us track you down in Siberia (no fooling) to work your manuscript magic. Peter Kispert, thank you for keeping us all on track, and thank you to Tina Constable, Campbell Wharton, Jessica Brown, Megan Schumann, Ayelet Gruenspecht, and the entire Crown publishing team. You have truly been my dream team.

Thank you to the entire Kourtesi/Kardakari family for showing me a way of living, being, and eating that has—obviously—shaped the course of my life. You will always mean the world to me. Thank you to the Wingerts, Ana Maria, Mayra, and the Common Hope crew for giving us an extended family in Guatemala.

Thank you to the colleagues who have inspired and encouraged me—Bruce Aidells (little did you know what an impact you had on my life!), Antonia Allegra, Kathleen Flinn, Nancy Hopkins, Sally and Lisa Ekus, Barry Estabrook, Jennifer Walters, Jennifer Brown, Maggie Baxter, and so many others. An extra special shout-out to Alison Ashton, the yin to my yang, the cumin to my coriander—I absolutely couldn't do what I do without you, nor would I ever want to. Thank you to Megan Farina, Karen Eldridge, and Chris Davis too for all the work you do to get the Nourish message out to the world.

I owe a huge debt of gratitude to the recipe testers who took time out of busy lives to make sure every one of these recipes was up to snuff: Robin Bort, Suzanne Russell, Amanda Eubanks, Joanna Strohn, Amy Gerrits, Rénee Haas, Sheila Sandford, Mickey Bickerstaff, Marie Blanc, Patti Pyle, and Rachel Mullins.

Thank you to the amazing women who carried me in prayer through this whole process: Linda Albert, Kelly Cole, Kelly Costa, Julie Curtin, Peggy Dyslin, Lucy Gierhart, Mary Loebig Giles, Megan Katerjian, Kelly Lyndgaard, Carrie Morris, Joanna Quintrell, Leigh Rodriguez, and Sister Michaela.

A shout-out to dear friends and family for being the ground beneath my feet and the sun above my head. Julie Curtin, to this day I ponder daily how on earth I was so blessed to meet you all those years ago. You are a foundational piece of my life, past, present, and future, and I love you to the ends of the earth. Kelly Cole, Kelly

Costa, Janis Milham, Catherine Knepper, Mary Loebig-Giles, and Andrea Sparks, thank you for being women who inspire me in so many ways. Jann and Gerry Forth, Honore Comfort, Chris Fitzgerald, and Joann Ferguson, you taught me what welcome looks like and how much love is to be had around the table. Bill Cleaver, thank you for saving our marriage, saving my sanity, and being the incredible human being you are. To my mom, my dad, and Russ for always believing in me, even when I didn't see it.

And the most special thanks of all to Christopher and Noemi, who tirelessly and selflessly picked up the slack while I was working on this book, and gave me the space to birth it. Christopher, I am so blessed to be yoked to you on this crazy, amazing journey we're on, and it just keeps getting better. Noemi, my sweet, funny, fierce daughter, you make everything in life brighter. I love you both oceanloads.

A final thank-you to the "God who sees things that are not as though they were." Thank you for seeing *Nourished*, and all the goodness in my life, well before I did.